ROUTLEDGE LIBRARY EDITIONS: MANAGEMENT

Volume 51

MANAGEMENT BUY-OUTS

MANAGEMENT BUY-OUTS

MIKE WRIGHT & JOHN COYNE

LONDON AND NEW YORK

First published in 1985 by Croom Helm Ltd

This edition first published in 2018
by Routledge
2 Park Square, Milton Park, Abingdon, Oxon OX14 4RN

and by Routledge
711 Third Avenue, New York, NY 10017

Routledge is an imprint of the Taylor & Francis Group, an informa business

© 1985 John Coyne and Michael Wright

All rights reserved. No part of this book may be reprinted or reproduced or utilised in any form or by any electronic, mechanical, or other means, now known or hereafter invented, including photocopying and recording, or in any information storage or retrieval system, without permission in writing from the publishers.

Trademark notice: Product or corporate names may be trademarks or registered trademarks, and are used only for identification and explanation without intent to infringe.

British Library Cataloguing in Publication Data
A catalogue record for this book is available from the British Library

ISBN: 978-1-138-55938-7 (Set)
ISBN: 978-1-351-05538-3 (Set) (ebk)
ISBN: 978-0-8153-6585-3 (Volume 51) (hbk)
ISBN: 978-1-351-26004-6 (Volume 51) (ebk)

Publisher's Note
The publisher has gone to great lengths to ensure the quality of this reprint but points out that some imperfections in the original copies may be apparent.

Disclaimer
The publisher has made every effort to trace copyright holders and would welcome correspondence from those they have been unable to trace.

MANAGEMENT BUY-OUTS

Mike Wright & John Coyne

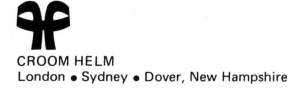

CROOM HELM
London • Sydney • Dover, New Hampshire

© 1985 John Coyne and Michael Wright
Croom Helm Ltd, Provident House, Burrell Row,
Beckenham, Kent BR3 1AT
Croom Helm Australia Pty Ltd, First Floor,
139 King Street, Sydney, NSW 2001, Australia,

British Library Cataloguing in Publication Data
Wright, Michael, *1952-*
  Management buy-outs.
  1. Corporations – Great Britain – Purchasing
  2. Executives – Great Britain
  I. Title
  658.1'6   HD2741
  ISBN 0-7099-3616-8

Croom Helm, 51 Washington Street, Dover,
New Hampshire 03820, USA

Library of Congress Cataloging in Publication Data
applied for.

Printed and bound in Great Britain by
Biddles Ltd, Guildford and King's Lynn

CONTENTS

Preface/Acknowledgements

List of Tables

List of Figures

1.	THE BUY-OUT PHENOMENON	1
2.	PRACTICAL ASPECTS OF MANAGEMENT BUY-OUTS .	11
3.	ECONOMIC ASPECTS OF MANAGEMENT BUY-OUTS ..	41
4.	GENERAL CHARACTERISTICS OF MANAGEMENT BUY-OUTS	64
5.	MANAGERIAL ASPECTS OF MANAGEMENT BUY-OUTS.	82
6.	INDUSTRIAL RELATIONS AND THE BUY-OUT	110
7.	PERFORMANCE IN MANAGEMENT BUY-OUTS	130
8.	CASE STUDIES	160
	Case 1: Panache Upholstery: A Management Buy-out of an Independent Company in Receivership	159
	Case 2: Mansfield Shoe Co. (1981) Ltd: A Management Buy-out from a Parent in Receivership..........	170
	Case 3: Lanemark Thermal Systems: A Management Buy-out from a Parent Still Trading but needing to Reorganise.....................	184

v

Contents

	Case 4:	Dennis and Robinson Limited (Trading as 'Manhattan Furniture') a Management Buy-out from a Parent still Trading......	194
	Case 5:	DPCE Holdings PLC: A Management Buy-out from a Foreign Parent still Trading...................	208
	Case 6:	A Management Buy-out on Retirement of the Previous Owners, which was eventually acquired by another Company......	222
	Case 7:	National Freight and Victaulic: Some Early Experiences in Two Staff Buy-outs from Nationalised Industries......................	227
9.	CONCLUDING REMARKS.......................		237
INDEX	....		**249**

LIST OF TABLES

CHAPTER 2
Table 2.1: Example of Topics to be Covered in a Company Appraisal in the Case of Buy-out from a Parent Company.
2.2: Main Buy-out Arrangements
2.3: Examples of Financing Institutions and Management Buy-outs Completed
2.4: Ranking of Main Sources of Finance

CHAPTER 4
Table 4.1: The Growth of Management Buy-outs
4.2: Source of Management Buy-outs
4.3: Industry Distribution of Management Buy-outs (Principal Activity)
4.4: Diversification in Management Buy-outs
4.5: Number of Subsidiaries Bought-out
4.6: Number of Sites Occupied
4.7: Price Paid to Purchase Company
4.8: Size of Management Buy-outs (Full-time Employees)
4.9: Management Buy-out Size Distribution and UK Size Distribution Compared
4.10: Management Buy-outs Compared with All Companies in Manufacturing Industry
4.11: Management Buy-outs and the Stock of Companies in the Region

CHAPTER 5
Table 5.1: Size Distribution of Buy-out Team
5.2: Correlation Between Size of Team and Employment
5.3: Number in Buy-out Team and Equity Stakes
5.4: Finance Participation by Employees

List of Tables

    5.5: Correlation between Price, Number of Financial Institutions and Managerial Equity Stakes
    5.6: Distribution of Management Functions in Buy-out Team
    5.7: Age Distribution of Buy-out Team Members
    5.8: Years Worked for Company Before Buy-out
    5.9: Managerial Changes by Source

CHAPTER 6

Table 6.1: Representation of Trade Unions
    6.2: Management Buy-outs and Multi-Unionism - Pre-Buy-out
    6.3: Trade Union Recognition
    6.4: Changes in Trade Union Recognition
    6.5: Source of Management Buy-outs
    6.6: Strength of Trade Union Representation
    6.7: Industrial Relations Disputes in Twelve Months Prior to Buy-out

CHAPTER 7

Table 7.1: Employment Changes in Management Buy-outs
    7.2: Changes in Employment Levels by Region
    7.3: Employment Changes by Different Size
    7.4: Improved Trading Relationships by Percentage of each Source of Buy-out
    7.5: Trading Relationships Between Ex-Parent and Bought-out Company Before Buy-out
    7.6: Attempts to Reduce Trading Dependence on Parent
    7.7.A: The Introduction of New Products in Buy-outs
    7.7.B: The Ending of Production in Buy-outs
    7.8: Investment Behaviour in Management Buy-outs
    7.9: Actual Performance - Buy-outs Two Years Old or More
    7.10: Actual Performance Compared with Expected-Buy-outs Less than Two Years Old
    7.11: Factors Affecting Profits for the Last Completed Financial Year
    7.12: Sources of Management Buy-outs and Cash Flow Problems
    7.13: Cash Flow Problems Before the Buy-out
    7.14: Cash Flow Problems After the Buy-out
    7.15: Some Key Performance Statistics

List of Tables

CHAPTER 8

Table 8.1.1: Panache Upholstery - Initial Financing
8.2.1: Mansfield Shoe Performance in the Period Leading up to the Buy-out
8.2.2: Mansfield Shoe Employees
8.5.1: DPCE Initial Financing Arrangements
8.5.2: Financial Performance of DPCE 1978-1983
8.7.1: The National Freight and Victaulic Staff Buy-outs in Summary

LIST OF FIGURES

CHAPTER 1

Figure 1.A: The Growth of Management Buy-outs: The Number of Buy-outs per Year

CHAPTER 8

Figure 8.2.A: Parent Company Life Cycle
8.3.A: Dunlop Holdings Divisional Return on Turnover
8.4.A: Dennis and Robinson Limited: Senior and Midale Management Organisation Chart: Before
8.4.B: Dennis and Robinson Limited: Senior and Middle Management Organisation Chart: After
8.5.A: Illustrative Management Structure DPCE 1984

PREFACE/ACKNOWLEDGEMENTS

This book is the result of an interest in management buy-outs which goes back to 1980 when one of the authors, Mike Wright, at the time working on divestments with Brian Chiplin noticed that a number of companies were being divested by means of a sale to the management. At the time, they had identified the phenomenon they did not know what to call it, an ignorance they shared even with many of those managers who had actually concluded a buy-out. Thus an interest in 'the phenomenon with no name' was born, as is so often the case in academic research, out of a desire to answer the questions posed by earlier work. It was in the early discussions following the discovery that the title 'management buy-outs' was introduced, at the Industrial and Commercial Finance Corporation (ICFC) so providing a convenient title for both the phenomenon itself, and subsequently this book.

The idea for further and more detailed research was formed following the first national conference on management buy-outs which was held at Nottingham University in March 1981, and jointly organised by the University and ICFC. The conference, which attracted a very large number of professional and industrial delegates, including many A.N. Others and John Smiths taking a day off from managing their respective subsidiary companies, clearly demonstrated that the buy-out was both a significant development on the UK commercial scene, and an activity worthy of detailed attention.

John Coyne had been attracted to the conference by the parallels which the management buy-out seemed to offer to the work on small firms and new enterprises with which he was at that time concerned. Thus, in mid-year 1981 a working partnership was formed which set out to look more

xi

Preface/Acknowledgements

closely at the buy-out phenomenon, and via a number of diversions and subsidiary issues on the way this study is one product of that collaboration.

In its current form the study is the product of a very intense eighteen months of research activity which has involved the administering of questionnaires (and the analysis of 111 responses), and the visiting of a very large number of companies, financial institutions, chartered accountants etc. Indeed, the authors spent so much of their time during the winter of '83/4 visiting companies that their frequent departures from the Industrial Economics department must have led their colleagues to believe that they were running the companies not just studying them! This intense research period was financed by the then Social Science Research Council (now the Economic and Social Research Council) under the auspices of its then Panel on The Economics of Industry, now disbanded and reconstituted. The authors wish to express their gratitude for this research support, and wish to state that they accept no responsibility for the fact that the committee that gave them the money was wound up, and that the overall research body had to change its name!

The current volume has benefited greatly from the very open and generous support given by so many companies, institutions and individuals over the past three years. It is impossible to examine an area such as this without making very real demands on the people actively involved in it, and the authors are very appreciative of how helpful people have been. It is a testimony to the supportive way in which this research has been received that of all the approaches made over the entire period of the work only one outright refusal to cooperate was received. It is difficult to pick out names from this general body but some people do merit particular thanks.

The whole study may never have got off the ground at all had not Paul Brooks, then of ICFC's Nottingham office (now of Charterhouse Developments) not been so receptive to the idea from the off. His encouragement not only in supporting the initial conference but in effecting introductions gave the research the start it needed. His then colleagues Sue Palmer and David Millom gave invaluable advice and recommendations in the early stages of research design and effected introductions to a large sample of ICFC clients, asking them to assist in our study.

Other individuals who ensured that the study got

Preface/Acknowledgements

off on the right track in those early stages, and who merit a particular mention are David Hutchings at Midland Equity, Ron Arnfield then of Nottingham University's Industrial and Business Liaison Office, and George Bloomfield, managing director of Melville Technology acting in his office as chairman of the Management Buy-out Association (which was formed just in time to help!).

The executives of the 111 companies who gave so generously of their time in completing the long, and sometimes complicated, questionnaire have provided the basic ingredient, information, without which the study could not have proceeded at all. Those who further subjected themselves to a site visit from the authors can be acclaimed for service beyond the call of duty, and those who then let their 'story' be told in these pages have contributed greatly to enable the understanding of the process of which they have been a part. Thus Bob Williams at Panache, Ray Pointer at Mansfield Shoe, Jim Downs at Manhattan, Harvey Tordoff at DPCE, Brian Cottee at NFC, David Stewart at Victaulic and John Spencer at Lanemark, by letting their companies' experiences be documented have made a valuable contribution to the assessment of the buy-out phenomenon as a whole.

In the later stages the development and presentation of material has benefited from discussion with a number of people, professionally involved in buy-outs from whom Adam Mills, partner in Spicer and Pegler's Birmingham Office, who has advised over 30 companies on buy-out perhaps merits a particular mention. Papers covering various aspects of this study have been presented at the University of Oxford, University of York, Paisley College, and the European Institute for Advanced Studies in Management (in Brussels), and on each occasion the participants' comments have proved pertinent and valuable.

Due acknowledgement must also be given to the contributions of the authors' colleagues in the Department of Industrial Economics, Accountancy and Insurance at the University of Nottingham who have at best offered advice and assistance, and at worst tolerated the authors during their endeavours. Valuable research assistance at crucial times has been given by Heather Lockley who seems naturally to possess those organisational qualities the authors strive for. The scribblings of the authors, who have been in competition to produce the most indecipherable piece of script, have been expertly typed into something resembling sense by Patsy

Rayner whose typographical brilliance gave momentum to the preparation of the final manuscript. One thing the authors have learned in their study of buy-outs is where the buck stops! Regrettably all the above named must be absolved of any responsibility for the final text - the buck stops with the authors.

Finally, a note of sincere thanks to those who have suffered most during the gathering of research material, and the preparation of this typescript - John's wife, Julie and daughter Emily, and Mike's wife, Maryse. They have suffered the absence and the irritation, and have done the chores the authors were not available to do. New research will have to be found if the authors are to continue to avoid doing the garden, washing the car, and painting the house!

Chapter One

THE BUY-OUT PHENOMENON

I. INTRODUCTION

The management buy-out is without doubt a major part of the current industrial and commercial scene. It is a means of effecting a change of ownership from absentee shareholders, or a parent group, to those currently managing the enterprise, which has grown rapidly in popularity over the past six years. There is little doubt that there have always been instances where management have bought their own companies, but what makes the current growth of buy-outs significant is the extent to which those numbers have grown and continue to grow, the way in which venture capital suppliers are looking specifically to finance such deals, and the positive mood of encouragement which permeates all the way down from government. The name "management buy-out" is newer than the concept, indeed many of the early phase of managers had completed the deal only to be told some time later than they had conducted a buy-out. So, what are the specific characteristics which constitute a buy-out?

II. WHAT IS A BUY-OUT?

For a buy-out to have taken place requires that some representatives of the management of the company, usually a small buy-out team, have negotiated to purchase the company from its current owners (including the receiver) and organised the finance to support the purchase. The transfer of ownership should be completed with the former owners having no substantial further ownership interest in the newly formed company. The management team, on average about four in number, are required to supply part of

1

the purchase price from personal funds, and will usually have a substantial equity stake in the company. The management buy-out must be distinguished from other means by which a new independent company may arise from an existing entity and which tend to have some characteristics in common. A 'leveraged' buy-out, a term much used on the American scene, is where a company is bought-out using loan capital and is thus highly geared but it is not usually the existing management that makes the purchase. A 'hive down' is where a company may transfer selected assets to a new company which it then registers as an independent entity prior to sale, but again the management would not necessarily be purchasers when it is eventually sold. Finally, a 'spin-off' is where a new company is formed by employees, often using assets and experience already acquired whilst working for a parent company. A spin-off often takes only part of the personnel, and part of any assets whilst the company from which it is spun-off continues. Thus, though it may have some of the management it does not constitute the sale of a complete entity. Spin-offs have been particularly common in high technology areas, or where sub-contracting is a feature of the operation and the new company often trades quite heavily with the parent from which it emerged.(1) The specific details on how management buy-out transfers may be undertaken and the consequent financial arrangements are the subject of Chapter 2. The size, shape and involvement of the buy-out teams is discussed in Chapter 5.

The essential difference between the bought-out company before and after the transfer is the extent to which the ownership and all the motivational consequences which flow from it, have been put firmly together. Those managers at the head of the company, once they own a controlling or substantial equity interest in the company, have a great personal incentive to ensure that it succeeds; at best in order to enhance personal wealth, and at worst to safeguard their often substantial personal investment in the company. As Keith Meadows, managing director of DPCE, the first management buy-out to get a full listing on the Stock Exchange, has said of his company's success:

> 'Without the buy-out we would not have achieved what we did because the motivation would not have been the same.' (2)

The Buy-out Phenomenon

The act of buying-out releases management from previous constraints, and enables them to make decisions, and exercise financial judgements totally on their own. The decisions they make will be determined by the nature of their financing commitments, and their attitude to risk, but philosophically what is important is that they are arrangements which they have chosen.

Gordon Warrington, chairman and chief executive of Welco sums up the feeling when he says,

'We would not have done as well without the buy-out. [Sales up 50%, large loss turned into large profit!] What we have now is the freedom to take decisions and take risks.'

That freedom to act is a recurrent theme throughout management buy-outs. The phenomenon has placed new emphasis on the role of the entrepreneur in industry, adding new credibility and new respect.

Thus, the management buy-out remarries ownership and control within industry, and encourages independent, entrepreneurial decision making. These issues are discussed in a wider context in Chapter 3.

The size of the buy-out team organising the purchase and taking equity stakes obviously varies depending upon the size of the company and the desires of those involved. In some instances the entire workforce has been invited to take part and under such circumstances the term employee buy-out is used. In the strictest sense a management buy-out, insofar as managers are a specific sub-group of employees, is a sub-set of employee buy-outs although the latter are more rare. The best known of the employee buy-outs is the National Freight Consortium which by its sheer size (23,000 employees, £53.5m price) attracted a great deal of popular attention. A similar, though generally unpublicised transfer took place when British Victaulic bought-out from British Steel, and issues arising from employee involvement in both cases are examined in Chapter 8, Case 7. It is unusual, even when offered the opportunity, for all the employees in a company to take an equity stake. For reasons no doubt directly related to personal wealth and a lack of experience of the financial world employees tend to be hesitant about committing themselves, and where they do so it is for modest sums. It is important to emphasise that in those instances where employees do subscribe it gives them no rights in law other than

3

those of a conventional ordinary shareholder. It is not a passport giving them rights to participate in management, nor does it set them apart from other employees who may not have subscribed when it comes to the exercise of day-to-day workloads and the acceptance of authority. Management buy-outs with some employee involvement, and fully fledged employee buy-outs must in no way be confused with worker cooperatives. In a cooperative the principles of organisation, decision making, and the distribution of rewards follow a distinct pattern which is unlike the 'conventional capitalist' firm. The buy-outs are wholly within the conventional pattern of UK limited companies. The management buy-out should therefore be seen as an extra dimension in the evolution of a traditional industrial economy, strengthening the principles of enterprise on which it is based, rather than being a departure from it. That this form of evolution has developed in the late 1970s and continued apace during the economic recession is a function of the growth of buy-out opportunities, and the availability of finance during this period.

III. A DEVELOPING MARKETPLACE

The growth in numbers of buy-outs is recorded in Figure 1.A. This has been compiled from the records of those financial institutions known to be financing deals, and has been cross-referenced through examination of press releases. In both respects there are possibilities for error. First, the number of bodies financing buy-outs has increased over time, so any trawl may not pick up <u>all</u> those providing finance. This problem is becoming more acute as the phenomenon receives wider publicity and attracts new providers of finance. The press release cross-reference can rectify some of these problems but there are sufficient circumstances under which no publicity is given to the deal for this to be an imperfect check. Nevertheless, the estimates are as precise as it is possible to make them for the period up to 1983. The difficulties are increasing over time, particularly as more ways are being found to finance the buy-out process with greater initiatives in recent times from commercial banks and the factoring companies. In addition, the creation of funds under the government's Business Expansion Scheme, and the development of the private Over The Counter Market,

The Buy-out Phenomenon

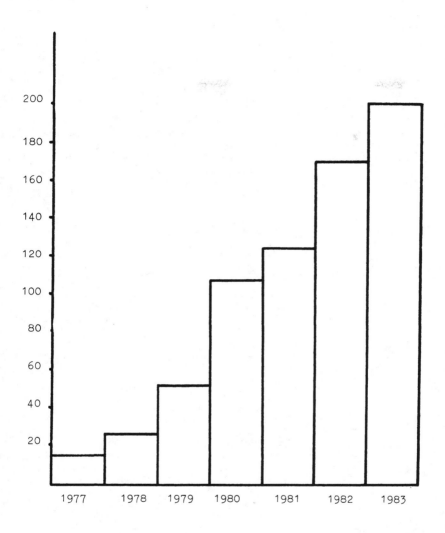

Fig. 1.A: The Growth of Management Buy-outs: Number of Buy-outs per Year

Source: Authors' survey of the lending institutions and the Financial Times.

The Buy-out Phenomenon

have both given added impetus and greater flexibility to the market.

In total, the five year period 1979-1983 has seen 650-700 buy-outs, including the staff buy-outs and probably involves something of the order of £750-850m of assets changing hands (at current prices). A feature of the early buy-outs was the size of the discount on net assets which management were often able to negotiate which may be justified on the grounds that the management team itself represents an important part of the assets. For the West Midlands, for example, it has been estimated that the typical discount in an engineering buy-out was 45%.(3) The size of any discount will obviously vary considerably depending upon the relative bargaining strength of the parties. As this market has evolved, as the successes of the early buy-outs have been publicised, and as new financiers have entered the market the size of discounts have tended to be eroded by the operation of conventional market forces. There is also a belief that many of the 'best' deals, where the management could extract the most favourable discounts, have been identified and completed so that increasingly the new deals have to be bid away from the current owners. Nevertheless, there is little indication that the number of buy-outs is beginning to fall yet. There is still a growing awareness of the opportunities and advantages which buy-outs can offer, not only to the managers for whom it represents the chance to own their own busines, but also to the boards of groups of companies which may see the buy-out route as an extra option in their own strategies for reshaping their business. For any buy-out to take place a desire and opportunity to buy has to be matched by a desire to sell, and these issues are discussed in Chapter 2, Sections II and III, and Chapter 3, Section V.

In the normal course of business development the processes of acquisition and diversification, and the equally important divestment and disintegration, will produce a fluidity in the economy which we would expect to continue to generate buy-out opportunities. There is no limit to the number of deals that could be done in sight yet, especially when one considers that if 1000 deals have been done it only represents a tiny fraction of the total stock of companies. The buy-out is not simply a phenomenon of the recession which has brought it to prominence. It is the result of a complex of forces which have been working their way

The Buy-out Phenomenon

through industry - the need for efficiency, the frustration of entrepreneurship, changes in company law, a favourable climate of encouragement from government, and developments in the venture capital market - which have all contributed to the emergence of the phenomenon and caused it to evolve.

The complexity and diversity of the buy-out marketplace is one of its most significant features and it has become increasingly varied over time. It is therefore unlikely that any two buy-outs will be the same in terms of size, financing arrangements, reasons for sale etc. The market has displayed great versatility in accommodating a wide variety of circumstances, and some of these arrangements are outlined in Chapter 2, Sections V and VI.

One aspect of the market's diversity and evolution can be seen in the growth of financing institutions. The traditional lender, and market leader has been the Industrial and Commercial Finance Corporation (ICFC) the subsidiary of Investors in Industry (3i) responsible for lending to small companies. In the late 1970s they pioneered the management buy-out as part of their portfolio of lending to smaller companies and were encouraged to develop the market by the relative success of their early lending where failure rates were substantially lower than in equivalent lending to entirely new start-ups. As deals were proposed that fell outside the funding levels which they could handle they became involved increasingly in syndicated deals and many of their co-lenders became significant contributors in their own right, each trying to find for itself a specialist and attractive niche in the market. In 1982 and 1983 ICFC were involved in approximately 40-50% of all deals but have been joined by a host of other major lenders notably County Bank and Midland Equity, with Barclays Development Capital and Citicorp looking for the larger end of the market. The entry of new lenders, not usually involved in venture capital provision, such as commercial banks, local authorities, and pension funds are almost daily adding variety and new dimensions to the market.

Complexity is added with respect to the type of company and market in which a buy-out may take place. There is virtually no sector of British industry, private or public, where a buy-out could not take place. As is demonstrated by the breadth of industrial coverage of the firms in this study most parts of industry, whether expanding or declining, whether making a product or providing a service, may provide appropriate conditions. The general characteristics of the buy-outs which comprise this study and which are considered to be a reasonably representative cross section of the entire market are discussed in detail in Chapter 4. Though the general focus of this study is the private sector, and whilst the most highly represented sector is manufacturing, there is every reason to regard the management buy-out as an important option within the general framework of privatisation favoured by the present government. Buy-out teams have attempted to buy part of the hotels group from British Rail, and were active in the sale of Sealink. There are many parts of British nationalised industries which might lend themselves to either a management buy-out or an employee buy-out.(4)

IV. THE ISSUES

The study of management buy-outs provides an almost unique opportunity to examine some important issues in the performance of companies and the economy. These issues are both general, for example the role of buy-outs in the process of change in an economy, and specific, for example the effects of incentives on efficiency and the relationships between management and employees. Introspectively the organisation of the new company, the attitudes and background of management and the way they adapt to their new independent roles is of interest not only to the buy-out but may also offer some generalised insights into the effective operation of all companies of a similar size and in similar industries.
   These issues are taken up in the survey which has been conducted and which gives access to information on 111 buy-outs concluded between 1976 and 1983. The detailed background to the survey, and distribution of firms investigated is contained in Chapter 4, which details the companies by size, source, industry and regional location. The chapter places the sample studied in context and enables a more intelligent appraisal to be made of the conclusions from Chapters 5, 6 and 7, in which the managerial, industrial relations, and performance issues are taken up in detail.
   The performance of bought-out companies is naturally a major focus of attention. In this study there is a division into three broad areas, each the subject of a chapter, though the combined effect is

The Buy-out Phenomenon

crucial. No single approach can be taken to assess the totality of the buy-out but each element contributes to the overall picture. Though it is not spelled out explicitly in the chapter on Performance the managerial changes, and attitude to industrial relations must underpin whatever economic and financial improvements have been effected in the company. For example, the shortening of the chain of authority as detailed in Chapter 5, and the increased worker involvement as outlined in Chapter 6 will have added considerably to the benefit of the company even if the specific contribution is difficult to measure objectively.

The aspects of existing knowledge to which an examination of management buy-outs may add, in both the economic sphere, and the managerial, are the subject of attention in Chapters 3 and 5. The buy-out has been placed in context with other developments in economic and managerial analyses of the firm so that the current phenomenon can be firmly rooted for comparison purposes.

V. THE EXPERIENCES

Throughout this study the analysis of bald statistical data has been tempered by the inclusion, wherever appropriate, of the experiences which lie behind the numbers. Where possible the analysis has been extended, and illustrated by reference to circumstances from the 111 companies within this study. For reasons of confidentiality it has not always been possible to name the people or the companies involved but reference to the actual circumstances surrounding a particular point is unavoidable if a true picture of this very 'alive' phenomenon is to be given. However, the examination of actual practice has been extended by the inclusion of a number of case studies in Chapter 6 which examine particular buy-outs in some detail. For the six cases from the private sector a consistent approach has been adopted which enables both the similarities and differences between particular circumstances to be seen. It is always difficult to select appropriate case material and the choice is largely to allow comparison rather than to effect study of one aspect in depth. In these case studies the companies are named.

The focus of this study is very much on the experiences of the companies themselves and

9

therefore the lending institutions, the ex-parents, the receivers and the body of professional advisers do not get separate attention. Their contribution is always contained within the framework of the study of the company but that is not to deny that their contribution is important. Their specific roles are perhaps most succinctly dealt with in Chapter 2 but no attempt has been made to include specific case material from within a lending institution or a professional advisory body. Perhaps such an examination may form the basis of a further study.

VI. CONCLUSIONS

The study of the buy-out phenomenon is dissembled into its constituent parts in the following chapters. Within each, every attempt has been made to address the issues in a 'free standing' way but it is absolutely inevitable that the whole analysis, and a full understanding of the process and all its ramifications, cannot be completely examined without treating the elements as complementary. Within the chapters, cross-referencing will be found to point out those areas where a very specific and obvious link exists. The loose ends, implications for policy and the future significance of the study are brought together in the final chapter, but it is inevitable in such a rapidly developing phenomenon that they will represent simply the conclusions to be drawn from a very specific snap shot. However, though the management buy-out cavalcade may move on, it is vital that the experiences of these early 'pioneers' be fully appreciated if the economy is to derive the full benefit from what is clearly a very important development in industrial life.

NOTES

1. Garvin, D.A.: "Spin-offs and the New Firm Formation Process", California Management Review, 2, January 1983.
2. From Anslow, M.: "Faster Growth for Buy-out Managers", Your Business, July, 1984.
3. Quoted in Anslow, M., op. cit.
4. See Coyne, J. and Wright, M.: "Staff Buy-outs and the Privatisation of Nationalised Industries", Department of Industrial Economics Discussion Paper, May, 1982.

Chapter 2

PRACTICAL ASPECTS OF MANAGEMENT BUY-OUTS

I. INTRODUCTION

The fast moving nature of the management buy-out market place and the different circumstances surrounding each buy-out make it difficult if not impossible to present the definitive statement on the practical aspects of management buy-outs. The more modest aim of this chapter is to give a broad overview of management buy-outs which provides the context within which the survey reported in later chapters may be discussed.

The chapter is divided into four main sections. The first section briefly outlines the circumstances under which management buy-outs can occur. In the second section the reasons why the vendor of a company would wish to sell to management in preference to someone else are tackled. This is followed, in section three, by a discussion of the ingredients for success; that is the trading conditions which must be satisfied for a management buy-out to be feasible. The fourth section discusses in detail the principal issues involved in the negotiation of the buy-out deal and the ways in which the financial package can be put together.

II. WHERE DO MANAGEMENT BUY-OUTS COME FROM?

There are five major circumstances from which buy-outs will generally arise: four in the private sector and one from the public sector. These are:

- Receivership of an independent company, in which the buy-out may be the only means of continuing the company although it may necessitate a much reduced and reorganised form (see for example the

Practical Aspects of Management Buy-outs

case of Panache Upholstery in Chapter 8).
- Receivership of the parent company, in which a viable subsidiary (or group of subsidiaries) is bought out whilst the remainder of the parent is liquidated (see for example, the case of Mansfield Shoe Co. in Chapter 8).
- Retirement or death of the current owners, in which a management buy-out may be an attractive way of ensuring that the company continues as an independent entity (see for example the retirement case presented in Chapter 8).
- Divestment of a subsidiary by a parent company still trading, where for reasons to be returned to below and in Chapter 3, the parent no longer wants the subsidiary and the management are the preferred buyers (see for example, the cases of Lanemark, DPCE and Dennis and Robinson in Chapter 8).
- Privatisation of all or part of a nationalised industry, where a management buy-out, or more probably, given the value of assets generally involved, an employee buy-out, is a more attractive or feasible proposition than immediate flotation on the Stock Exchange.

To date, the majority of management buy-out activity has been concentrated in the private sector, and it is here that the survey results presented in later chapters concentrate. However, there have been some public sector buy-outs and with the government's privatisation programme still in progress the buy-out option remains a real possibility in some cases.(1) So far the only public sector buy-outs to take place have been those of National Freight Consortium, British Victaulic (a former subsidiary of British Steel), Tyne Ship Repairers (a former subsidiary of British Shipbuilders) and Keighley Foundries (one of BL-Austin-Rover's four foundry plants). The pertinent issues raised by this kind of buy-out are discussed in the cases of NFC and British Victaulic in Chapter 8. The possibility of a management/employee buy-out has also been floated in respect of British Airways, British Transport Hotels, Sealink, Jaguar(2) and British Steel.(3) However, the buy-out option appears to have been ruled out as inappropriate.(4) The suggestion that British Steel becomes an employee buy-out does not at present seem appropriate given the sheer size of

12

Practical Aspects of Management Buy-outs

the operation and its capital intensive nature. The management of British Transport Hotels failed in their attempt at a buy-out, and the hotels were eventually sold to various purchasers. Though Sealink was eventually sold to Seacontainers, it had been suggested that NFC would purchase it.(5)

III. WHY SELL TO MANAGEMENT?

For a buy-out to take place requires the coincidence of desires on the part of vendor and purchaser. There must be a willingness to sell on the part of the vendor, and a desire to buy on behalf of the management team. However, the management group may be only one of a number of prospective purchasers and so we must assess the advantages and disadvantages of sale by means of a management buy-out in order to understand the rationale behind the phenomenon. This is particularly so when one considers that until fairly recently there were severe financial, legal and taxation barriers which managers buying out had to overcome. It often took great will to find a way, though these practical difficulties have eased considerably of late and are discussed in more detail below.

The rationale for sale to management will tend to vary depending upon the material circumstances from which the opportunity to purchase arises. From the vendor's point of view there are certain general criteria which are of importance -

- to get the best price
- to facilitate an easy sale
- to safeguard their shareholders interests which may be further compounded in certain instances by:
- the need to preserve a corporate image/corporate confidence
- the potential competition which an independent may pose
- a desire for a quiet, no fuss sale
- the knowledge that management are an important part of the bundle of assets which constitute the firm and have a lower value when disaffected.

The management team may therefore be in a strong position when purchasing because of:

13

Practical Aspects of Management Buy-outs

- asymmetric "inside" information on assets and potential
- the knowledge of their own value in the company
- alertness to the opportunity, and full information at all stages

There is clearly the potential for conflict over the objectives of the parties, and in most instances the issue will be resolved by the balance of bargaining power between the two sides, often bolstered on management's side by the attitudes of the institutions expected to finance the deal, whose interests will tend to ensure that unacceptable risks are avoided. It is useful to examine some of these issues in more detail, and in relation to the material circumstances under which they arise.

In the case of companies in receivership it is the receiver's legal duty to obtain the best deal for the creditors for whom he acts and much will depend on how he perceives this can best be achieved. For example, whether the first inclination is to break up the business, or to sell as much as possible as a "going concern". Management will be in a good position to know what can be salvaged from the receivership and may want to purchase only part of the assets to reform a company. However, once the intention is declared it is in the receiver's interests to force management to purchase as much as possible to avoid being left with an unsaleable residue of assets. In these circumstances management may be forced to take more than they want and have to accept responsibility for disposing of assets in restructuring immediately post buy-out. The exact bundle of assets, and purchase price will depend upon the balance of power, though management may have quite a strong hand if they are the only interested purchaser.

The sale of an independent company or a subsidiary which is a going concern raises other important issues. An important factor in both types of company is the threat of management veto or resistance if a sale is made to another group. The consequences of resistance by management to being absorbed into a larger, unfamiliar organisation may be serious, particularly if management skills are an important contributory factor to the net worth of the company (eg this point may be especially true in computer software companies). Though this problem may strengthen management's hand in negotiations, the vendor has to be mindful in striking a price that the interests of the current owners are not unduly compromised; that is, the vendor needs to ensure that the threat of management veto does not lead to sale of the company at an excessive discount. This problem may be compounded by the behaviour of management, who realising their strong bargaining position, may deliberately depress the performance of the company for a period prior to buy-out in the expectation of acquiring it at a substantial discount though this is a dangerous strategy. Dissatisfaction from shareholders with this kind of behaviour may lead, in the extreme, to a general unwillingness to invest in any company, an outcome which would be most unwelcome when many companies are seeking to attract external equity participation. The response in the USA to this conflict of shareholder/manager interest is to obtain a valuation by independent accountants and then to put the company out to tender from other parties. Though this may obtain a fairer price in the eyes of the vendor, it may create other problems. First, such a scheme may introduce delay, unwelcome publicity and increased costs which may prejudice the long-run success of the company. Second, if the process results in an external purchaser acquiring the company, in an 'auction' at an excessive price but with a disaffected management it may generate its own difficulties in surviving once trading independently. This provides another aspect of asymmetric information and is returned to in more detail in Chapter 3.

Management veto apart, the parent's corporate view will strongly influence its willingness to sell to management. For example, a subsidiary may be put up for sale because it does not fit with the parent's corporate strategy. Such a mismatch can arise in several ways: a change in direction by the parent so that the subsidiary is no longer required; the subsidiary may have been acquired "by accident" as part of another acquisition; there may be rationalisation by the parent where excess capacity exists; the parent may need to effect a sale to realise cash for projects considered more central to corporate strategy; the subsidiary may require funds for investment which the parent is not prepared to divert from elsewhere; a supplier/customer relationship may still exist but the parent company may consider the management of the subsidiary requires expertise in areas beyond their competence etc. Where excess capacity exists the parent may prefer to close a geographically distant subsidiary in order to concentrate and strengthen production nearer its home base. Where supplier/customer relationships still exist, sale to the management may avert the threat of loss of supplies or markets which sale to another group may produce. In the other circumstances outlined above, the position is perhaps more ambiguous. Parents may play down or ignore the problem of managerial veto and sell the subsidiary for the highest price it can obtain externally. Bringing good calibre subsidiary management into the parent before the sale may help remove the problem of resistance without the potential external purchaser being aware of the loss. Alternatively, the subsidiary may be disposed of to another group by means of an asset swap. However, there are conditions under which a sale of the subsidiary to the management may be preferred - where no external purchaser is willing to pay the required price; where the managing directors of the parent and of the subsidiary come to a personal arrangement for a buy-out; and where sale to the management may better guarantee the maintenance of the subsidiary in being and so maintain the good name of the parent in a particular locality. The corollary of the last mentioned, is that a parent may not wish to sell to a weak management if there is a possibility the buy-out will fail, leaving the ex-parent to pick up the pieces.

Though the parent may thus consider a sale to the management, it is necessary for management to want to buy it and for financial institutions to be convinced they ought to support it and so provide an appropriate financial package. It is therefore necessary to address the conditions under which a successful management buy-out may occur.

IV. INGREDIENTS FOR SUCCESS

If a management buy-out is to take place, the conditions discussed in this section need to be satisfactory to both management and the financing institutions, and the resultant price offered for the company, must meet the vendor's requirements.

The ingredients for success broadly divide into three main categories:

- the potential buy-out company's (Target company) economic viability
- the capabilities of the incumbent management
- the financability of the change in ownership

Practical Aspects of Management Buy-outs

Each of these categories are now examined in detail.

i) Economic Viability of Target Company

Disappointing performance may be an obvious and important reason for the sale of a company, and in the case of receivership it is almost certain that the target company has not been earning profits. However, disappointing performance may be relative not absolute and may merely mean that returns have been less than desired under the current ownership. A change of owner may provide the opportunity to effect changes, but the underlying position must be economically sound. Attention focuses on four main elements of viability.

First, the present or likely future product range must clearly have some attractions in the market place. If the existing market faced by the firm is in long-term decline and the product range is obsolete, "end game",(6) important questions need to be asked. The reason for sale may be a very weak market position, in which case, if a deal is to be pursued, it is vital that the price paid is heavily discounted. If the market position is fairly dominant, a cushion may be provided during which time new products may be developed. Clearly, the greater the reliance on one product the more severe this problem will be. The ability of the managers as owners to change previous policies and introduce new products and explore new markets will determine the success of the enterprise.

As will be seen in the empirical section, management buy-outs occur in a wide variety of product areas. Leaving aside the problems of investing in declining industries, which may nevertheless contain attractive product areas, a question arises over the risk involved in investing in fast-growing high technology areas. In a fairly stable low to medium technology industry funds may be required for investment after the buy-out, particularly if the subsidiary had previously been used as a 'cash-cow' by its parent. (The problems here are very well illustrated by the case of Dennis and Robinson in Chapter 8.) However, in fast-growing high technology industries a continued need for funds after the buy-out is likely to be present. Given the volatility of such industries, there may be a high level of uncertainty surrounding the ability of the company to generate sufficient resources to finance its continued development or to

17

grow fast enough to the point at which a stock exchange listing could be sought. Whilst this problem may be containable within a group structure it may lead some financial institutions, especially those looking for an exit within five years (see below), to shy away from supporting such a proposition. However, there have been a number of successful deals in the high technology areas, as Chapter 4 and the case of DPCE in Chapter 8 show. American institutions investing in leveraged buy-outs appear to prefer 'mundane' product areas, where there is less risk, less need for research and development expenditure and a good chance of the institutions being able to sell-out within three to five years.(7) The Hoare Candover fund was set up in January 1984 specifically to finance these kinds of opportunities in the UK.

Whatever the industry an important aspect of viability is relations with customers and suppliers. Of particular importance here is the stability and potential of the order book. Two main problems may be identified. In the case of buy-outs from receivership it is necessary to ensure the continuation of supply and that customers will not have gone elsewhere. Those buy-outs from receivership that were interviewed as part of the study made strenuous efforts before the crash, when the writing was on the wall, to maintain good relationships with both customers and suppliers in order to ensure support on independence. For the most part both have been very supportive of the management team and few have lost customers or suppliers.(8) In the case of divestments, over-dependence on the ex-parent for custom may present a potential problem area. Although in the companies in our survey over-dependence on the parent was rarely a problen it is not unknown. In such cases the financing institution may insist on a purchase/supply agreement at least for the short-term as a condition of extending funding. A good example of this type of arrangement is the case of Progress Foundry which initially sold eighty per cent of its output to its ex-parent, Wheelabrator Fry.(9) The purchase/supply agreement then gives management the stability from which they can seek new markets or suppliers.

Complementary to all of the foregoing is the fourth influence on viability - cost levels and their controllability. If the target company is part of a group it will be necessary to introduce independent and appropriate local cost control procedures across the whole range of activities - possibly for the first time. In many instances subsidiaries are subject to central systems and procedures imposed upon them by central managements more concerned with their appropriateness across the whole group rather than whether they meet a specific local need. Subsidiaries often also suffer from the imposition of blanket charges centrally for "management services" which may not be regarded as particularly good value at local level. There may be a saving from the removal of these central charges and procedures but this must be balanced against the costs of installing an effective and comprehensive local system.

It is evident that the four elements of viability, important though they are, cannot exist effectively on their own. The role of management in their co-ordination is crucial to the success of the business.

ii) Management Expertise

The management team should contain an individual or group of individuals exhibiting two principal qualities. First, the ability to co-ordinate the activities in the business so as to keep it running from day-to-day. Second, the ability to perceive opportunities in the market place and to act upon them to provide customers with what they demand. In short, the second quality is entrepreneurship. If either of these two qualities is missing the chances of commercial success are limited.

Management that have been part of a larger organisation, where they may not have had direct and sole responsibility for strategic decisions may have been good co-ordinators. But, they may not necessarily make successful entrepreneurs when the parent's protective umbrella is removed or they have to start deciding for themselves where the company is going. Even as co-ordinators they may not have been concerned with the complete range of functions necessary for running the business, but rather with fulfilling remote, central, corporate plans. Very often, their expertise may be limited to one particular area, such as production. The manager without entrepreneurial skills may be at a disadvantage in seeing business from its broadest perspective and indeed may hold a fundamental misconception about what business the firm for which he works is in. Simply stated a firm exists to make money. It is an appreciation of the way in which the business makes its money that is crucial. Take as an actual example, a company using copper wire with which to make cables. The profitability of the firm depends to a lesser degree on the technical aspects of its making and selling cables, than on the buying of copper wire at favourable prices. A management team looking for funding would find it difficult to attract the financing institutions' commitment if they failed to appreciate what it was about the business which generates the profits. It is difficult to monitor how often this factor features as a reason why some buy-outs do not take place as failed negotiations are seldom reported. An exception was the case of the proposed buy-out of Richard Shops and John Collier which failed. Here the management team were the favoured candidates of the divesting parent, Hanson Trust. However, in contrast to the management buy-out of Timpson Shoes, also from Hanson Trust and which was successfully completed, the Richard Shops and John Collier team were considered to be lacking, especially in the buying department which is crucial in a retail clothes company.(10)

These two companies also illustrate two further points concerning management expertise.

Firstly, in a buy-out, emphasis is on skills possessed in the team as a whole rather than just an individual. It is necessary, therefore, for the team to cover ably all important functions. If it is weak in one area then the deal may fail. The likelihood of failure becomes particularly acute if the weakness is in a specialised area, where scarce skills may be difficult to replace as in the buying department of Richard Shops. Other functions, particularly finance, may not exist in the fullest sense in subsidiaries but may be relatively easily introduced, as is shown in Chapter 5.

The second point concerns the management's ability to operate as an independent team. Although the team may be well motivated and able to work together under a parental umbrella, they may be ineffective when forced to act on their own. Conversely, if an ailing subsidiary becomes the subject of a buy-out proposal it is necessary to ask whether the shortcomings in performance are due to poor capability of management or those restrictions imposed by the parent which will be removed on

Practical Aspects of Management Buy-outs

buy-out. In the two cases cited above it is interesting to note that although the behaviour of the parent company has been considered as restrictive, the management team at Timpsons had adapted and increased its market share in the six years prior to buy-out, whereas the Richard Shops and John Collier team did not adapt and lost considerable ground in the market over the same period of time.(11)

Both these points have emphasised the quality of the team as a whole, which is the particular feature of buy-outs. But it is important to note, as is apparent from the survey results reported in Chapter 5, that buy-out teams are rarely characterised by collective leaderships. What is required is a 'leading light' with the energy and expertise to 'manage' the buy-out team and effect the change of ownership which sets the company on its way as an independent entity. The "leading light" may not be part of the team managing the company prior to the buy-out as is observed in a number of the studied firms.

Though it may not improve the calibre of the management team the contribution of their own funds to purchasing the company may be important in introducing and maintaining a high level of commitment to the success of the buy-out. The institutions certainly regard management funding as an important influence on their willingness to extend finance. It is difficult to be precise about the level of management contribution that is required, but Spicer and Pegler estimate that for buy-outs in the price range up to £1.5 million the management team should seek to find at least ten per cent of the total price.(12) For larger deals, it becomes difficult for management to find such a high proportion of funds from their own resources and it is necessary to structure financing so as to give them a degree of control whilst safeguarding the interests of the financing institutions. One solution may be for management to take-up partly-paid ordinary shares, giving them a large equity stake, with the balance of the share price being paid when the company is floated on the Stock Exchange. A more common solution is for the size of the buy-out team to be extended from the four or five managers occupying the key senior functions to the next level of the organisational hierarchy. Such a move has the advantage of deepening the level of commitment to the success of the buy-out. It does become necessary, however, to define clearly which

Practical Aspects of Management Buy-outs

group has the ultimate decision-making power, both for the running of the company and to satisfy the financing institutions.

The management team's contribution is but one part of the much larger issue of the financability of the buy-out towards which attention is now directed.

iii) Financability

Essentially, the price paid for the company determines its financability. The price determines the amount of finance required and the corresponding level of funds which need to be generated to service the financial package. If the net revenue generated by the business is insufficient to cover interest and dividend payments then the price must be regarded as too high. Realistically, net revenue should be viewed in terms of what is left over after provision has been made for funds required for working capital, fixed asset replacement, research and development and possibly taxation. Net revenue must also be viewed in terms of what is actually generated by the trading activities of the business rather than including items of a 'one-off' nature which arise from grants or various schemes for relief on overhead costs. Funds required for fixed asset replacement may be quite substantial, particularly if the company has been drained of resources by its former parent company (see, for example, the case of Dennis and Robinson in Chapter 8). It is important to make due allowance for this replacement at the outset rather than attempting to renegotiate funding some months after the transfer of ownership has been completed.

In theory, the price to be paid should be based on the opportunity cost of the assets. If the company is in imminent danger of liquidation or is in a declining industry, the correct price to pay is based on net realisable value.

In such circumstances, net book value, which has tended to be the basis for the valuation of buy-outs in the US or the purchase of American subsidiaries operating in Britain is largely irrelevant. When coupled with the revenue generating ability of a business faced with these circumstances, a price substantially below book value should be looked for. However, a problem may be raised here because of the obligations placed upon the agent selling the company to obtain a fair price for the owners. A parent disposing of a subsidiary may be unable to bear the loss incurred by selling at a heavy discount, whilst a receiver is obliged to look after the interests of the creditors. The behaviour of receivers in some buy-outs was an issue raised in the study reported later. One manager buying-out was moved to remark ruefully that the price paid in such cases was closely related to which receiver happened to be dealing with the case and the number of other receiverships he was dealing with at the same time.

If the firm is neither in danger of liquidation, nor in an industry in long-term decline, then managers involved in a buy-out should expect to pay a higher price based on the earnings potential of the assets. To some extent, the actual price to be paid may be adjusted to recognise the value to the company of the intangible input of the management team's cumulative efforts over a number of years. Where the management team is the only possible purchaser or is able to exercise a veto should competing purchasers appear, this downward pressure on the price to be paid may be most in evidence. If the vendor is not being forced to sell because of the precarious state of the business or management's veto against an external purchaser is ineffective, then a discount on book value may be out of the question. At the time of writing (July 1984) the balance in the market appears to be moving in this latter direction, after a period of three or four years in which management generally held the upper hand. Distress sales and purchases at a discount may still be expected, but not as frequently as has been witnessed in the past.

Given favourable interest and dividend coverage ratios, the business as noted already should be able to service its financing package. The structuring of the type of funds to finance the buy-outs is discussed below. However, the following conditions need to be dealt with before the deal can be finalised. First, the extent to which management can provide funds and their willingness to do so needs to be clarified. Second, the financial institution will usually expect to invest part of their funds as an equity stake so as to be able to participate in the rewards which flow from taking the risk of investing in the company. Third, the financial institution will require security for the loan funds it puts into the deal. Fourth, where employees benefited from a pension scheme in the previous company, appropriate arrangements will have to be made to safeguard the benefits so derived. Each of these four conditions contains potential problems which can affect the feasibility of a buy-out taking place.

The willingness by management to provide funds is regarded by the financial institutions as an important indicator of their commitment to the success of the buy-out. For someone of limited financial resources such a decision cannot be taken lightly, especially given the disastrous consequences should the company fail. The institutions like to feel that the buy-out team's exposure to risk is such as will ensure a coincidence of interests. In those buy-outs where sufficient funds can be raised from certain members of the team other key personnel may be included in the team even though initially they are unable to contribute financially. Since the introduction of the 1981 Transfer of Undertakings (Protection of Employment) regulations it has been more difficult to create the necessary break in employment which had previously been important in triggering redundancy payments which could then be used by employees to finance their contribution to the buy-out.

The taking of an equity stake by the institutions introduces the problem of dilution of ownership, but this may be unavoidable if the buy-out, particularly one at the larger end, is to be feasible. One safeguard for the management in these circumstances, where a consortium of institutions may be involved, is to ensure that each institution's holding is separate from those of the others. For some of the smaller buy-outs the problem is increasingly being resolved by recourse to the clearing banks.

The long-term debt finance they provide does remove the problem of equity dilution, but introduces the difficulties associated with high servicing costs in the early years. The clearing banks, in common with the other financial institutions, will also require security for their funding. Problems may arise here in respect of the valuation to be placed on the assets used as security and conflict between institutions as to who takes a charge on which asset. In appropriate circumstances, arrangements may be made under the Loan Guarantee Scheme, which provides for up to £75,000 of advances to be guaranteed by the Department of Trade and Industry.

The problem with pension arrangements arises in particular in buy-outs from parent companies which have group pension funds. Once the buy-out takes

Practical Aspects of Management Buy-outs

place the employees will no longer be eligible for the group scheme and it becomes necessary to ensure that the funds to be transferred from the former parent's scheme are sufficient for the new company's scheme to be actuarially sound. If the parent's scheme has been substantially under-funded the resources required to rectify the problem may be beyond the buy-out's ability to pay, putting the viability of the new company at risk. The most spectacular case of pension scheme under-funding involving buy-outs was that of National Freight Consortium, where of the £53m price paid for the company, some £47m was required to put the pension fund on a sound footing.

V. THE DEAL

This section discusses the completion of the deal itself in two parts. The first examines the negotiations, and outlines the possible ways of effecting the transfer of ownership. The second examines the structuring of the financing package. It must be stressed that what appears here is only a flavour of the general issues as experience teaches that each case is likely to be different in some respects. Those considering a buy-out are always well advised to seek the opinion and services of a specialist intermediary.

i) The Negotiations Themselves (13)

A new relationship arises between the management of the target company and its current owners as soon as a buy-out is in prospect. The delicacy of this relationship, particularly with respect to open conflicts of interest emphasises the need for a professional intermediary to act on behalf of the purchasing team. In many buy-outs the intermediaries will be a team usually consisting of an accountant, a solicitor and a representative of the financial institution providing funding; all highly experienced in negotiating buy-out deals. For more effective negotiating a leader should be clearly identified. Skilled negotiators can help prevent management being out-manoeuvred by receivers who are used to driving hard bargains or by bosses taking advantage of a superior hierarchical position. Not unimportant are the roles that the intermediary can play in protecting management from fears regarding

25

job security should the buy-out not proceed and also in protecting management from themselves when in their anxiety to acquire the business they are prepared to pay more for it than the minimum the vendor is willing to accept.

Although opinions differ on the first stage in negotiations it seems preferable for a management team considering a buy-out to approach an intermediary or a financial institution to outline the proposition. A fairly informal approach such as this will often give a clear indication to all concerned as to whether a deal is feasible and at what price and whether the management team have the calibre to see a deal through. Only after this preliminary screening is it worthwhile progressing. This process is not costless so management should be comitted to the enquiry and be prepared to sink some funds in the examination of the preliminary stages.

This initial stage may take place either where management are making preliminary enquiries without any firm discussions having taken place with the vendor or at the stage when discussions have begun around the vendor's original asking price. The former circumstances may be more common now as managers become more aware generally of the possibility of a management buy-out.

Ideally, once the initial screen has been completed and the decision is taken to proceed, fuller discussions can take place on agreeing a price. However, before a final price can be agreed which an institution would be willing to finance, it is necessary to produce a detailed proposal including a thorough appraisal of the company. The detailed proposal can be most important in negotiating a satisfactory price at which the business will be able to generate sufficient net revenue to service the financial package. The items that the report should cover are itemised in Table 2.1 and cover the seven main areas - the company's history, its markets and marketing policies, its past and expected performance, the assets to be acquired, the existing financial resources, the company's manpower resources and its present and proposed organisation structure. Such detail is necessary both for assessing performance potential and for identifying areas of weakness which will need to be rectified.

In the more marginal deals, there may be difficulty in attracting finance from the first institution approached. The report on the company then becomes useful in approaching alternative

Practical Aspects of Management Buy-outs

TABLE 2.1
Example of Topics to be Covered in a Company Appraisal in the Case of a Buy-out from a Parent Company

TOPICS

1. Company Histories
    - of subsidiary to be bought-out
    - of parent

2. Markets and Marketing
    - the overall state of the market in which the subsidiary is operating
    - the subsidiary's marketing policy
    - the subsidiary's customers and suppliers
    - seasonal trading characteristics

3. Performance (Past and Expected Future)
    - summary of past five years audited accounts
    - profit forecast for first three years after buy-out
    - cash flow forecast for first year after buy-out
    - statement of assumptions on which forecasts based
    - production and sales statistics for previous five years

4. Assets to be acquired
    - fixed assets
    - stocks and work in progress

5. Existing Financial Resources
    - long-term capital structure and shareholders
    - working capital (including detailed debtor and creditor position)
    - taxation aspects

6. Manpower
    - directors and their personal histories
    - union representation
    - workforce size and characteristics (including charges)
    - key employees and management and their effectiveness

7. Organisation of the Company
    - organisation chart
    - how the company is managed and controlled
    - how effective is the current management and control of the company
    - state of industrial relations

sources of funding - its credibility much enhanced, as far as the companies studied here were concerned, if it were produced by an accounting firm with a national reputation.

Some would counsel against hawking a proposal round a number of institutions without making amendments based on the comments received.(14) However, rewriting a proposal may incur extra expense and loss of time. More importantly, it is necessary to bear in mind that assessments and risk preferences do vary between institutions so that the first one approached may not be the most appropriate in all circumstances. It is necessary to listen to what an institution has to say, especially when the proposal may have an underlying soundness, but the deal is only feasible at a much lower price. It is better not to go ahead with a buy-out than to agree on a price which requires an unserviceable financial package.

The case of Meatpak, a buy-out from the US-based Esmark group, illustrates the above issues.(15) A price close to book value was placed on the subsidiary by the parent. The subsidiary itself was reported to have a 'patchy' profit record, to have a narrow customer base (eighty per cent of sales were to one customer), to have a management team which had worked together for less than a year and to have been starved of investment funds by its parent. At the parent's asking price, the buy-out proposal was unattractive to a number of institutions. Indeed, funding was refused by no less than eight of them before Sharp Unquoted Midland Investment Trust (SUMIT) was persuaded that the deal was viable. It is worth noting that the level of determination by the management team and a five year purchase commitment by the major customer were highly important factors influencing the decision to proceed.

Despite the problem of a high initial asking price, the above case did not have to contend with the two common problems which affect buy-out negotiations - the need for a deal to be completed quickly and the existence of competing potential purchasers. The need for speed may itself be occasioned by the threat from the vendor to offer the business to external buyers if an arrangement with the management is not achieved within a specified period of time. The existence of a time constraint introduces the twin problems that on the one hand the buy-out team may be tempted to pay too much for the company and on the other hand they may be forced into accepting a financing package which is inappropriate and costly. The latter problem may also be evident if competing purchasers exist, particularly for buy-outs on receivership where the management have no alternative employment possibilities. The threat of competing purchasers appearing may be reduced by conducting negotiations in secret, which in many cases may involve clandestine operations to ensure that even the vendor is unaware of what is happening until an offer is made. Where open competition cannot be avoided, the management may have two powerful vetoes at its disposal. First, the team itself may make it clear that they would not work with an external purchaser. This threat can be most effective where the performance of the business depends largely on the particular expertise of the incumbent management. The second veto derives from a refusal by a major customer or supplier to deal with anyone other than the management team. This veto has been used very effectively in managements' favour in buy-outs of distributorships.(16)

Assuming that negotiations with the vendor do proceed to an advanced stage, consideration needs to be given to the complex legal and taxation aspects of the transfer of ownership. The specific arrangements vary considerably from case to case as unique elements of a particular purchase need to be accommodated. The details are becoming more complex as new ways of utilising the arrangements provided for in successive Finance Acts are sought. The use of appropriate, and experienced professional assistance is vital to ensure that the most beneficial format is agreed.

Readers wishing to pursue these issues in greater detail are referred to the references contained in the Further Information section at the end of this chapter. For the purposes of this study it will suffice to present a broad overview of the main types of buy-out arrangement. The five main ways in which a buy-out can take place are summarised in Table 2.2. On examination of the table it will be evident that there are two basic means of effecting the transaction; a transfer of shares or a transfer of assets. Although all the methods shown in Table 2.2 are legally possible, for taxation reasons the transfer of shares routes are normally considered to be the most advantageous to both vendor and purchaser.

Prior to the introduction of the Companies Act 1981 there were serious problems in the buy-out of

Practical Aspects of Management Buy-outs

TABLE 2.2

Main Buy-out Arrangements

1. *Independent Company Still Trading*

    New company formed by management which obtains finance to purchase shares in Target company. After the acquisition the preferred route from a taxation point of view is for the target company's trade to be transferred to the New Company, possibly followed by liquidation of Target Company.

2. *Subsidiary Company of a Parent Still Trading*

    Target Company pays a dividend to its parent and shares in the Target Company are then acquired by New Company or by the managers. This scheme requires that Target Company has sufficient distributable reserves. Alternatively, the financier can replace a loan from the parent company to Target Company.

3. *Company in Receivership (or for Purchase from a Group)*

    Subsidiary of Target Company is formed, with trade of Target being transferred to new subsidiary ('hived down') on loan account. Financier replaces loan and New Company or managers personally purchase shares in Target's new subsidiary. For purchasers from Receiver, hive down must take place before liquidation of Target and sale of its subsidiary. For purchase from a group, new subsidiary must commence trading before sale takes place.

4. *Purchase of Assets from Vendor Company*

    New Company is formed and used to purchase assets of Target Company. [Note: Although in principle a very simple method it can, if purchase is at a discount, often cause serious conflicts of interest between the vendor and the purchaser in terms of liabilities and allowances for taxation. As a result one of the previous three methods may be preferred.]

5. *Purchase of Target Company when Management Team already Own Some Shares*

    Either shares in Target Company can be distributed as dividend to buy-out team and their shares in the distributing company become worthless (a 'demerger' as provided for in the Finance Act 1980) or Target Company purchases for cash shares of outgoing shareholders leaving managers in control (as provided for in the Companies Act 1981)

Source: Adapted from J.P. Hardman and M.R. Young: 'Management Buy-outs', <u>Accountants Digest No. 133</u>, Spring 1983

an existing company rather than the acquisition of the assets of that company. The difficulties arose because Section 54 of the Companies Act 1948, which was designed to protect creditors, prevented the use of the assets of the company as security to obtain funding. Although Section 54 of the 1948 Act has been repealed, Section 42 of the 1981 Act still maintains the general prohibition against a company giving financial assistance for the purchase of its own shares. Assistance may take the form of giving loans, guarantees or security based on the assets. It is the exception contained in Section 43 of the 1981 Act, removing a number of the difficulties in the case of private companies, which has made it easier to use a company's assets as security in funding a buy-out. Even so, the problems in agreeing securities noted above still need to be borne in mind.

ii) The Financial Package

There are a large, and increasing, number of sources from which the buy-out may be funded. Typically, finance may be obtained, often in combination, from the management, the employees, the former owners, government funds and most importantly from one or a consortium of financial institutions. The precise combination of these sources of finance will depend on the size and type of buy-out. Management will always be expected to invest some of their own funds which apart from giving them an equity stake is viewed as an important means of testing and sharpening their commitment to the success of the venture.

Most financial institutions claim that they tailor the financial structure to the circumstances surrounding each individual deal. This claim is true within limits. That is to say, the institutions vary in their emphasis on the proportion of loan, preference shares or ordinary shares in the financing arrangement. In addition, the type of structure adopted will also depend upon the perceived risk involved, the size of the deals and the time horizon that an institution envisages for its investment in a buy-out.

Some of the leading institutions in financing buy-outs are shown in Table 2.3. It is clear that ICFC is the market leader with a tendency to specialise in smaller buy-outs, although Moracrest and CIN also have particular interests at the lower

TABLE 2.3
Examples of Financing Institutions and Management Buy-outs Completed

Institution	1981 No	1981 Average Size	1982 No	1982 Average Size
Barclays Development Capital	4	2.75	3	2.00
Candover Investments	5	6.18	2	8.07
Coal Board Pension Fund (CIN)	2	na	6	0.63
Citicorp	7	0.47	5	3.04
County Bank	16	0.38	13	1.09
ICFC	80	0.50	85	0.50
Midland Equity (Moracrest)	13	0.40	13	0.52

NB: The Institutions and deals represented in this table are meant to be illustrative of the sizes of buy-outs looked for by different financiers. The information presented must not be taken as an exhaustive survey of the market place. The deals reported are where the named institution was the leader in setting-up and financing the buy-out. During 1983 and 1984 the number of institutions offering to support buy-outs has extended both within the traditional financial sector, through BES funds, to County Councils. The choice open to prospective purchasers is now wider than ever.

end of the market. Moracrest, which is jointly owned by Midland Bank, British Gas Central Pension Schemes and the Prudential Assurance Company invests in buy-outs in the form of equity finance and has a policy of confining its investment to a minority stake. ICFC on the other hand tends to prefer to lend loan capital with a supplementary minority equity stake. The case of CIN is interesting as its buy-out activity tends to focus on opportunities in mining areas. County Bank are another institution which predominantly prefers to finance deals where their major financial input is debt capital. Candover Investments tends to specialise in the larger buy-outs concentrating on putting together syndicates of institutions with itself contributing a minor share of the finance and looking for a USM or full stock market listing for the buy-out within five years. Barclays Development Capital tends towards the larger deals and was the leading institution behind the NFC and British Victaulic buy-

Practical Aspects of Management Buy-outs

outs. All the institutions named here are likely to syndicate larger deals and ICFC and County Bank in particular are likely to syndicate deals where the equity stake, were they to finance the buy-out on their own, would be above about thirty per cent. Increasingly deals tend to be syndicated, which makes it difficult to determine precisely the extent of buy-out activity and the numbers of buy-outs in which a particular institution was the leader. In addition, the passing of the Companies Act 1981 has meant that more buy-outs are funded by loan capital from the clearing banks, as the Act makes it easier for them to take a charge on the assets. Besides the types of institutions already named local authority enterprise boards are increasingly becoming involved in backing management buy-outs. The tendency has been for deals to be arranged from receivership or in declining industries. For example, the West Yorkshire Enterprise Board joined with Guidehouse merchant bank in financing the buy-out of Keighley Foundries from BL-Austin-Rover. The danger in these cases is that deals may be clouded by political and local employment issues with less regard to the underlying commercial viability. A financial institution contemplating syndication with an Enterprise Board would need to reassure itself as to the potential viability of such a buy-out.

Returning to the issue of the form of financial structure adopted in any particulat deal, it is necessary to be more precise about the options available. Whether a deal is more equity or loan biased has different implications for the annual inescapable commitment of repayments to the providers of finance. On the face of it the choice is simple. A package biased towards loan funding means regular fixed payments, whilst that biased towards equity means dividends are liable to be paid only when profits are being earned. However, in practice, the position may not be quite so straightforward.

The main sources of finance used in buy-outs are summarised in Table 2.4, together with the direction of increasing risk. In the event of failure it is the ordinary shareholders as the proprietors of the company who suffer the greatest risk of loss. Cumulative shares mean that unpaid dividends must be carried forward and made up out of future profits before any distributions can be made to shareholders further up the hierarchy. Convertible shares and debentures may be converted at a later date to ordinary shares upon agreement by the ordinary

33

TABLE 2.4
Ranking of Main Sources of Finance

RISK	Source
↑ Direction of Increasing Risk	Ordinary Shares
	Deferred Ordinary Shares
	Cumulative Convertible Redeemable Participative Preferred Ordinary Shares
	Cumulative Convertible Redeemable Participative Preference Shares
	Redeemable Preference Shares
	Unsecured Loan or Debenture
	Secured Loan or Debenture

shareholders. Redeemable shares may be repaid at a given date at par or at a premium. Participative shares are entitled to an additional dividend in certain circumstances. It is unlikely that any given company's financial structure will possess all of the sources of finance shown in Table 2.4. Given the nature of buy-outs it is usual for secured and unsecured loans to provide the bulk of funding, with this source being shared with preference shares or preferred ordinary shares in cases where the financial institutions involved emphasise this type of funding. Though there is a multiplicity of ways in which the deal may be structured it is rare for the financing institution to hold straight ordinary shares. Usually shares will be of the cumulative convertible, redeemable, participative types. Although the burden of payments to the provider of finance whilst profits are not being earned, is reduced, unlike debt finance, these types of shares can carry quite a sting in the tail as the following example of the conditions attached to such finance shows:

> 'The Preferred Ordinary shares are entitled to a fixed cumulative cash dividend each year of ten per cent of the total subscription price, payable half yearly, with one year's grace.

The Preferred Ordinary shares are also entitled to a cumulative cash dividend each year of such sum (if any) as when added to the fixed cash dividend shall equal six per cent of the net pre-tax profit of the company.

Thereafter, subject to the payment of a dividend on each ordinary share equal to the aggregate amount paid on each preferred ordinary share dividends are to be payable on both classes as if they were of the same class.'

One of the over-riding problems has been that in a number of cases management teams have not been prepared to accept the kind of reduction in their equity stake which would be a consequence of an appropriate capital structure. Such reluctance to accept equity dilution is a common occurrence in smaller companies.

Though these are the main sources of finance others may be used in some circumstances for 'topping-up' purposes. Government grants, made under the provisions of the Industry Act 1972, or local authority grants may be available under certain circumstances, especially for buy-outs on receivership. Indeed, one company in this study was refused loan funding by the local authority because the risk was thought to be too high but was given a grant by the same body. The buy-out turned out to be one of the most successful we have encountered. One of the problems with some of the early buy-outs was a lack of awareness on the part of managers buying-out and those administering the schemes as to precisely what was available. Some buy-outs have received part of their finance with the support of the loan guarantee scheme. The premium charged can make this type of finance expensive but at the margin it may make the difference between a deal going through or not. Smaller buy-outs come within the scope of many of the government's initiatives on small businesses, though problems may arise in identifying what is available and the speed at which it can be obtained. Speed of access to funds always seems to be important and is also a problem with finance that may be available from the EEC or the ECSC.

One recent innovation in financing buy-outs has been to use funds set-up under the Government's Business Expansion Scheme (BES) which provides for tax relief to subscribers to such funds. The BES was introduced in the Finance Act 1983 to encourage more new equity investment in a variety of unquoted companies. In a management buy-out through share purchase shares simply change hands without new equity funds being raised. One way of circumventing this problem has been to arrange a large overdraft, use it to purchase the target company and subsequently use BES funds to repay borrowings. Such deals have to receive qualifying company clearance from the Inland Revenue and the vendor must not receive directly the proceeds from any new equity raised. From the point of view of management buying-out, BES funding, because of the tax relief available, may allow a competitor to be outbid, but because the funding is equity-based management's equity stake may be very limited.

The remaining important sources of funding for buy-outs are the company's employees and its parent. In many buy-outs, from a parent still trading, the necessity for secrecy in negotiations makes it impossible for employees as a body to be involved in the initial funding although employees' redundancy payments have been used in some instances of buy-outs from receivership. However, this possibility has been limited by the Transfer of Undertakings (Protection of Employment) Regulations 1981 which were designed to protect employees from unfair dismissal on the change of ownership. It is now difficult for a break in employment to be created which would entitle the employee to a redundancy payment which could be invested in the business. Where this problem arises it may thus be necessary to adjust the purchase price of the company accordingly. Where redundancy payments would not be available in any case, as in buy-outs on divestment or retirement, lack of personal resources limit the employees' ability to buy shares in or make loans to the company for which they work. However, the Companies Act 1981, provides for companies to make loans to their employees in order that they may purchase shares. This change was particularly important in NFC, where the deal was delayed until the Act was passed so that advantage could be taken of its provisions. Employee share ownership has also been made more attractive by the introduction of tax relief on loans taken out by employees to buy shares. The initial requirement was that qualifying companies must be at least seventy-five per cent employee controlled, though this has been reduced to fifty per cent in the Finance Act 1984. However, punitive taxation rates still remain which may hinder a number of potential employee buy-outs. For example, it is often the case that the vendors require that the marketability of shares is restricted so as to prevent a takeover. In these circumstances, an income tax surcharge can arise on the increase in value of the shares in a period of up to seven years.(17)

Where employees have not been given the opportunity to purchase shares at the time of the buy-out it may be possible to extend share ownership to them at a later stage through share incentives schemes or share option schemes as in other conventional companies. The attractiveness of such schemes from a personal taxation point of view was increased in the Finance Act 1984.

An increasingly common method of including employee shares is for a transfer of ownership to be structured as a cooperative. Such conversion cooperatives are beyond the scope of this book and are dealt with in detail elsewhere.(18)

Finally, it is possible in some deals that the ex-parent company will provide finance, though often this may take the form of accepting payment spread over a number of years.

In those fairly rare cases where the former parent maintains a long-term equity stake the danger of parental interference in decision-making may arise, especially if trading relationships exist with the former subsidiary. Such interference may inhibit the ability of management to diversify customer or supplier relationships away from dependence on the former parent. However, in some cases, the link may be beneficial at least in the short-term, in that a fairly new subsidiary with a developing product line can obtain a range of parental support and a level of finance which may not be available externally. Moreover, it may provide the only means by which management can obtain a substantial equity stake in the business for which they work.(19)

As regards short-term finance, an overdraft arrangement is likely to be employed in most cases. Alternatively, or in addition, a factoring arrangement may be insisted upon, leasing of machinery and vehicles or a sale and lease-back transaction.(20)

VI. CONCLUSIONS

The management buy-out market place is fast-moving and requires many complex legal, financial and taxation issues to be taken into account for a buy-out deal to be successfully completed. The closeness of the management team to both the target company and the vendor means that a new dimension is added to the already complex procedures which must be completed in order to effect a sale. The purchase needs to be taken not in a state of euphoria over the opportunity to buy one's own company but in the light of cold calculated financial reality. Some aspects of this reality have been outlined in this chapter in a manner which emphasises the range of entrepreneurial skills which the buy-out team must possess if the deal is to lead to a successful company. Just how these factors translate into practice is reported in Chapters four to eight where the results of a survey of management buy-outs are presented. The following chapter discusses the theoretical economic issues which surround management buy-outs.

FURTHER INFORMATION

Whilst not intended to be exhaustive, the following list provides some practical sources of information for those contemplating a management buy-out:

I. General Brochures

   i) 'The Management Buy-out', 2nd Edn, Spicer and Pegler Chartered Accountants, February 1984.
   ii) 'Management Buy-outs', Price Waterhouse Chartered Accountants.

In addition most of the other large accounting firms also publish a brochure on management buy-outs. Brochures available from any branch office.

   iii) 'Management Buy-outs', Investors in Industry (ICFC) - available from any regional office.
   iv) Moracrest Investments Ltd (Midland Bank Equity), 'Management Buy-outs'.

In addition, most of the equity arms of the major clearing banks also publish brochures on management buy-outs, as do other institutions interested in this area e.g. Candover Investments, CIN etc.

Practical Aspects of Management Buy-outs

II. Detailed Guides

- J.P. Hardman and M.R. Young: 'Management Buy-outs', Accountants Digest No. 133, Spring 1983.
  Written by accountants, mainly for accountants, but a concise and comprehensive guide to all practical issues.
- R.V. Arnfield, B. Chiplin, D.M. Wright and M.G. Jarrett: 'Management Buy-outs Corporate Trend for the 80's?', Nottingham University, Dept Industrial Economics, 1981.
  Proceeds of the First National Conference on Management Buy-outs. Contains very useful case material as told from the viewpoint of the management themselves.
- L.R. Blackstone et al: 'Management Buy-outs', Economist Intelligence Unit, Special Report No. 115 (1984). Update of an earlier EIU report. Contains practical guidelines, some survey results of management buy-out funding institutions and a list of the institutions interested in financing buy-outs together with their particular focusses.
- Accountancy 'Special Feature on Management Buy-outs', December 1981.

NOTES

1. See J. Coyne and M. Wright: 'Staff Buy-outs and the Privatisation of Nationalised Industries', University of Nottingham, Dept Industrial Economics, Discussion Paper, May 1982.
2. For British Airways, Sealink and Jaguar there have been various newspaper reports and questions in Parliament.
3. See J. Aylen: 'Prospects for Steel', Lloyds Bank Review, April 1984.
4. See e.g. I. Owen: 'Tebbit Rules out NFC-style Staff Buy-out at Jaguar', Financial Times, 1.3.84.
5. It is not appropriate to deal with the rather specialised nature of this kind of buy-out in any further detail here. For detailed treatment of the issues and the cases of British Victaulic, British Transport Hotels and Sealink, see A. Bruce: 'Divestment from State Enterprises' in M. Wright and J. Coyne (Eds), Divestments and Strategic Change, Philip Allan, forthcoming.
6. See K.R. Harrigan, Strategies for Declining

39

7. *Businesses*, Lexington, 1980.
   See N. Wallner: '*The Leveraged Buy-out Manual*', La Jolla, California, The Wallner Company, 1980, p. 60.
8. For details see Chapter 7.
9. 'Progress Foundry', *in* R.V. Arnfield *et al*: *Management Buy-outs: Corporate Trend for the 80's?* Nottingham University, Dept of Industrial Economics, 1981.
10. R. Maugham: 'Fashioning a New Image', *Financial Times*, 5.10.83, M. Brown: 'Family is Back in Step', *Sunday Times*, 18.9.83.
11. D. Churchill: 'Buy-out Proposal, Seeks to Tailor Fresh Image for Retail Chains', *Financial Times*, 9.9.83.
12. 'The Management Buy-outs', 2nd Edition, *Spicer and Pegler Chartered Accountants*, 1984.
13. For an excellent summary of the process of negotiating a buy-out from the intermediary's viewpoint see D.S. Haggett: 'Negotiating the Deal', *in* R.V. Arnfield *et al.*, *op. cit.*
14. J.P. Hardman and M.R. Young: 'Management Buy-outs', *Accountants Digest*, No. 133, Spring 1983.
15. See T. Dickson: 'A Growing Force, but the Price is Getting Steeper', *Financial Times*, 13.3.84.
16. See e.g. R.V. Arnfield *et al.*, *op. cit.*, p. 45.
17. See Deloitte, Haskins and Sells: *The Budget*, March 1984: *Personal Tax Supplement*, 1984.
18. See N. Wilson: 'Conversion Cooperatives', *in* M. Wright and J. Coyne (eds) *op. cit.*
19. These kinds of spin-offs of subsidiaries with products with a high growth potential but which are peripheral to the parent's interests have been common in the USA; see e.g. S. Sabin: 'At Nuclepore, They Don't Work For GE Anymore', *Fortune*, December 1983.
20. See J. Coyne and M. Wright: 'Short-term Finance and the Factoring Decision', *Management Accounting*, April 1984, for discussion of when factoring may be an appropriate short-term financial source.

Chapter 3

ECONOMIC ASPECTS OF MANAGEMENT BUY-OUTS

I. INTRODUCTION

The study of management buy-outs can make a contribution to a number of major debates within the field of economics. Study of the act of buying-out itself, and examination of the pre and post buy-out record of the firms involved provides a rich source of information from which to address these issues. This chapter outlines some of these debates and through an examination of current thought identifies those aspects which the study of buy-outs may elucidate, and places the buy-out concept in context. It is difficult at such an early stage in the life of the 111 buy-outs in this study to form any definite conclusions but a picture is beginning to emerge which enables some perspective to be given to the issues involved.

There are four predominantly 'economic' questions which are of direct relevance to this study and into which it is possible to integrate the distinctive contribution which the buy-out phenomenon may offer.

- Evolution of the Economy - where buy-outs fit into the evolution of firms and industrial economies.
- Entrepreneurship - the role of the entrepreneur in firms, the economy and the buy-out.
- Efficiency and Competitiveness - what is necessary for efficiency and how buy-outs can contribute.
- The Firm, The Market and Organisation - how the buy-out can exist alone and what organisational forms may spawn them.

These four broad categories encompass a wide range of ideas and topics so treatment here is necessarily selective from an extensive literature. Each of the debates is examined in turn with the implications for buy-outs considered as appropriate. appropriate.

II. EVOLUTION OF THE ECONOMY

The buy-out can be viewed as a product of the economy in which it emerges. Whilst the immediate pressures which lead to a company being sold come from within there is little doubt that the general circumstances prevailing in the economy are important in determining the environment which causes the sale to emerge. The existence of the buy-out phenomenon may be one aspect of the maturity of an economy which is adapting to particular events. There are two distinct sets of factors which are of importance: first, the general economic climate, possibly affected by government policy, which produces the need to rationalise, adapt, or readjust on the part of those purchases arising from divestment, or the bankruptcies which lead to those purchases from receivership, either of the parent company or the target company bought out. The fourth private sector category used in this study - buy-out on retirement of previous owners - may be expected to be more independent of the economic climate and related more to the age of existing owners although there will be a secondary influence on the decision to go early or delay exit. The second important set of factors concern the specific elements of government policy and institutional support which makes it either easier or more difficult, at certain periods, to effect particular kinds of ownership transfer. So we may expect buy-outs, in aggregate, to be related to general factors which lead firms to seek to adapt, thus creating opportunities for changes of ownership of all kinds, and secondly, to those specific aspects of government policy either philosophical, ideological or financial which favour managers seeking to buy-out their own company. These factors may explain in large part why we observe different cycles of economic adjustment, and different forms of adaptation in countries seemingly broadly similar in industrial structure and performance. Thus, for the late 1970s and early 1980s the buy-out route of ownership change was a specifically UK phenomenon no doubt encouraged by the depth of the UK recession which began slightly ahead of our Western European partners, and encouraged by the ideological preference for, and attention given to, independent small business by the current government.(1) Leverage buy-outs in the United States, a phenomenon not dissimilar to the buy-out in the UK in terms of institutional funding and a new management equity stake and high degree of control, have been a part of the US business scene for much longer, and the peak of their fashion, the late 1970s now seems to have passed with only one major US bank, Citibank, still actively seeking to promote leverage buy-outs in the States.(2) There is some evidence to indicate that the buy-out route is now becoming more prevalent in Germany and in France.(3) The formation of the "second marché" in France, which gives access to finance, and the possibility of a less expensive listing and market for equity in the way that the Unlisted Securities Market has done for the UK may well give a further boost to French activity.(4) Institutional factors such as the legal framework, the distribution of share ownership, and the development of venture capital markets all contribute to the differing European experience, and compounded with the preponderance of family interests in Italian business, have contributed to the non-emergence of buy-outs in Italy.(5)

The buy-out may therefore be seen as one aspect of the realignment of firms, as an economy evolves, and may emerge irrespective of national characteristics providing the underlying forces requiring firms to adjust are present. One aspect of the development of Western industrial economies which is common to all is the development of the public company with consequent divorce between the ownership and management of enterprises. Aspects of this divorce will be examined in more detail below but it is necessary to point out here that this divergence may have implications, in its ultimate development for the shape of the economy. Schumpeter noted as early as 1934 and developed in later work the idea that economies would develop until they were deminated by a small number of giant corporations each administered by large bureaucratic committees. The managerial classes would thus take over from owners of capital as the guiders of industry. These ideas of growth and corporatism perhaps seemed entirely (6) prophetic as the post war economy in the UK grew and subsequent merger booms led to greater concentration of industry. Attention was firmly placed on acquisition and merger activity in the economy, and was supported ideologically from within government where a general belief in economies of scale seemed to suggest that big was efficient and best, and the technical evidence on decreasing costs per unit as output was increased was extended throughout the totality of the multi-product firm. The scale of the phenomenon can be seen from the evidence on firm "deaths" during the late 1950s and 1960s. Up to 1950, if a firm ceased to exist it was most likely to be because of liquidation, but between 1954 and 1960, and for 1966-68 approximately 77% of deaths were caused by takeovers and a further 4% by mergers.(7) Between 1964 and 1970 a UK manufacturing firm had a one in three chance of being taken over during the period, with a peak of activity in the period 1965-1978.(8) The trends in corporate organisation, notwithstanding the monopolies and restrictive practices legislation, was towards large firms adding new growth through acquisition, very often of a diversifying nature leading to many conglomerate companies.(9)

This trend has been significantly reversed during the 1970s and into the 1980s and much of the buy-out activity may in fact be part of the reaction to this period of acquisitive activity. Many conglomerates are now dismantling and attention has been focussed on the divestment activities of UK companies rather than on their merger and acquisition activity.(10) The reaction has come partly as a result of the disappointment which many acquirers have felt at the profitability of the group post acquisition.(11) In other respects managerial diseconomies have emerged which have highlighted the difficulties in maintaining control of diverse wide spread conglomerates.(12) At the same time there has been a re-emergence of interest in the small firms' sector of the economy which has managed to arrest its decline and is now much more to the forefront of government thinking.(13) A new respectability has been given to the role of small firm proprietor, which for definitional purposes is generally taken to be the owner/manager of a company employing less than 200 people in manufacturing.(14) Under the guidance of the Minister for Small Firms the Government has introduced since 1979, coincidentally with the rise of the buy-out phenomenon a whole series of measures to assist the promotion of small firms including the easing of administrative procedures and the introduction of the Loan Guarantee Scheme.(15) Thus the combination of reaction to poor performance, the emergence of managerial diseconomies, and the more favourable climate for independent small business have all contributed to the role of the buy-out as part of the evolution of the structure of the economy.

III. ENTREPRENEURSHIP

Perhaps the over-riding characteristic necessary for the buy-out to take place, and for the new entity to trade successfully is the exercise of entrepreneurship. In the sample of companies discussed in this study the existence of entrepreneurial skills proved to be the prime determinant, and most important single element in the entire phenomenon. Entrepreneurship is worthy of closer attention to define precisely what it is, and how it contributes to the modern corporation. It is easy to think of entrepreneurship in terms of an individual entrepreneur - to associate the 'role' with a particular person who may then conform to some 'cameo' which society holds about such individuals. However, it is the role itself which is the vital element, and which requires the completion of certain functions within any firm if it is to survive and progress. It may be a collective role, where the outcome is a function of inputs by a group of people, central to an organisation, who exercise the entrepreneurial judgements required. In this respect the "buy-out teams', in each of the companies, in this study may be considered to be the locus of entrepreneurship. Yet, in the majority of cases it is necessary to return in practice to the overriding role of one individual within each of the teams which suggests that individual qualities of personal leadership are an essential pre-requisite to the exercise of entrepreneurship.

The essential ingredients traditionally associated with entrepreneurship are the collection and application of assets and funding to produce a product or service in response to a perceived consumer demand, the assessment of, and acceptance of risk associated with the enterprise, and the guidance of change within organisation. From earliest writings a distinction has been made between skills of coordination and those of risk taking and it is only when the latter is also present that true entrepreneurship is found.(16) In the first effective 'job description' of the entrepreneur the skills of "superintendance and administration" are noted, and J.B. Say attributed

45

the rise of the industrial economy in Great Britain to "the wonderful practical skills of her entrepreneurs".(17) When viewed in relation to the modern corporation these elements of coordination "superintendance", risk taking and risk assessment, are perhaps the most essential feature of companies. Nevertheless, one has to look very hard indeed within the discipline of economics for a discussion of the contribution of the entrepreneur to the firm. In most models of the firm, which in the neo-classical paradigm is assumed to be profit maximising, there is no room for an entrepreneur because the solution to the economic problem has been reduced to a matter of mere calculation. This almost total neglect of entrepreneurship in many formal treatments by economists has possibly led to the widespread misunderstanding of the role of entrepreneurs within companies and their contribution to overall economic growth and prosperity.

One notable exception to this general statement is the work of the "Austrian School" of economists whose work, almost unbroken for over a century, has always placed the exercise of entrepreneurship at the forefront of their analysis in understanding the workings of market economies.(18) In the Austrian view, markets are not certain, equilibrating mechanisms. The market for any commodity is regarded as a "discovery process", to use Hayek's term, where the opportunity to make profit is there for all who are alert enough to observe the opportunities and to act upon them.(19) Markets are characterised by uncertainty, where it is necessary to exercise judgements, and to make decisions on the basis of expectations about the likely outcome of future events. Life is much more complicated in the real, and uncertain world of commerce, than the simple textbook models of economics would suggest.(20) As Israel Kirzner puts it:

'Making the "right" decision ... calls for far more than the correct mathematical calculation; it calls for a shrewd and wise assessment of the realities (both present and future) ... a correct decision calls for reading the situation correctly; it calls for recognising the true possibilities where none exist; it requires that the possibilities should not be overlooked, but that true limitations should not be overlooked either.'(21)

So, entrepreneurship is about alertness, and the exercise of judgement; it is about acting in response to opportunity.(22)

One final aspect of entrepreneurship which must be noted, and which naturally extends from alertness and perception is the role of entrepreneurship in the process of innovation; the bringing of new ideas to the market. Entrepreneurship consists not simply of reactive behaviour, but also pro-active. Opportunity can be created by the introduction of a new product, the radical redesign of an existing product, or the development of new, and superior modes of production. Entrepreneurship is thereby the mechanism of change, and entrepreneurs are innovators. This view predominates in the work of Schumpeter where it possibly overshadows, detrimentally, the other aspects of the entrepreneur's role discussed here.(23) The entrepreneur, in a Schumpeterian sense is concerned with major changes in markets, yet much of the contribution of successful entrepreneurship in a day to day sense is in the effective observation of, and acting upon, small changes in markets.

When all these elements are combined it is possible to produce a comprehensive definition of entrepreneurship, which may also appear quite flattering to those individuals to whom it may be applied. It might certainly make one wonder why entrepreneurs are not held in higher esteem in society. The essential characteristics are of alertness, judgement and action; of skills of co-ordination and management; the ability to assess risks and the preparedness to take them, of perception, and determination; to be a force for change in business.

What incentive does any individual have for wishing to exercise entrepreneurial skills? The simple answer is the pursuit of profit and personal gain. When assessing the essential institutional characteristics which must exist within an economy in order to encourage the development of such skills it is generally recognised that the structure of personal incentives, and the ability to act, within the law, free from undue government interference are paramount. Whilst it is not beyond the individual entrepreneur to act in a benevolent or philanthropic way, the prime objective is the pursuit of a personal objective, or in the case of the 'buy-out team' a common objective.(24) Even in companies where the buy-out has also included a substantial involvement of the workforce the leaders of the buy-out team have often been at great pains to point out that personal gain, the opportunity to generate personal wealth, has been foremost in their minds, and has provided the essential incentive. As one, anonymous, member of a buy-out team put it:

'If the workers can benefit as a result of the buy-out then that's fine by me - but don't get me wrong. I saw this opportunity, and I wanted to do it for myself!'

If entrepreneurship requires alertness and responsiveness there first has to be a structure of incentives which makes it worth the individual's time looking in the first place.

A further aspect of entrepreneurial skills is their acquisition. Where does one 'learn' entrepreneurship? What kind of people become entrepreneurs?

Much of the work on the background of entrepreneurs has tended to focus on the creation and development of new small firms and to examine the professional and personal backgrounds of new firm founders. These entrepreneurs tend to come disproportionately from 'disadvantaged' groups,(25) being 'the non-conformist and the odd-man-out'(26) or from ethnic minority groups.(27) Small firms are much more likely to generate new small firm proprietors than large firms, an observation which has been found in both the UK and the United States.(28) In all studies the 'organisation man' who comes from a conventional large business background and has gained all his experience within the bureaucracy of a large company does not figure prominently at all. However, the buy-out entrepreneurs, particularly in those instances of buy-out on divestment, or where the parent is in receivership, are typically former 'organisation men' coming out from under the larger corporate umbrella for the first time.(29) The reasons usually put forward for their lack of prominence in previous studies are threefold; first, the security of employment provided by large companies during a relatively stable economic climate does not encourage individuals to go out and take risks; secondly, the division of labour within large corporations means that one individual may not be exposed to all the range of activities and skills necessary for entrepreneurial evaluation; and finally, that the remoteness of the entrepreneurial role in large companies does not allow learning by observation. It is noteworthy that the companies examined in this study are likely to have been managed previously in a relatively independent manner, but, even so, some vital functions, notably finance, were often missing and needed to be implanted post buy-out.

If the entrepreneur himself does not possess all the qualities essential to successful entrepreneurship then, providing he has organisational and delegation skills, he can complement his own abilities and cover for any deficiencies by the employment of persons delegated to fulfill particular tasks.(30) In this case, he must establish a means of delegation and a structure appropriate to the circumstances which ensure that his objectives are met. An alternative solution may be the assembly of a team, each member of which has a personal stake in the business and is in every sense a part of the entrepreneurial function. The incentives and delegation problem is set aside by broadening the function but the cost is that decisions by committee or by teams may be less efficient than when made by individuals.(31) The assembly of the buy-out team by the buy-out leader may be seen both as the exercise of one aspect of the leader's own entrepreneurial skill - to select complementary human assets - and a need to spread the entrepreneurial function either to make it more effective, to maximise the probability of commitment to success, or simply to spread the risks.

Entrepreneurship is thus a vital ingredient in the success of any firm, and is an important part of the economy under-represented in conventional economic analysis. It is probably more evident, and more critical than ever, in the case of management buy-outs where the group of entrepreneurial manager/owners are striking out on their own account for the first time.

IV. EFFICIENCY AND COMPETITIVENESS

It is self-evident that in order to be successful a company must produce products or services efficiently and price them competitively. However, it is how they become efficient, and under what conditions they have the incentive to seek efficiency, that is of concern here. There are many aspects of the pursuit of efficiency which encompass the co-ordination of resources, choice of appropriate technology, the management of inputs, marketing, etc. All is overlain by the understanding and implementation of the firm's objectives - does it wish to maximise profit, sales or growth, or is it simply content to attain 'satisfactory' levels of performance? Whilst all aspects, functional or objective are of importance in the management buy-out two specific aspects will be focussed upon here. First, the influence of ownership on the objectives of the firm and the potential consequences of a remarriage of ownership and control, including the role of the right to first claim on profit as an incentive, and, secondly, the need for flexibility in the use of resources.

i) Ownership and control
The relationship between ownership and control and the consequences of various distributions has been one of the most important debates within organisation theory since the publication of Berle and Mean's seminal work which showed that in 1929 of 200 large corporations which they studied in only 22 did any individual or identifiable group of persons control more than 50% of the voting shares.(32) This work, which challenged the standard treatment in economics of the coincidence of ownership and control led to consideration of the different objectives which particular groups, notably shareholders and managers, may have and how they may be reconciled. The extent of the divorce between ownership and control for the UK has been illustrated by Prais, who found that in 1972 in only 11 out of the top 100 firms did the directors' personal holdings exceed more than 10 per cent, and in only 27 did it exceed 2 per cent.(33) Given that ownership is distributed amongst shareholders but the company is managed by professional managers under the direction of the appointed board of directors how can the shareholders exercise control over the company to ensure that their objectives are met and what other control mechanisms exist? There are four issues which must be examined in answering this question. First, the proportion of the shareholding required for control may be quite small; second, a small proportion of the equity may still be sufficient to ensure that the managers' objectives are the same as the general body of shareholders; third, the rise of institutional shareholding may lead to more direct pressure from expert and active fund managers, even though they have traditionally been reluctant to interfere in the day-to-day management of companies in which they

Economic Aspects of Management Buy-outs

have a stake, and finally, the extent to which the takeover mechanism exerts indirect control.

Beed has suggested that between 1 to 5 per cent of the shareholding may be sufficient for control in large companies,(34) and boards of directors are quite stable despite small proportionate holdings,(35) which suggests that the power of boards of directors may be more complete than the simple figures suggest. This is particularly the case when proxy voting is considered, with the widespread practice of vesting the proxy vote in the hands of directors at shareholders annual meetings, which are in any event seldom well attended.(36) Where an individual manager's shareholding is a small proportion of the overall company shareholding it may nevertheless form a substantial portion of his personal wealth and the dividend he receives from his equity may be a significant part of his personal income. The essential role of the rights to profit and the need to effectively monitor company performance is developed in the work of Alchian and Demsetz.(37) In addition, the widespread use of stock option schemes may further reinforce the incentive significance of shareholdings however small.(38) It may not be necessary for the holding to be large at all for the incentive to be felt. One point of potential difference depends upon the wants of shareholders. It is suggested that because capital gains are taxed at lower marginal rates than unearned income the shareholder may prefer reinvestment to boost the share price, rather than dividend payment, to maximise the long-run capital gain. It is very difficult for owner/managers to act in the same way because a decision to sell from within the company, besides gradually diluting the manager's holding, could also spark off a downward movement for the shares in the market. Thus any gain on realisation may be matched by a loss in value of the paper still held if all the holding is not liquidated at once.(39)

These two issues are of importance to managers buying-out when the topic of equity stakes, equity dilution and the attentuation of control are discussed in negotiating the financial package. Managers on buy-out are naturally concerned that the benefits of the risks that they take, and the efforts which they put in should be rewarded by their possession of the maximum amount of equity possible. Many are unwilling to see dilution because it may lessen control, but more normally because they do not like to see the benefits of capital gain being taken by 'outsiders'. However, where the alternative is unrealistic gearing ratios and a high degree of indirect control, in so far as the need to meet interest and capital repayments often dictates short-term policy and at best constrains it, they may be well advised to spread the equity a little more widely and so be in a position to use cash generated for growth geared investment. In any event the equity held by the management does not have a ready market in that very few of the buy-outs have attained a listing. To July 1984 only two had attained full quotation on the London Stock Exchange (DPCE and Sarasota) although others were on the Unlisted Securities Market or funded through the Over The Counter Market. The incentive effect of shareholdings in the small owner/managed company is seldom an issue of concern as compared with the fear of limitation of control.

The increasing role of institutional shareholdings in companies has been the subject of much enquiry in the academic literature, and the institutions' involvement has intensified in the 1980s as the competitive environment has led to traditional bodies extending into new financial markets.(40) The holdings in UK companies by insurance companies and the like accounted for almost 42% of UK equity in 1970.(41) This proportion had risen to over 47% by 1975, had exceeded 50% in 1978, and was predicted to be more than 70% by 1990.(42) Besides the increase in activity in the purchase of quoted shares the 1980s has brought a much greater willingness to provide venture capital for smaller unquoted companies, sometimes for entirely new start-ups (where the high technology sector, electronic and biological, has been the favourite area), and particularly for the issue under investigation here, for management buy-outs. The insurance companies and pension funds have been particularly involved, almost exclusively as part of syndicated deals, in the funding of buy-outs discussed in this study. In the buy-outs there has been no indication whatsoever that these institutional investors have so far tried to exercise managerial control but the managers have felt that they could go to the institutions for advice if necessary. In a number of cases sizeable external shareholdings by the institutions have led to a non-executive directorship at the nomination of the lender.

Finally, for control there is the general observation that if efficient capital markets exist

Economic Aspects of Management Buy-outs

then the takeover mechanism, whereby the value of inefficient companies falls and they are taken over by other companies with the managers responsible for the poor performance being replaced, should always ensure that the shareholders' wishes guide management action. For the control to be effective requires that markets approach perfection, that shares are traded and that potential purchasers are alert to opportunity. The markets in reality are seldom completely efficient so that wide discrepancies may be necessary to trigger change.(43) The resultant effect is that the discipline provided by the mechanism is weak.(44) Singh has observed from his major study that it is almost impossible to distinguish, a priori, from performance indices alone, between takeover predators and victims.(45) In a similar test Kuehn also found it difficult to distinguish predators and victims (46) though Firth has noted that share price performance of the two groups does vary in the period before the takeover date.(47) Singh concludes that the safest companies tend to be the largest irrespective of performance. Size is therefore an important factor in remaining independent.

Buy-outs are at present somewhat outside this issue although as more come to the market then they will face very real threats from larger predator companies. Quite surprisingly of the companies in this study it is the company looking to be taken over that has been more evident rather than looking to defend itself from a bid. In one company in particular the leader of the buy-out team saw takeover as advantageous in three respects; it enabled early liquidation of equity for the buy-out team without becoming a quoted company, it would remove the onerous debt provisions, and it would provide opportunity for managerial development for the more talented executives.

ii) Flexibility
The contribution to the firm of resource flexibility can be quite considerable. Whenever a company wishes to operate efficiently it must use all available assets optimally and thus must ensure that there is the minimum amount of 'down time' per unit of output. The managers in small firms, and the majority of buy-outs in this study come into that category, must also be flexible themselves in their ability to contribute to a number of functional areas of the firm. It is quite natural when selecting a piece of capital equipment to assess its

53

full range of capabilities and evaluate its contribution in that light. A decision to purchase can be made in the full knowledge that if required to perform to those specifications the capital will do so. Management has not always been allowed the same flexibility in its use of organised labour. Individuals, skilled in one particular task may be reluctant to perform other jobs required by management, and trade unions will defend vigorously negotiated job boundaries and demarcation.(48) Trade unions may thus affect the productivity of companies through the application of these restrictive practices.(49) It generally requires some major change in the management-union relationship to fundamentally alter the working practices and many managements have been unwilling in the past to engage the unions in direct confrontation on these issues.(50)

In all three aspects of flexibility - managerial, use of capital and use of labour the buy-out has effected improvements. The specific labour relations changes are discussed in Chapter 6 in greater detail but suffice it to say here that many companies have made significant improvements in labour flexibility without the wholesale removal of trade union representation. The nature of the relationship has changed but the mechanics of representation remain. Such gains as quality control, job boundaries widening, and absorbing supervision into productive jobs, have been made.

V. THE FIRM/THE MARKET/ORGANISATION

The buy-out produces a 'new', independent owner managed company in many cases trading for the first time free from the parent. In other cases the bought-out company may be returning to independence having previously been taken over by a parent (as in the case of DPCE, and Dennis and Robinson in Chapter 8). It is therefore pertinent to examine in a little detail precisely what is required for a firm to exist, and how trading relationships may be affected by such ownership transfers. It is necessary therefore to touch upon the nature of the firm, integration, diversification, conglomeration and the appropriate organisation form.

The conditions under which a firm can exist were first outlined in a seminal paper by R.H. Coase.(51) He examined the allocative role of the price mechanism to contrast the market with the internal organisation of a company as an allocator of resources. The price mechanism is not costless, exchanges must be contracted for, transfers may take time, and information is imperfect. Under certain circumstances the cost of using the market would exceed internal costs and so those activities would be brought into the firm. Thus, the optimal firm is a collection of interrelated operations which can be more economically conducted by organisational decision making than by the use of the market. The ideas of Coase have been much developed in subsequent work without ever moving from this fundamental concept - if it is cheaper to buy in than to organise internally - use the market. Williamson has fleshed out the analysis by distinguishing the various types of transactions involved under conditions of uncertainty about the future.(52) This transactions cost analysis emphasises also the strategic nature of certain decisions to organise internally where the firm is ensuring supplies into the future at each stage of a vertical process. Judgements must be made on the strategic importance of these uncertainties and priced in the analysis.

Elements of this approach are invariably found in the decision to buy-out where a divestment is involved. The potential vendor must assure himself of the peripheral nature of the activity to his main business and that he is not releasing any element which will either increase the costs of operations remaining, lead to the interruption of strategically important supplies, or offer competition to products and services which remain with the parent. One would expect to observe buy-outs taking place which satisfy the transactions cost approach and that where trading relationships continue between the ex-parent and the newly bought-out company we would expect both to attempt to reduce dependence, and for the buyer of resources in the medium-term at least to require strict contracts. These issues are taken up for this study in Chapter 7.

One reason for transaction costs being sufficiently high internally for the company to be offered for sale is the existence of diseconomies in managing large, diverse organisations. The costs of management are crucial.(54) We need to ask under what conditions these diseconomies may arise in order to suggest the type of parent organisation which may generate buy-outs. The literature on appropriate organisational forms is both extensive and controversial and does not warrant full

55

exposition here.(55) What we may expect to see from buy-outs is a greater tendency for them to arise from diverse parents who have previously engaged in widespread acquisitive activity. A previously hierarchical control form may have generated the conditions of asymmetry in information which leads the centre to undervalue an operating division although a holding company or matrix management structure leads to the existence of an almost complete management team already 'in situ' and with profit responsibility.

The concept of asymmetry of information is useful in understanding how the opportunity to buy-out may arise from different valuations of the assets. In any bargaining relationship the possession of information is an important weapon with the advantage in the hands of those with most information. The consequences of an uneven distribution in the market has been explored extensively since the seminal article by Akerlof which succinctly placed the problem in context in a model analysing the purchase and sale of secondhand cars.(56) In insurance markets too there may be problems of market failure owing to this asymmetry as the bad risks force up the price and drive out the good.

Within the large firm there may be an uneven distribution of information about the markets in which products are sold, the techniques of production, the utilisation and opportunity cost of assets etc. Local management may be able to disguise any operational inadequacies and inefficiencies from the centre to the extent that at group board level there may be a distorted view of the true value of a subsidiary's assets. Judgements may be made on balance sheet information which does not fully represent the potential of the assets. At the same time those managing in subsidiaries or divisions will not be party to the debate on strategic policy for the group as a whole which may nevertheless fundamentally affect them. In the normal course of business politics, as distinct from business efficiency, both may have very good reasons for wishing to maintain secrecy in their own spheres.

As a consequence of this potential misinformation and indeed distortion, a decision to divest a subsidiary for earning an inadequate return may be made notwithstanding that local management believe the potential exists to meet a target rate. In an instance such as this the value which local management place on the assets of a target company

Economic Aspects of Management Buy-outs

would exceed the value which central management place on it, and the basis for a mutually advantageous deal exists. The buy-out team is at an advantage because the asymmetry which exists internally would extend beyond the company's boundaries so that external predators may also be misinformed.

The costs of bringing the return on the assets up to an acceptable level may also be higher for an outside purchaser who would need to spend time on internal appraisal.(57) So asymmetry may benefit local management in providing the opportunity to purchase, and may mitigate against a competing takeover raid.

The broader the diversification of the parent the greater the probability that central management expertise will be spread thinly across operating subsidiaries, which may also increase the opportunities to buy-out. In these instances the age of the industry and products and the overall strategic thrust of the parent must be considered - they are unlikely to sell emergent products in 'fashionable' venture areas related to their overall strategic plan. (See the Smiths Industries - Dennis and Robinson case in Chapter 8.)

Overall diversification and conglomeration in one period may well generate the conditions which contribute to a spate of buy-outs in a later period as companies disentangle themselves.(58) The buy-out provides an extra option in this process of divestment and may offer certain advantages to the parent as has been discussed in Chapter 2. For the business bought-out the act may provide the necessary spur to the pursuit of efficiency which had been less evident in the mature firm. Indeed it may well be that the process conforms very closely to the life cycle model of growth maximisation and manager welfare outlined by Mueller.(59) Whilst the traditional life cycle models emphasis growth and acquisition the analysis is also susceptible to interpretation on conditions for sale.(60) We may also observe a compressed form of the life cycle in the bought-out firm in the period immediately following independence but although the first phases can be seen fairly clearly the phenomenon is not yet old enough for a comprehensive picture to emerge.

The bought-out firm is generally too small (average size 170 employees) for the choice of an appropriate organisational form to be much of a problem. A simple hierarchical model is followed by most with emphasis on flexibility of personnel.

57

Though the managerial aspects are dealt with elsewhere (Chapter 5) it is worth noting here that the companies do tend to exhibit a reaction against the management structure of their previous existence. They often identify aspects of the previous company which they seek to avoid at all costs in their new existence whether it be with respect to communication, employee involvement, financial procedures or whatever.

VI. CONCLUSIONS

The buy-out provides a distinct opportunity to examine evidence pertinent to a number of major issues in industrial economics and organisation theory. The act of buying-out can be seen to be consistent with many of the predictions of received economic analysis and indeed it may be something of a surprise that the phenomenon did not occur earlier. Study of the consequences of buy-out will provide a useful extension to our level of appreciation and understanding in the areas discussed. This study cannot begin to answer all the questions which it poses but will indicate the direction which future work might take.

NOTES

1. For a review of UK policy towards small firms as a whole see Curran J. and Stanworth J. 'The Small Firm in Britain: past, present and future' European Small Business Journal, 1, 1982.
2. See Wallner, N.: 'The Leveraged Buy-out Manual', The Wallner Company, 1980. Citibank information given in private communication.
3. The authors earlier writings on Management Buy-outs have generated interest in West Germany.
4. Fairley, A.: 'Second Marché is Walking in the Right Direction', Accountancy Age, 14 June 1984.
5. Baronchelli, A.: Communication from unpublished dissertation, European School of Management, Paris, Frankfurt, Oxford, 1984.
6. This is a line of argument found throughout Schumpeter's work. See for instance J.A. Schumpeter: 'Capitalism, Socialism and Democracy', Harper, New York, 1950.
7. For period to 1950 see Hart, P.E. and Prais, S.J.: 'The Analysis of Business Concentration: A

Statistical Approach', *Journal of the Royal Statistical Society*, Series A, Vol. 119 Part 2, 1956, and for the later period Singh, A.: 'Takeovers: their Relevance to the Stock Market and the Theory of the Firm', Cambridge, 1971.
8. Singh, A.: 'Takeovers, Economic Natural Selection, and the Theory of the Firm: Evidence from the Postwar United Kingdom Experience', *The Economic Journal*, Vol. 85 No. 339, 1975.
9. Utton, M.A.: 'Diversification and Competition', Cambridge University Press, Cambridge, 1979, and Utton, M.A.: 'Large Firm Diversification in British Manufacturing Industry', *Economic Journal*, 87, 1977.
10. Chiplin, B. and Wright, M.: 'Divestment and Structural Change in UK Industry', *National Westminster Bank Review*, February 1980.
11. Meeks, G.: 'Disappointing Marriage - A study of the Gains from Mergers, 'Cambridge 1977; and O'Brien, D.P.: 'Mergers - Time to Turn the Tide', *Lloyds Bank Review*, October 1978.
12. The existence of managerial diseconomies is recognised in most texts see e.g. Bates, J. and Parkinson J.R.: 'Business Economics', 3rd edn. Basil Blackwell, Oxford, 1982.
13. Bannock, G.: 'The Economics of Small Firms: Return from the Wilderness', Basil Blackwell, Oxford, 1981.
14. The definitions vary depending upon sector. For a summary of the small firms sector see Binks, M. and Coyne, J.: 'The Birth of Enterprise', Institute of Economic Affairs, Hobart Paper 98, April 1983.
15. For a discussion of the Loan Guarantee Scheme see Coyne J. and Wright M. 'Loan Guarantees: The First Year' *Accountancy*, Nov. 1982.
16. The essential characteristic of risk bearing appears first in the work of Cantillon, R.: 'Essai sur la nature du Commerce en Général', Fletcher Gyles, London 1755. The 'coordination' role of the entrepreneur forms the backbone of Mark Casson's 'The Entrepreneur', Martin Robertson, Oxford, 1982.
17. Say, J.B.: 'A Treatise on Political Economy', translated from the 4th edition of C.R. Prinsep, J.B. Lippincott and Co., Philadelphia, 1854, Vol. I, p.54.
18. The 'school' encompasses the work of Von Mises, Bohm Bawerk, Hayek and more recently Kirzner. For a review of 'Austrian' economics see S.C. Littlechild, 'The Fallacy of the Mixed Economy',

59

IEA. 1977
19. Hayek, F.A.: 'Competition as a Discovery Procedure', in 'New Studies in Philosophy, Politics and the History of Ideas', University of Chicago Press, Chicago, 1978.
20. As Frank Knight pointed out in his seminal work over 60 years ago - Knight, F.H.: 'Risk, Uncertainty, and Profit', Houghton Mifflin, Boston, 1921.
21. Kirzner, I.M.: 'The Primacy of Entrepreneurial Discovery', in 'Prime Mover of Progress: The Entrepreneur in Capitalism and Socialism', IEA Readings 23, Institute of Economic Affairs, London, 1980.
22. These themes are developed further in Kirzner, I.M.: 'Perception, Opportunity and Profit', University of Chicago Press, Chicago and London, 1979.
23. Schumpeter, J.A.: 'The Theory of Economic Development', OxfordUniversity Press, New York, 1934, re-issued by OUP, Oxford, 1961.
24. See Pearce, I.: 'Reforms Required for the Entrepreneur to Serve Public Policy', in 'Prime Mover of Progress', op cit.
25. Bannock G. and Doran, A.: 'Small Firms in Cities', EAG for Shell UK Ltd., London, 1978.
26. Bannock, G.: 'The Economics of Small Firms: Return from the Wilderness', Basil Blackwell, Oxford, 1981, p.38.
27. Roberts, E.B. and Wainer, H.A.: 'Some Characteristics of Technical Entrepreneurs', IEEE Transactions on Engineering Management, Vol. E.M.18, No.3, 1971.
28. See Johnson, P.S. and Cathcart, D.G.: 'The Manufacturing Firm and Regional Development: Some Evidence from the Northern Region', Regional Studies, Vol.13, 1979, for evidence on the UK and Cooper, A.C.: 'The Palo Alto Experience', Industrial Research, 1970, for the United States.
29. The specific details on background and experience of the buy-out teams in this study are given in Chapter 5.
30. Casson, M.R.: 'The Entrepreneur', Martin Robertson, Oxford, 1982.
31. These issues are examined in some detail in Casson, M.R. op cit which is a superb and comprehensive treatment of the entrepreneur.
32. Berle, A. and Means, G.: 'The Modern Corporation and Private Property', New York, 1932.
33. Prais, S.J.: 'The Evolution of Giant Firms in

Britain', Cambridge University Press, 1976. The evolution of this position is confirmed by comparison with Sargant Florence's findings. In his study of 102 large firms in 1936 the average percentage of equity owned by the directors was 3%, and in 1951 was 1½%. Sargant Florence, P. 'Ownership, Control and Success of Large Companies', London, 1961.
34. Beed, C.: 'The Separation of Ownership and Control', Journal of Economic Studies, Vol. 1, 1966.
35. Marris, R.: 'Economic Theory of Managerial Capitalism', MacMillan, London, 1964.
36. Midgley, K.: 'How Much Control Do Shareholders Exercise?' Lloyds Bank Review, October 1974. Midgley calculated the average attendance at less than 1% of shareholders.
37. Alchian, A. and Demsetz, H.: 'Production, Information Costs, and Economic Organisation', American Economic Review, 62, 1972; Williamson, O.E.: 'Hierarchical Control and Optimum Firm Size', Journal of Political Economy, 75, 1967.
38. Llewellyn, W.: "Management and Ownership in the Large Firm', Journal of Finance, 24, May 1969; see also Meeks, G. and Whittington, G.: 'Director's Pay, Growth, and Profitability', Journal of Industrial Economics, 24, No.1, September 1975.
39. The converse case of buying in to a corporation and mounting a takeover bid through share purchase and the effects on dilution and distribution of profit is discussed in Grossman, S. and Hart, O.: 'Takeover Bids, the Free Rider Problem, and the Theory of the Corporation', The Bell Journal of Economics, 11, 1980.
40. Note in particular the increased extent of the insurance companies' investment activity.
41. Moyle, J.: 'The Pattern of Ordinary Share Ownership 1957-70', D.A.E. Occasional Paper 31, CUP, Cambridge, 1971.
42. Prediction is from Dobbins, R. and Greenwood, M.J.: 'The Future Pattern of UK Share Ownership', Long Range Planning, 8, No.4, august 1975.
43. See Fama, E.: 'Efficient Capital Markets: A Review of Theory and Empirical Work', Journal of Finance, 25, 1970. An evaluation of the capital asset pricing model is contained in Jensen, M.C.: 'Capital Markets: Theory and Evidence', Bell Journal, 3, 1972.
44. Williamson illustrates this weakness in several

aspects of his work wither with respect to managerial discretion, (see Williamson, O.E.: 'The Economics of Discretionary Behaviour', Chicago, 1967) or organisational form (see Williamson, O.E.: 'Managerial Discretion, Organisation Form, and the Multi-Divisional Hypothesis'. in Marris, R. and Wood, R. (ed.): The Corporate Economy, London, 1971.
45. Singh, A.: 'Takeovers, Economic Natural Selection and the Theory of the Firm', Economic Journal, 85, 1975.
46. Kuehn, D.A.: 'Takeovers and the Theory of the Firm', London, 1975.
47. Firth, M.: 'The Profitability of Takeovers and Mergers', Economic Journal, 80, 1979.
48. This issue is treated in most basic textbooks on industrial relations.
49. Addison, J.T. and Barnett, A.H.: 'The Impact of Trade Unions on Productivity', British Journal of Industrial Relations', 20, 1982.
50. A fuller discussion of the effects of Trade Unions from a managerial standpoint is to be found in 'Trade Unions: Public Goods or Public Bads?' Institute of Economic Affairs, Readings 17, 1975, and Burton, J." 'The Trojan Horse', IEA.
51. Coase, R.H.: 'The Nature of the Firm', in AEA 'Readings in Price Theory', London, 1953, reprinted from Economica, 1937.
52. Williamson, O.E.: 'The Vertical Integration of Production: Market Failure Considerations', American Economic Review, Papers and Proceedings, 51, 1971.
53. On vertical integration and strategy see Penrose, E.: 'The Theory of the Growth of the Firm', Basil Blackwell, Oxford, 1959. See also Wright, M.: 'The Make Buy Decision and Managing Markets: The Case of Management Buy-outs', Mimeo, Industrial Economics, University of Nottingham, 1984.
54. Management costs were first introduced into economic analysis by Kaldor, N.: 'The Equilibrium of the Firm', Economic Journal, 44, 1934.
55. For a review see Caves, R.: 'Industrial Organisation, Corporate Strategy and Structure', Journal of Economic Literature, 18, 1980; and also Buck, T.W.: 'Institutions Beyond the M-Form', Industrial Economics Discussion Paper 91, University of Nottingham, 1984.
56. Akerlof, G.: 'The Market for Lemons: Qualitative

Uncertainty and the Market Mechanism', <u>Quarterly Journal of Economics</u>, 84, 1970.
57. Grossman, S. and Hart, O.: 'The Allocational Role of Takeover Bids in Markets with Asymmetric Information', <u>Department of Economics Mimeo</u>, University of Pennsylvania, 1979.
58. See Chiplin, B. and Wright, M., op. cit.
59. Mueller, D.C.: 'A Life Cycle Theory of the Firm', <u>Journal of Industrial Economics</u>', 20, 1972.
60. For a review see Marris, R. and Mueller, D.C.: 'The Corporation, Competition and the Invisible Hand', <u>Journal of Economic Literature</u>, 18, 1980.

Chapter 4

GENERAL CHARACTERISTICS OF MANAGEMENT BUY-OUTS

I. INTRODUCTION

The discussion of the practical and theoretical aspects of buy-outs in Chapters 2 and 3, respectively, has raised a number of empirical questions about what has been occurring in management buy-outs in general. In this and the remaining chapters an attempt is made to answer some of these questions. Here the more general demographic topics are dealt with.

The first section explains how the survey was carried out and analysed. The results that are presented in the remaining part of the chapter enable a general picture of buy-outs to be constructed. Specifically, an attempt is made to quantify answers to the following questions:

- What is the age distribution of buy-outs?
- What are the relative proportions of their sources?
- In which industries do buy-outs occur?
- Do buy-outs operate in narrow product areas or are they diversified, and if so to what extent?
- How big are management buy-outs, both in terms of price paid and employees and in relation to other firms?
- Where are management buy-outs located?

Each of these questions is examined in turn whilst subsequent chapters focus on what has been happening inside buy-outs in terms of management changes, industrial relations and financial and economic performance.

II. THE SURVEY

The results reported in this chapter and the rest of this book are based on a survey of management buy-outs carried out by the authors in the summer of 1983 onwards. The survey was conducted in two parts. First, a mailed questionnaire was sent to a sample of surviving buy-outs. Secondly, detailed case studies were undertaken of a sub-sample of these companies. From telephone surveys of the financial institutions and searches of the financial press, it has been estimated that up to the time that the sample for the survey was drawn (Spring 1983) 580 buy-outs had been completed.(1) There are no available statistics on the buy-outs which fail but it has been reported that of those financed by ICFC (the market leader) the current failure rate is one in ten.(2) Hence, the surviving population that the sample was drawn from was about 520. As relatively few buy-outs are reported in the Press, since many deals are rather sensitive, the financing institutions are the only effective source of the names and addresses of these companies. Accordingly, the financing institutions were approached and asked to supply contact names in their client companies. All agreed to contact their clients to ascertain whether they wished to participate in the study. Some institutions provided us with names and addresses, others preferred to mail the questionnaires direct so as to maintain confidentiality in cases where the client did not, after all, wish to take part. This procedure resulted in 191 questionnaires being sent out, with usable replies being received from 111 buy-outs, producing a response rate of 58.1 per cent without a reminder being administered. It should be noted that the main reasons that questionnaires were sent to only a minority of the buy-outs thought to have taken place were that many of the earliest buy-outs (pre-1981) were often not termed as such or had disappeared; secondly, some had received so much press attention that they had decided enough was enough and, thirdly, some were in a precarious position and did not wish to have attention drawn to the fact.

In assessing the reliability of the survey results, these caveats need to be set against the fact that no other remotely reliable source was available. Given the sensitivity of many buy-out deals, approaching those known buy-outs directly without the agreement and recommendation of the

65

institutions would very likely have produced a near zero response rate. Although we must stress that the buy-outs in our sample are survivors it is still of value to study these companies since it may provide insights into the types of problems that managers buying-out have to face and overcome if they are to succeed.

The second stage of the survey involved visits to twenty companies to discuss issues relating to the buy-out in more detail. These cases were chosen from our 111 respondents so as best to illustrate the kinds of changes and problems that had occurred.(3) Throughout the following chapters we draw upon this case study material to illustrate particular issues. Chapter 8 also reports some of the case material in full.

In addition to our sample of more conventional buy-outs, two employee buy-outs from nationalised industries, National Freight Consortium and the Victaulic Company, were also surveyed. The results for these two companies for the purpose of comparison and because of the interesting issues they highlight are presented in the Case Study chapter, but otherwise they are excluded from the rest of the survey material.

III. AGE DISTRIBUTION OF BUY-OUTS

As has already been noted in previous chapters official published information on ownership transfers in general is not very reliable, particularly for the sales of subsidiaries.(4) However, there are no officially published statistics on management buy-outs. A minority of buy-outs are reported in the Financial Times, but the absence of any systematic reporting, and a tendency for some deals to prefer a quiet transfer meant that it was necessary to obtain the figures for the first column of Table 4.1 from a survey of those institutions financing buy-outs. The institutions were asked to provide the number of buy-outs they had supported in each year in which they were the lead institution which was then checked to avoid double-counting. However, it became evident when the survey was being conducted that there was some ambiguity over which was the leading institution in certain deals; some regarding themselves as leader if they put the most money in, others if they put the consortium together. Hence, though the trend in buy-outs in Table 4.1 is very

General Characteristics of Management Buy-outs

TABLE 4.1

The Growth of Management Buy-outs

	Overall No.	No. in Survey Sample No.	%age
1967-1976	43	1[1]	0.9
1977	13	1	0.9
1978	23	2	1.8
1979	52	1	0.9
1980	107	14	12.6
1981	124	40	36.0
1982	170	37	33.3
1983 (estimated)	205	15[2]	13.6
TOTAL	737	111	100.0

Source: Authors' survey of the lending institutions and management buy-outs.

Notes: 1. 1976
2. First nine months

clear, the data must be regarded as broad estimates rather than precise numbers. The age distribution in our sample tends to under-represent a little the years prior to 1981. The main reasons for this problem are firstly, that in the earlier period many buy-outs were not termed as such and are thus difficult to identify precisely, and secondly, they are more likely to no longer exist as independent units since some will have been acquired or sold to other buyers and others will have gone into liquidation. (One buy-out that had been acquired was included in our survey and is reported in Chapter 8.)

As the majority of buy-outs have occurred in the last four years their experiences that we are able to report are necessarily short-term ones. The longer term effects of buy-outs still remain uncertain. However, the shorter time-scale does present the off-setting advantage that respondents are more likely to remember what has happened.

IV. SOURCE OF MANAGEMENT BUY-OUTS

It is important to analyse management buy-outs by their four main sources as they may be expected a priori to lead to different post-buy-out experience.

General Characteristics of Management Buy-outs

TABLE 4.2
Source of Management Buy-outs

Source	No.	%
- Independent Company in Receivership	5	4.5
- Parent Company in Receivership	15	13.5
- Parent Company Divesting a Subsidiary	68	61.3
- Previous Owner on Retirement	23	20.7
TOTAL	111	100.0

We might anticipate in particular that employment levels, profitability and sales growth would differ depending upon the bases from which the buy-out commenced. The relative magnitudes of each source, as represented in our sample, are shown in Table 4.2. As can be seen from the Table the main sources are buy-outs of independent companies from receivership, buy-outs of subsidiaries of parent companies either in receivership or still trading and buy-outs from companies where the previous owners wish to retire. Buy-outs from receivership provide opportunities for resurrection in firms that might otherwise have been completely closed. Less than a fifth of buy-outs in our sample were from receivership. It is possible, however, that in those companies divested an alternative course of action for parents may have been to close the subsidiary rather than offer it to an external purchaser had management not been prepared to buy it out. Clearly, though, of the large number of company closures which have taken place since 1978 few have been resurrected as management buy-outs. Leaving aside the serious obstacle placed by the rational desire of parent companies still trading to remove excess capacity in order to maintain their overall viability, there appears to be a serious need to consider more closely those cases which perhaps, with major restructuring, could continue. The number of buy-outs from receivership which were previously subsidiaries of larger companies is noteworthy in this context. It is evident that companies which are not profitable in a larger form may contain viable parts which are able to survive and succeed outside the restrictions imposed by a troubled parent.

However, the largest single source of the management buy-outs in our sample is from parent companies still trading divesting a subsidiary, for the kind of reasons that have been discussed in Chapters 2 and 3. In some of these cases the parent has, despite the sale of its subsidiary, been unable to avoid the inevitable and has subsequently gone into liquidation.

The proportion of buy-outs from owners retiring seems higher than might be expected. One reason for this result may be because only survivor buy-outs have been examined. A priori it would be expected that in these cases the owner is more likely to sell for reasons of age or personal health rather than the health of the company. In many of these cases the company may be converted into a workers' cooperative rather than remaining as a conventional capitalist firm.(5)

V. INDUSTRIES

The general impression that may be gleaned from reading those buy-outs reported in the Press is that they occur across a wide spread of industries. The evidence from our survey, reported in Table 4.3 provides some indication of the relative magnitude occurring in each industrial sector.

In the table, the main activity of each buy-out, as shown in the questionnaire, is allocated to the relevant 1980 Standard Industrial Classification CLASS (2-digit) headings. These class headings are then summarised for the broad industry Division headings. The 1980 SIC comprises ten Divisional headings which are then split into sixty class codes and then further sub-divided into product group (three-digit) and product (four-digit) classifications.

The main activities of the buy-outs in our sample are seen from the table to occur in seven out of the ten possible industrial divisions and in twenty-two out of the possible sixty 2-digit class codes.

The major divisions where buy-outs are absent are Agriculture, Forestry and Fishing; Energy and Water Supply and Other (mainly governmental and local) Services as might be expected.

General Characteristics of Management Buy-outs

TABLE 4.3

Industry Distribution of Management Buy-outs (Principal Activity)

2-digit Code (CLASS)	Description	No. of firms	%	No. of firms	%
22	Metal Manufacture	5	4.5		
24	Non-Metallic Mineral Product Manufacture	4	3.6		
25	Chemicals	3	2.7		
2 Manuf. Metals, Mineral Products and Chemicals				12	10.8
31	Other Metal Goods Manuf.	6	5.4		
32	Mechanical Engineering	13	11.8		
33	Manuf. of Office Machinery and Data Processing Equipment	5	4.5		
34	Electrical and Electronic Engineering	5	4.5		
35	Motor Vehicles and Parts	8	7.2		
37	Instrument Engineering	2	1.8		
3 Metal Goods, Engineering and Vehicles				39	35.2
42	Food, Drink, Tobacco	3	2.7		
43/44	Textiles	4	3.6		
45	Clothing and Footwear	4	3.6		
46	Timber and Wooden Furn.	6	5.4		
47	Paper, Printing, Publishing	10	9.0		

TABLE 4.3 *(continued)*

48	Processing of Rubber and Plastics	4	3.6		
4 Other Manufacturing Industries				31	27.9
50	Construction	6	5.4	6	5.4
61	Wholesale Distribution	8	7.2		
63	Commission Agents	1	0.9		
64/65	Retail Distribution	6	5.4		
6 Distribution, etc.				15	13.5
72	Transport	1	0.9	1	0.9
83	Business Services	4	3.6		
84	Hiring	3	2.7		
8 Finance and Business Services				7	6.3
TOTAL		111	100.0	111	100.0

The main product areas where buy-outs are more likely to occur are in metal goods and other manufacturing industries - in particular in mechanical engineering and printing and publishing. Other noteworthy areas are motor vehicle components, furniture, wholesale and retail distribution and other metal goods manufacture. It is also interesting to observe that buy-outs occur with some frequency in heavier metal industries such as foundrying as well as in industries concerned with the manufacture of electronic and computer equipment and the provision of computer services. There are thus not only viable opportunities for buy-outs in what are generally regarded as buoyant sectors of the economy, but profitable market niches also exist in those areas which have witnessed the demise of a great many traditional firms.(9)

The viability of a company depends very much upon the longer term prospects for the product being marketed. The greater the reliance on a single product the more vulnerable will be a company if its longer term market prospects are declining. The extent of diversification in buy-outs may therefore shed further light on their prospects for survival. Diversification may be considered along a continuum from broad to narrow spectrum diversification. Broad spectrum diversification occurs where a company produces goods or services in more than one industrial Division; narrow spectrum diversification is observed when goods and services are provided in more than one four-digit category (i.e. product group). Given the relatively small size of management buy-outs, it might be expected that the extent of diversification would be limited to narrow spectrum, if indeed it existed at all. The evidence from the survey is presented in Table 4.4

It is evident that where diversification does exist it predominantly takes the form of a spreading of interests into fairly closely related areas. However, the extent to which buy-outs do operate in more than one class (36.9 per cent) or division (25.2 per cent) is quite surprising. Further detailed examination of this question is not possible given the data available (for example, we have no information on the precise percentages accounted for by each product group within a firm). But there is a strong suggestion that many buy-outs are either substantially vertically integrated or engaged in conglomerate activities. For the 50.5 per cent of the buy-outs in our sample who were reliant on a single activity, the issue of broadening their

General Characteristics of Management Buy-outs

TABLE 4.4
Diversification in Management Buy-outs

No. of Industries involved in	Division (1-digit) No.	%	Class (2-digit) No.	%	Group (3-digit) No.	%	Activity (4-digit) No.	%
1	83	74.8	70	63.1	66	59.5	56	50.5
2	24	21.6	30	27.0	28	25.2	35	31.5
3	3	2.7	10	9.0	12	10.8	12	10.8
4 or more	1	0.9	1	0.9	5	4.5	8	7.2
TOTAL	111	100.0	111	100.0	111	100.0	111	100.0

TABLE 4.5
Number of Subsidiaries Bought-out

No. of Subsidiaries	No. of Firms	Percentage
1	77	69.4
2	14	12.6
3	4	3.6
4	6	5.4
5	3	2.7
6	3	2.7
8	1	0.9
More than 10	3	2.7
TOTAL	111	100.0

TABLE 4.6
Number of Sites Occupied

No. of Sites	Before Buy-out	After Buy-out
1	55	48
2	27	36
3	10	9
4	6	4
5-10	9	10
11+	4	4

product base may become an important one if survival in the long-term is to be assured.

A substantial majority of companies on buy-out were single entities usually occupying a single site (see Tables 4.5 and 4.6). But in approaching one third of cases more than one subsidiary was bought-out and in half of the cases the company occupied more than one site. Though some companies closed some of their sites there was a general tendency after the buy-out for the company to be located in more than one place. An important reason for this change is seen when acquisition and disposal activity is examined. Six companies disposed of parts of their activities whilst nineteen companies acquired interests in at least one other company following the change in ownership.

The discussion in this section thus suggests two very different types of buy-outs. First, those which are single activity and single entity. Second, those which are effectively small-groups of companies.

VI. SIZE

Management buy-outs differ from new small firms in that they do not face the problem of starting a business totally from scratch. Though certain of them have had to relocate or introduce management functions previously supplied by the parent (see Chapters 5 and 7), the market and the workforce at the very least already exist. However, the size of companies purchased by their managers may bring them more into line with established smaller firms.

There are a number of ways to measure size - for example, assets, turnover, employees, price paid etc. From the questionnaire survey it is only possible to measure the size of buy-outs by the price paid and their full-time employment at the time of purchase.

In many cases, the price paid for the company is a very sensitive issue for the management, especially if the assets were acquired at a substantial discount. When taken in conjunction with the gearing ratio it enables some estimate of the management team's personal wealth to be made. In order to avoid the serious possibility of widespread non-response the questionnaire asked only for the range in which the price fell to be identified. The price distribution is as shown in Table 4.7. Almost a half of firms cost less than half a million pounds, whilst less than five per cent cost over £5

General Characteristics of Management Buy-outs

TABLE 4.7
Price Paid to Purchase Company
(Current Prices)

Price Range (£)	No. of Firms	%
0-100,000	9	8.1
100,001-250,000	26	23.4
250,001-500,000	20	18.0
500-001-1,000,000	23	20.7
1,000,001-2,000,000	16	14.4
2,000,001-5,000,000	11	9.9
Over 5,000,000	5	4.5
Not stated	1	0.9
TOTAL	111	100.0

million. A size distribution of this nature is to be expected given the level of resources that are likely to be available to most managers. However, the possibilities available for varying the numbers in the management team, the size of the management team's equity stake, the gearing ratio and the number of financing institutions mean that some quite large companies can become candidates for management buy-outs. The correlations between these factors as shown by the survey results are dealt with in more detail in the next chapter. The number of employees in a company is not subject to the same sensitivity as price, and, given the numerous factors which can affect the price of a bought-out company, probably provide a more reliable indicator of size. The average number of employees, which is

TABLE 4.8
Size of Management Buy-outs (Full-time Employees)

	Before Buy-out	After Buy-out
Mean	171.84	159.24
Standard Deviation	174.5	181.5
Median	102.5	99.9
Minimum	6	9
Maximum	900	1,240
Range	894	1,231
Total Employment	18,903	17,517
Base	110	110

General Characteristics of Management Buy-outs

TABLE 4.9

Management Buy-out Size Distribution and UK Size Distribution Compared

Size of Companies by Number Employees	No. of Enterprises	%	No. of Employees	% of Total Employees
(i) *Management Buy-outs**				
1-99	51	46.4	2598	13.7
100-199	26	23.6	3754	19.9
200-499	25	22.7	7371	39.0
500-999	8	7.3	5180	27.4
1000+	-	-	-	-
TOTAL	110	100.0	18903	100.0

*At time of buy-out

(ii) *UK Manufacturing Enterprises (1979)*			(000s)	
1-99	84229	93.9	1137.8	17.5
100-199	2609	2.9	360.4	5.6
200-499	1543	1.7	474.9	7.3
500-999	609	0.7	425.3	6.6
1000+	751	0.8	4086.6	63.0
TOTAL	89741	100.0	6485.0	100.0

seen to fall substantially after the buy-out, hides a wide degree of dispersion in the size of buy-outs as may be gauged from the standard deviation and range shown in Table 4.8.

Whilst some 70 per cent of buy-outs (Table 4.9) fall within the generally accepted small category for manufacturing of having less than two hundred employees, the rest, accounting for two thirds, of buy-out employment, clearly do not. This distribution, though weighted towards the bottom end is considerably more even than for all manufacturing companies in general, as the Table shows, and for whom the average size of firm is only seventy-two employees.

The question of the size of management buy-outs as compared to all companies can also be analysed by industry. Table 4.10 provides such an analysis at the sector level of aggregation and also shows a broad indication of buy-out propensity by industry.

General Characteristics of Management Buy-outs

It is clear from Table 4.10 that the overall greater average size of management buy-outs already noted, also extends to the industry level. Only in chemicals, manufacture of office and data processing equipment, and motor vehicles and parts, are buy-outs on average smaller than companies as a whole.

As would have been expected the proportion of companies bought in a particular industry is very low indeed. However, it is noteworthy that the manufacture of office and data processing equipment industry shows a relatively high buy-out propensity.

VII. REGIONAL LOCATION

As may be seen from Table 4.11, although all government standard regions have experienced buy-outs, there is a very marked difference in the numbers occurring in each region.

However, in order to place any meaning on this distribution it is necessary to make a comparison with some measure of the overall distribution of industry in each region. Table 4.11 uses the regional stock of all companies to make the desired comparison. It is apparent that on this basis, a different picture emerges as to which regions seem to be under or over-represented in the number of management buy-outs. By inspection, the South East region is slightly under-represented, whereas the West Midlands and the South West in particular are greatly over-represented. Given the pattern of industry and the nature of closures in the West Midlands it is encouraging that this region is so well represented. For the South West, a minority of the management buy-outs are to be found in those areas most affected by unemployment.

The relatively low level of buy-out occurrence in the remaining regions may be partly attributable to the London-based location of the majority of the financial institutions. However, the principal reason, which has regional policy implications, may be an unwillingness by some parent companies in industries with large excess capacity to see management buy-outs as an acceptable form of restructuring. They may prefer instead to protect themselves by the removal of excess capacity through closure. In many cases this behaviour may involve a retreat from those parts of the country into which previous regional policies had forced them when their preference had been to expand nearer to their

77

General Characteristics of Management Buy-outs

TABLE 4.10

Management Buy-outs Compared with All Companies in Manufacturing Industry

2-Digit Code	Description	Average Employment Size MBOs	Average Employment Size All Companies	MBOs as Proportion of the Industry Companies	MBOs as Proportion of the Industry Employees
		(No.)	(No.)	(%)	
22	Metal Manufacture	215.6	165.5	0.24	0.31
23	Extraction	–	21.3	–	–
24	Non-metallic minerals	168.0	53.6	0.08	0.24
25	Chemicals	108.7	117.6	0.10	0.09
26	Man-made fibres	–	1035.5	–	–
Class 2 total		173.0	90.6	0.12	0.21
31	Other metal goods manufacture	124.7	39.4	0.05	0.15
32	Mechanical Engineering	229.7	55.3	0.07	0.28
33	Manufacture of Office Machinery and Data Processing Equipment	77.0	181.1	1.90	0.82
34	Electrical and Electronic Engineering	178.4	120.7	0.09	0.13
35	Motor Vehicles and Parts	169.5	203.1	0.33	0.28
36		–	210.8	–	–
37	Instrument Engineering	185.0	44.0	0.08	0.35
Class 3 total		175.9	74.6	0.09	0.23
41		–	90.5	–	–
42	Food, Drink, Tobacco	423.3	143.3	0.13	0.38
43/44	Textiles	141.3	102.5	0.10	0.14

TABLE 4.10 *(continued)*

45	Clothing and Footwear	365.0	42.5	0.04	0.35
46	Timber and Wooden Furniture	216.8	20.8	0.05	0.53
47	Paper, Printing, Publishing	152.2	38.8	0.07	0.29
48	Processing, Rubber and Plastics	259.8	70.6	0.11	0.40
49			30.5	–	–
	Class 4 Total	230.9	50.8	0.07	0.33

Source: Authors' Survey and Census of Production 1979.

General Characteristics of Management Buy-outs

TABLE 4.11

Management Buy-outs[1] and the
Stock of Companies[2] in the Regions

	MBO's		Stock of Companies	
	No.	%	No.	%
South East	36	32.7	408,000	35.8
East Anglia	1	0.9	35,200	3.1
South West	23	20.9	111,300	9.7
West Midlands	17	15.5	106,400	9.3
East Midlands	10	9.1	78,000	6.9
Yorkshire/Humberside	11	10.0	96,600	8.4
North West	3	2.7	122,600	10.8
North	1	0.9	48,300	4.2
Wales	2	1.8	55,200	4.8
Scotland	6	5.5	80,300	7.0
TOTAL	110	100.0	1,142,800	100.0

Source: Authors' survey of management buy-outs and A. Ganguly: 'Regional Distribution of Births and Deaths of Firms in the UK in 1980', British Business, 2 April 1982, p. 648.

Notes: 1. N. Ireland was omitted from our study, but management buy-outs are known to occur there, see G. Sargeant: 'The Management Buy-out as an Alternative Strategy: Some evidence from N. Ireland', Dept of Geography, Queen's University, Belfast, mimeo 1983. There were 111 companies in our sample, one did not declare its location.
2. Stock of companies in 1980, excluding agriculture.

headquarters in the Midlands and the South.

If we try to focus more sharply on problem areas for unemployment by identifying the number of buy-outs in Assisted Areas, we find that only 15 (13.5%) are in areas with this status.

VIII. CONCLUSIONS

This chapter has outlined the nature of the survey which forms the substance of this study and identified the pertinent characteristics of the bought-out companies. It is evident that the sample contains a very diverse group of companies in terms of size (however measured), industry, and regional location. The information presented adds weight to

General Characteristics of Management Buy-outs

the view that there is no typical management buy-out but a large number of aspects by which they may vary. Buy-outs are found in all of the Standard Industrial Classification groups 2 to 8, but with a preponderance in essentially manufacturing groups 3 and 4, in all regions, vary in size from 6 employees to over 900, and have varied considerably in their product diversity and acquisitive behaviour.

The next three chapters look within the companies in the sample and examine in turn the managerial aspects, the industrial relations issues, and overall performance.

NOTES

1. See Wright, M. and Jarrett, M.: 'New Initiatives in the Financing of Smaller Firms', National Westminster Bank Review, August 1982, and Coyne, J. and Wright, M.: 'Industrial Restructuring and Finance for Smaller Firms', Paper presented to EIASM, Brussels, May 1983.
2. See Brown, M.: 'Buy-outs Become Big Business', Sunday Times, 9.10.83. It is estimated that this rate may rise to one in five, which would still be below the one in three failure rate reported for new start-ups.
3. Neither the mailed questionnaire nor the case study checklist are reproduced here. Copies are available on request from the authors. The mailed questionnaire results were analysed on the University of Nottingham ICL 2906 Computer using the Statistical Package for the Social Sciences (SPSS).
4. See Chiplin, B. and Wright, M.: 'Divestment and Structural Change in UK Industry', National Westminster Bank Review, February 1980.
5. See Wilson, N.: 'Conversion Co-operatives', in Wright, M. and Coyne, J. (eds): Divestment and Strategic Change, Philip Allan, forthcoming 1985.
6. See Coyne, J. and Wright, M.: 'Buy-outs and British Industry', Lloyds Bank Review, October 1982.
7. See Porter, M.: 'Competitive Strategy", New York, The Free Press, 1980.

Chapter 5

MANAGERIAL ASPECTS OF MANAGEMENT BUY-OUTS

I. INTRODUCTION

The discussion of the general characteristics of buy-outs in the previous chapter has set the scene for an examination of their internal aspects. These are discussed in this chapter and the next two with the focus of attention here on management. In Chapter 6, employee and industrial relations are examined, followed in Chapter 7 by an appraisal of performance.

As with many other features of buy-outs, managerial aspects have hitherto been dealt with in various pen-pictures of how managers bought out the company.(1) These approaches have been most useful in drawing the attention of other managers considering buying their company to the problems they are likely to face in negotiating the deal. But, probably because of the newness of the phenomenon, there has been an almost total absence of detailed discussion on the management related changes that have followed the buy-out.(2) It is important to examine these changes for three principal reasons. First, to consider whether management personnel and managerial processes in buy-outs differ from those in other companies. Second, if there are differences, what form do they take? Third, how have these changes been brought about and what problems were encountered in introducing them? The evidence presented in this chapter which tries to throw light on these issues is drawn from the detailed case studies of buy-outs which supplement our questionnaire information. During these case studies, a number of recurrent themes did emerge that enable us to attempt some initial generalisations. Before these detailed changes are discussed it is necessary to draw on the results of our mailed questionnaire survey to try to present a general background picture of the important characteristics of buy-out teams. These results enable a picture to be built up of the size distribution of buy-out teams, the functions covered, the ages of management buying-out and their work experience.

II. CHARACTERISTICS OF THE BUY-OUT TEAM

The discussion in Chapter 2 concerning the preconditions for a successful buy-out referred, amongst other factors, to the existence of a well-balanced, well-motivated and able management team. One aspect of this balance is that the members of the team cover the essential functions of the business - sales and marketing, production and finance. In addition, particularly in industries where the competence of the design or technical function may be crucial to the ability of the company to adapt successfully to changing market conditions, one would expect to have this function represented within the buy-out team. Given the need for a chairman/managing director, who as will be seen below, is often the key person in the successful conclusion of the buy-out, it would be expected that the size of the buy-out team would be between three and five, depending on whether or not the chairman/managing director also dealt with another function.

TABLE 5.1

Size Distribution of Buy-out Team

Number in Team	No.	%
1	13	11.7
2	25	22.5
3	20	18.0
4	20	18.0
5	21	18.9
6	6	5.4
More than 6	5	4.5
Not stated	1	0.9
TOTAL	111	100.0

Average = 4; Standard deviation = 4.375;
Minimum = 1; Maximum = 42.

From the evidence in the survey, as reported in Table 5.1, it can be seen that although the average of four in the buy-out team conforms to this view, there is in fact a wide spread around this figure. Indeed, over the sample the range was from one to forty-two, with a standard deviation of 4.375. The buy-out with forty-two in the team was a company specialising in international stockbroking and financial services and was composed of sixteen directors and twenty-six employees out of a total workforce of 320 spread across twenty-five subsidiaries at the time of the buy-out. In terms of the functions covered, there were three chairmen/managing directors, eighteen sales, ten production, four finance and seven others. This buy-out apart, the range was from one to twelve in the team. In comparison, the buy-out teams at National Freight and the Victaulic Co, the two buy-outs from nationalised industries that we have studied, consisted of fourteen and nine managers, respectively. At the other extreme, it is somewhat surprising that an eighth of teams comprised one person only.

TABLE 5.2

Correlation Between Size of Team and Employment

Ratio of Buy-out Team to Pre-Buy-out Employment	Frequency	
%	No.	%
0.4 - 1.0	14	12.8
1.1 - 2.0	24	22.0
2.1 - 3.0	21	19.3
3.1 - 4.0	11	10.2
4.1 - 5.0	7	6.4
5.1 - 10.0	24	22.0
10.1 - 33.3	8	7.3
TOTAL	109	100.0

Mean = 4.3% Standard deviation = 4.4%
            Standard error   = 0.4%

Pearson Correlation coefficient of number in buy-out team against pre-buy-out employment = 0.218 significance level 1.1%.

Spearman Rank Coefficient = 0.512 significance level 0.1%.

Kendal Rank Correlation Coefficient = 0.381 significance level 0.1%.

Managerial Aspects of Management Buy-outs

There are a number of possible reasons to explain the variation in the size of buy-out teams. First, it may be argued that the number in the team varies with the size of the company as measured by its employees. For example, it could be that the larger the company the greater is the need to involve representatives from each department to generate commitment to the new form of ownership. Table 5.2 indicates little evidence for this proposition. Though the average size of the ratio of numbers in the team to pre-buy-out employment is 4.3 per cent, the range is from 0.4 per cent to 33.3 per cent with a standard deviation of 4.4 per cent. Most of the ratios do lie below the three per cent level and tests of correlation between the numbers in the team and number of employees, as shown in Table 5.2, do indicate a positive correlation which is strongly significantly different from zero.

However, the number of employees is clearly not the only explanatory variable for the size of the team. A second explanation lies in the price to be paid to buy the company.

It would be expected that, the higher the price the greater the funds that have to be found from outside the resources of a nucleus of three to five managers. A possible way in which extra finance might be raised without having to incur the servicing costs of outside funding is to increase the numbers in the buy-out team, even perhaps to the point of involving the body of employees in general. Undoubtedly, there is evidence that to some extent this line of action is taken by management. The Pearson, Spearman & Kendall correlation tests on the numbers in the buy-out team against the price of the company all produce significant differences at less than the one per cent level (see Table 5.5).

However, it does appear that when price increases the deal is likely to be struck with the introduction of more than one financing institution and/or a reduction in the equity stake held by the management team. Table 5.3 shows that the smaller is the team, the more likely is it to hold a majority equity stake, though it is in only about a quarter of cases that management does not have the majority equity stake anyway and in only 14.4 per cent of buy-outs does the buy-out team not hold the largest single equity share. Table 5.4 shows that participation by employees as a whole in financing the buy-out is restricted to ten per cent of companies in the sample.

When the relationships between price paid and the

85

TABLE 5.3
Number in Buy-Out Team and Equity Stakes

Number in Team	Total		Buy-out Team Majority Equity Stake	Has largest Single Equity Stake	Not largest Single Equity
1	13		11	2	0
2	26		24	0	2
3	19		16	2	1
4	19		13	3	3
5	22		12	3	7
6 or more	12		5	4	3
TOTAL	111	100.0%	81 73.0%	14 12.6%	16 14.4%

TABLE 5.4

Finance Participation by Employees

Type	Number of Firms	%
Equity	9	8
Loan	2	1.8
No participation	100	90.1
TOTAL	111	100.0

number of financial institutions and equity stakes are examined (see Table 5.5) there are strong indications that the higher the price the greater is the number of institutions involved, the less likely are management to hold a majority equity stake and correspondingly the greater the number of institutions involved the more likely are management to hold a minority equity stake. The number of financing institutions involved ranged from zero to twelve, with the ex-parent company providing finance in two cases.

All these results are not particularly surprising, but they serve to reinforce and quantify the impressionistic evidence that we have gathered from discussions with representatives of the financial institutions. Two points need to be emphasised. The first point concerns the question of the necessity for the management to have a significant equity share as an incentive to perform well. In a large company, the institutions would argue, a minority equity stake still represents a significant incentive package, and in any case, the managers will be left to have a free hand in running the company (this question of equity stakes and performance is returned to in more detail in Chapter 7).

There are parallels here with the position in new small firms. The resistance by entrepreneurs in these firms to outside equity participation is well-known.(3) However, given the generally larger size of management buy-outs that has already been noted (see Chapter 4) some outside financing is usually unavoidable and biasing funding too much towards loan-financing could lead to severe problems in servicing the debt.

The second crucial point made by the financial

TABLE 5.5

Correlation between Price, Number of Financial Institutions and Managerial Equity Stakes

	Correlation Test		
	Pearson	Spearman	Kendall
Price correlated with number of financial institutions	0.628**	0.714**	0.584**
Price correlated with management majority equity stake	-0.448**	-0.427**	-0.356**
No. of financial institutions correlated with management majority equity stake	0.324*	0.432**	0.394**
Price correlated with number in buy-out team	0.317**	0.378**	0.304**

Note: ** = significant at less than 1 per cent level.
* = 5% significant at 5 per cent level or better.

Managerial Aspects of Management Buy-outs

institutions is that the equity stake that is held must be in the hands of a clearly identifiable group which has responsibility for running the company. Should this not be the case the incentive effects of the equity-holding are likely to be dissipated and the focus of the objectives of the company may be shifted away from being commercial and profit orientated.

Both the above points therefore serve to emphasise a preference for a smaller rather than larger buy-out team.

The industry in which the firm is operating does not seem to be related to the size of the buy-out team, there being a spread of team sizes across all two-digit industries. Indeed, a chi-square test produced a value of chi-square of 29.7 which with 30 degrees of freedom is insignificant at the ten per cent level. There are, however, important behavioural factors which are also likely to influence the size of the team which it is difficult to quantify. First, the team may be smaller than expected if certain potential members are unwilling to join or are not invited to. Some may be unwilling to join the team as they are nearing retirement or have already found alternative employment. This latter point is particularly true of buy-outs from receivership, but we have found examples where the reverse has happened - managers who have found other jobs have been tempted back into the company on the re-start. Some managers may not be invited to join the team as they are simply not considered to be of sufficient calibre nor do they 'fit' in behavioural terms. These, clearly, are very delicate issues. In some cases it is a signal to the manager to look elsewhere for a job; in others it may mean that the individual concerned is excellent in a day-to-day management role but unsuited for dealing with more strategic issues. Either way, great skill is required in ensuring that the potential for disruption by the 'rejected' individual is minimised and some means must be found to ensure that the function is adequately covered by another member of the team.

One solution to this problem is to include the able day-to-day managers as a valued part of the buy-out team but not to give them strategic responsibilities. The extension of the buy-out team in this way reflects the view that key personnel in the company can reside at the second tier of management. If sufficient people of high calibre do not exist at this level to put into practice the

89

TABLE 5.6

Distribution of Management Functions in Buy-out Team

Number in Team	Chairman/MD No.	%	Sales No.	%	Production No.	%	Finance No.	%	Other (Technical) No.	%
0	9	8.1	52	46.8	56	50.5	48	43.2	71	64.0
1	81	73.0	46	41.5	45	40.5	61	55.0	32	28.8
2	15	13.5	10	9.0	7	6.3	1	0.9	4	3.6
3	6	5.4	2	1.8	1	0.9	-	-	1	0.9
4 or more	-	-	1	0.9	2	1.8	1	0.9	3	2.7
TOTAL	111	100.0	111	100.0	111	100.0	111	100.0	111	100.0

TABLE 5.7
Age Distribution of Buy-out Team Members

Age Range (Years)	Chairman/MD No.	Chairman/MD %	Sales No.	Sales %	Production No.	Production %	Finance No.	Finance %	Other (Technical) No.	Other (Technical) %
Less than 25	–	–	–	–	–	–	–	–	–	–
25-34	4	3.1	6	7.9	5	7.1	12	17.9	2	3.4
35-44	43	33.3	33	43.4	34	48.6	31	46.3	27	46.6
45-54	58	45.0	25	32.9	20	28.6	19	28.4	23	39.7
55-64	21	16.3	12	15.8	11	15.7	4	6.0	6	10.3
65 and over	3	2.3	–	–	–	–	1	1.4	–	–
TOTAL	129	100.0	76	100.0	70	100.0	67	100.0	58	100.0
Average Age	47.6		45.2		44.8		42.2		45.2	
Firms with Function	102	91.9	59	53.2	55	49.5	63	56.8	40	36.0

changes deemed necessary by the senior team, the success of the buy-out could be threatened. An interesting example of this problem arose in the National Freight buy-out, where it was realised that the public relations manager was a key figure in ensuring that the employees, in the company's 730 depots, were kept informed about the progress of the buy-out and in motivating them to feel part of the new structure.(4) As a result, the public relations manager became part of the fourteen-man buy-out team. The inclusion of the public relations manager also illustrates a further aspect of the composition of the team, that is, the need for secrecy which is so often prevalent during negotiations. By including the public relations manager inside the team the company effectively ensured that the control of information about the buy-out was in its hands. Clearly, in general, the smaller the team the less likelihood there is that there will be an unwelcome leak of information when negotiations are at a crucial stage.

A little more light on the managerial functions represented in the buy-out team is shed in Table 5.6. As might be expected there are few companies without a managing director, and a substantial amount without a representative of design or technical functions in the team. The key functions of sales, production and finance fall between these two extremes, with only two companies having more than one finance expert in the team. The existence of both a chairman and a managing director is shown in almost a fifth of buy-outs. Where more than one member of the team is in the sales, production or technical and design functions the company is probably operating in two or more very different markets where different expertise is required.

In general, whatever the size of the team the ability to cover all essential functions well is crucial to the success of the buy-out. Weakness in certain areas may discourage the financial institutions from backing the deal. For example, the lack of sufficient calibre in the buying department of Richard Shops has been suggested as having a strong influence on the proposed management buy-out not being completed.(5)

Apart from the need for all crucial functions to be ably covered, the longer term success of the buy-out may be greatly influenced by the age of the management team and their experience. The age of the team raises questions about when the need to replace certain individuals will arise and has implications

TABLE 5.8
Years Worked for Company Before Buy-out

Number of Years	Chairman/MD %	Sales %	FUNCTION Production %	Finance %	Other (Technical) %
From outside the Company	7.3	1.4	4.1	10.8	5.3
1-5	15.3	23.0	16.4	23.1	21.1
6-10	26.6	18.9	24.7	32.3	26.3
11-20	32.3	43.2	34.2	23.1	31.6
Over 20	18.5	13.5	20.6	10.7	15.7
	100.0	100.0	100.0	100.0	100.0
Average years worked for Company before buy-out	12.27	12.20	12.77	9.42	11.43

for the second and subsequent generations of management. Given the disruption caused by the ownership change it would seem appropriate that a team exists which can continue to work together for a number of years. The evidence presented in Table 5.7 suggests that for the most part buy-outs are not going to be faced with a succession problem in the immediate future, since at least three quarters of managers in each function are aged between 35 and 54. Some are clearly going to be faced with succession problems, particularly in respect of the chairman/managing director. This problem will be exacerbated the smaller is the team and the higher is the proportion of members in the highest age categories.

As might be expected chairman/managing directors tend to be older than other team members, whilst members dealing with finance are substantially younger on average. Indeed, almost eighteen per cent of heads of finance in management buy-outs are aged between 25 and 34. The main reason for this age disparity is likely to be the absence of a finance function in many buy-outs on divestment, resulting in a need for recruitment from outside the company (some indication of the extent of this is shown in Table 5.8). It may be that recently qualified accountants will be the most attractive proposition if only because they cost less.

In comparison with all senior managers, managers in buy-out teams are, if anything, generally slightly younger. Deeks (6) reports that the average age of all owner-managers in the furniture industry is 47.7 years. A study of senior managers across all industries and sizes of firms carried out by Ellis and Child (7) reports average ages for individual functions. The average ages of senior managers in Sales, Production, Finance and Technical Functions were 45.1, 45.2, 45.5 and 43.5 years respectively. Although sales managers are about the same age, technical managers are older and production and finance managers are younger in management buy-outs than in industry generally.

The evidence available on those entrepreneurs starting completely new businesses (8) indicates that they are more likely to do so in industries in which they have previously worked. For managers buying-out this is by definition true, apart from the minority who are brought in from outside to complete the team, as shown in Table 5.8. This minority group is more likely to comprise finance experts, as already noted, but may also include the chairman/managing director. From the discussions that we have had with the financial institutions and in the case studies, the chairman/managing director who comes into the team in this way has often been acting in a consultancy role for the parent or company itself before the buy-out and may play a leading part in setting up the deal (we say more about this point below). For those in the team who were previously working for the company, the range of experience is considerable, though in subsidiary companies some or almost all of this has been with the former parent. Over half of managers buying out had worked for their company for more than ten years in the chairman/managing directors, sales and production functions and over forty per cent had this experience in the remaining two categories. Correspondingly, around one fifth of chairmen/managing directors and production managers had worked for the company for over twenty years; whilst this was the case for only about ten per cent of finance managers. There is, therefore, a wide dispersion of experiences around the average number of years that managers had worked for the company in each function, with that for accountants being substantially different from the remaining functions and biased towards the lower end.

In terms of comparisons with other studies, the average length of time that managers buying out had spent with their company is less. Deeks reports (9) that all owner-managers in the furniture industry had been employed on average for 17.1 years in their firm. The average employment period with their current company for senior managers in the Ellis and Child study (10) was 14.51 years for sales, 17.93 years for production, 14.03 years for finance and 14.59 years for technical managers.

In general, the characteristics of buy-out teams that we have discussed suggest great variety in their composition. If there are stereotypes then the results of our survey and case studies would suggest two sorts. First, a team mainly comprised of managers who have worked for the company or its parent for many years and who view the buy-out as the only realistic way to retain their jobs (for buy-outs on receivership) and/or as the opportunity to demonstrate that they can run the company better without interference from more distant owners. Second, a younger team with less experience with the company but well qualified and able who see the buy-out as an opportunity for individual success. This latter group is probably more prevalent in faster growing markets.

Managers buying out are clearly in contrast to founders of entirely new firms. Although both became owners of firms in industries with which they are familiar, the new firm founder is much more likely to have previously been a craftsman with a consequential possible lack of managerial skills.(11) This difference may be crucial to the relative survival rates of new small firms and management buy-outs since mis-management is one of the most important indirect causes of bankruptcy. There is evidence to suggest that one half of business failures could have been avoided by appropriate business training for the founders before the position became hopeless.(13) Managers buying out, on the other hand, have by definition had managerial experience and where the buy-out is on divestment may well have been exposed to formal management training programmes. This means, as was evident in the case studies, that formal control systems and methods, particularly with respect to credit management, are likely to be well developed. For those buy-outs from independent companies in receivership the management may have been frustrated in their attempts to manage by the behaviour of the owner-founder or his family. This was certainly true of one of our case studies, that of a furniture manufacturer. On the other side of the coin, it may be argued that managers buying out may be less entrepreneurial, having been sheltered under the protective umbrella of the previous parent company or owners. To the extent that they are not forming a completely new enterprise to exploit a new opportunity, managers buying out are more akin to second and third generation owner-managers. As such they are likely to be less socially-marginal than founders of new enterprises and be more likely to accept the dominant business ideology with its stress on growth, acquisition activity and the professionally managed company.(14) However, to the extent that they have usually personally borrowed heavily to finance the buy-out they are certainly in the business of taking risks. Indeed, the managers that we have spoken to in our case studies clearly had profit as their major objective and were entrepreneurial in that they perceived that the business could be more efficient if it were removed from the dead-hand of parental control. In fact, rather than being sheltered by the parent their wish to be entrepreneurial was often frustrated by the need to follow inappropriate centrally defined objectives. In some companies, it is true, the entrepreneurial spirit was perhaps not very strong. In the case of Richard Shops,(15) mentioned earlier, this seems to have been a further contributory factor in the buy-out not taking place. In one of our case studies, a die-casting company bought out from receivership, it required the confidence and experience of one man in dealing with financial institutions to lead the remainder of the team, who though good managers had not been exposed to such external pressures. In fact, in all the case studies that were undertaken there was a clearly identifiable 'leading light' who was crucial in the successful negotiation of the buy-out and in ensuring satisfactory performance thereafter. In essence, it was this person who most closely resembled the entrepreneurial founder of the firm. However, unlike the founder of a completely new firm, who initially has only himself to deal with, in a management buy-out a workforce and often a management structure already exists. The 'leading light' must therefore possess a wide range of skills including both entrepreneurial and managerial ones. As has been noted elsewhere by Davis,(16) successful leaders must possess 'psychological maturity' which includes the traits of intelligence, social maturity, inner motivation and respect for human dignity or to be self-actualising in Maslow's terms.(17)

There are clear implications raised by these characteristics of buy-out teams for the managerial styles found in the companies after the change in ownership. These issues are discussed below using case study evidence after the managerial changes revealed by the questionnaire survey have been examined.

III. MANAGERIAL CHANGES IN MANAGEMENT BUY-OUTS

The managerial changes that may arise following the buy-out involve firstly the shape of the management structure and secondly the individuals contained within it. Changes in the management structure may be necessary for a number of reasons and can take various forms. Removal of a tier of management may be required as part of rationalisation and cost reduction following a buy-out from all four sources. From Table 5.9, nine per cent of companies in our sample are observed to have removed a tier of management. However, the evidence from our case

97

TABLE 5.9
Managerial Changes by Source

	Total		Receivership						Retirement	
			Independent		Subsidiary		Divestment			
	No.	%	No.	%	No.	%	No.	%	No.	%
No change	65	58.6	2	40.0	11	73.3	39	57.4	13	56.5
Change in Team	11	9.9	1	20.0	3	20.0	7	10.3	–	–
Divisionalisation	4	3.6	–	–	–	–	3	4.4	1	4.3
2nd Tier of management created	13	11.7	–	–	1	6.7	7	10.3	5	21.7
Removal of a tier of management	10	9.0	1	20.0	2	13.3	6	8.8	1	4.3
New Mgrs/Directors	10	9.0	–	–	–	–	8	11.8	2	8.7
Others	13	11.7	1	20.0	1	6.7	8	11.8	3	13.0
Base for %	111		5		15		68		23	

studies suggests that this figure may be understated since, in a number of instances, either companies bought out from receivership or on divestment from a parent still trading but where the subsidiary needed to be substantially reduced to be viable, non-working foremen were abolished. It became evident that this function was often not considered to be a managerial one. In one buy-out from a parent in receivership, which reduced its employment by 15 per cent to 150, specialist service functions including inspection, production control and personnel were removed so that the first two were in the hands of working foremen and the latter with the managing director.

At the other end of the spectrum, an extra tier of management may be created. For a buy-out on retirement of the previous owner this need may arise due to a lack of willingness on the part of traditional entrepreneurial previous owners to delegate responsibility, and was evident in a fifth of this type of buy-out. In buy-outs from divestment a new tier may need to be created simply because the function was previously carried out by the parent. For the four of our case studies where this occurred the function being introduced was finance or accounting orientated. In some instances the creation of an extra tier was related to the rapid growth of the company following the buy-out. This rapid growth was also the main reason behind the divisionalisation of the company.

Where changes in the buy-out team occurred this was either due to retirement or death of one or more members or because members for certain functions, especially finance, joined the company shortly after the deal had gone through. New managers and directors were appointed as new tiers of management were introduced or to replace some individuals who had not been brought across from the old company as previously constituted. Given the age distribution of the companies in the sample and the growth rates of some of them it is perhaps not surprising that a further nine companies were seriously planning to appoint new managers or directors and two were planning to introduce a new tier of management. Even where companies had not made these kind of changes there was nevertheless widespread evidence in the case studies of serious attempts to adjust the management structure. The aims of these adjustments were twofold, firstly, to emphasise the flexibility of both management and non-management employees in the tasks they performed, and, secondly, to make the structures more appropriate to the companies' needs than was possible under the restrictions enforced by the parent.(18) One buy-out, making switches, was planning to divisionalise the company to cover individual product groups whilst another in the furniture industry, had commissioned a firm of management consultants to analyse the management structure.

The above changes were supplemented in 45 companies (40.5 per cent of the sample) by a representative of the financing institutions taking a seat on the board of directors. This representative was usually present in a general financial advisory capacity, though in one company that we visited the representative performed a technical advisory role.

IV. MANAGERIAL STYLES

Owing to the nature of the mailed questionnaire survey, it was not possible to ask questions about managerial styles beyond what was covered in the previous section. The evidence that is presented in this section is drawn from interviews with the two employee buy-outs from nationalised industries and with fifteen buy-outs in the private sector. These fifteen buy-outs were chosen from our total sample so as to be illustrative of the range of changes taking place after the buy-out. The number of employees at the time of the interviews varied from twelve to four hundred and fifty. Seven of the buy-outs were from parents still trading, five were from parents in receivership, one was formerly an independent in receivership and two were buy-outs on the retirement of the previous owners.

Managerial or leadership style may be generally considered to run along a continuum from no participation in management by subordinates at one end to complete participation at the other. The influences on the appropriate leadership style in a company and the implied organisational structure have been discussed extensively in the management and related literature for many years. Recently, increasing unionisation, increasing demands for greater disclosure of company information, the EEC Fifth Directive, and government commissions have all produced greater pressure for more participation right across industry. A series of studies in the late 1950s and early 1960s purported to show that greater participation in decision-making in the workplace would produce greater satisfaction, greater motivation and improved performance by employees than did the more traditional coercive and authoritarian style of management. Hence, McGregor's Theory Y should be preferred to his Theory X style of management and similarly, Likert's management system type four was seen to be preferable to his other three.(19)

However, it should be borne in mind that the notion of participation does not mean the same thing to all who would advocate its adoption. At one end of the spectrum, it can mean a greater, even equal, say in the strategic objectives of the enterprise and how they are achieved, whilst at the other end it might involve greater disclosure of information or joint consultation on more routine matters. Studies of what kinds of decisions employees themselves are interested in participating more in suggest that there is less interest in financial or general business considerations, unless there is a direct effect on the shopfloor, and rather more interest in joint consultation, extensions of collective bargaining and greater economic participation through, for example, profit sharing.(20)

From the management point of view the consensus seems to be that increased participation is only acceptable if it does not impair the efficiency of the enterprise. For example, consulting subordinates over the quality of the material they have to work with may be advantageous as it may improve purchasing policy and reduce the levels of waste material. But the time taken to reach a decision and the inflexibility of formal participative procedures may have an adverse effect on efficiency. Even if participation does have a beneficial effect on efficiency it may be short-lived as the 'Hawthorn effect' on motivation begins to wear off.(21) It has been suggested, for example, using American experience, that this is a danger with participation in the form of quality circles,(22) which are often portrayed as bringing significant benefits to industrial efficiency.(23)

Recent studies of leadership styles have increasingly begun to focus on the idea that the appropriate style depends upon the context, so that what might be appropriate in one firm may not be true for another. The type of context is generally considered to be influenced by four main factors - the environment in which the firm is operating, its technology, its size and the type of ownership.(24)

In other words, each of these contingencies affect the type of problem that the leader has to deal with. The appropriate solution to these different problems may be argued to be along a two-dimensional scale which has the degree of necessary information available to the leader on one axis and the acceptability of the solution to subordinates on the other. Studies would suggest that when the leader possesses all the information necessary to solve the problem and the solution is acceptable to subordinates the appropriate leadership style omits participation. At the other extreme, when he does not possess all the necessary information and staff do not accept the decision then more participation is called for.(25) Hence, higher satisfaction, higher motivation and greater performance do not always go hand-in-hand. Indeed, the expectancy theory of motivation suggests that an individual's motivation towards doing a job depends on his perception that carrying out the task will bring him the desired reward and on his perception that putting in the effort will lead to the desired level of performance.(26) The means for maximising the individual's expectancies comes from obtaining that blend of leadership styles, job and payment structures which strengthens the link between effort, performance and rewards. The successful leadership style then is one that is responsive, in terms of greater or lesser participation, to the type of problem that is to be dealt with.

The implications of this theoretical discussion for management styles in buy-outs are as follows. It is useful at the outset to distinguish between the stages of the negotiation of the buy-out and those afterwards when the company is trading in its new ownership form. In the negotiation stage of the buy-out, a non-participative style of leadership would be expected, and indeed is observed as the need for secrecy precludes a wider base for making decisions. In the case of buy-outs from receivership where the attempts to buy-out are likely to be more widely known, especially if employees may be required to invest redundancy money, the extent of participation is also likely to be limited, although it is important that employees as a whole are in favour of management's attempts to purchase the company.

When the company begins to trade under its new form of ownership the appropriate leadership style needs to be seen at two distinct levels. To the extent that the firm begins to pass through the early stages of the life-cycle again, then a dominant entrepreneurial style is required to give the momentum for continued growth.(27) But since, unlike a completely new firm, an organisation, which may be quite large and formal, already exists a different style may be required to carry the workforce along.

The evidence from our case studies suggests that these differences are resolved by, on the one hand, management taking a clearly dominant role in setting the objectives of the company, which are invariably profitable growth orientated, and planning how these aims are to be achieved and on the other hand by a conscious effort to reduce any 'US versus THEM' attitudes. As has already been noted in the previous section, the plans to achieve the company's objectives often involve changes in the organisational structure with above all emphases on increased flexibility of working practices and reductions in chains of command. In the case studies the needs for these changes and the more dominant leadership styles are seen in those companies which are buy-outs from receivership or on divestment from a parent still trading where certain essential functions had previously been absent. They are also evident in two cases of divestment from parents still trading employing less than twenty people each where the more formal procedures in evidence under the group umbrella were inappropriate once independence was achieved. The remaining cases were previously fairly independent anyway.

At the second level, attempts to reduce the differences between management and employees generally concern attempts to involve employees more directly. This involvement relates to changes in the level and form of communication and in participation in decision-making at the more routine level. Overall there have usually been explicit attempts to develop the identification of the employee with the company rather than simply an employee or trade union member. The form of communication is influenced to a great extent by the size of the company. In the very small cases that we visited (twelve to thirty-five employees) there were regular meetings of all the staff in order that they could be informed about progress, and could raise particular issues. In the larger companies, communication took a variety of forms. For the most part it involved the use of notice boards and regular meetings of the whole workforce at which progress was outlined and questions were encouraged and answered. However, in seven of the cases there were regular meetings between management and a works committee, which was usually, but not always, made up of trade union representatives. In addition, two companies sent company newsletters/progress reports to all employees individually. A third company was planning to reintroduce this form of communication, whilst another made detailed performance information available to all employees if they wanted to see it and broadcast any recent changes over the tannoy system.

In terms of participation in decision-making, there was usually a recognition that each group of employees had its own skills which should be made use of to the full. As a result it was normal for management to let employees get on with the job and for them to take into account feedback from employees on problems or changes in the market where employees worked on the customer's site. On a wider level of decision-making, participation was more likely to arise through meetings between all employees and management, in the case of smaller companies, or between employee representatives and management for the larger ones. In these meetings the approach was normally for management to put forward proposals for discussion, but with management prerogative being made clear.

Managerial style in two of the buy-outs was in marked contrast to the preceding discussion. Both were buy-outs from retirement of the previous owner. In one, the company had subsequently been acquired as part of a group. As a result, management style in the company which employed sixteen people, had become more autocratic and removed from the subsidiary itself. In fact, a reversal of what was observed above in those buy-outs from parents which had kept their independence. In the other company, the management style was considerably more entrepeneurial, in the traditional sense. Power over all decision-making very clearly resided with the managing director, and there was emphasis on high-lighting the differences between management and employees generally. It is interesting to note that in this company, the buy-out team had had a very short experience in managing the company before the buy-out and may more realistically be regarded as a management buy-in.

In general, then, there does appear to be some indication that the leadership styles in management buy-outs are responsive to the type of problem to be dealt with. Although there is a strong demand for a style of leadership in the negotiation of the buy-out which excludes participation, though requiring support of employees as a whole, the style of leadership after the buy-out is required to be conducive to minimising the differences between management and the workforce so as to increase satisfaction and motivate all participants in the company to perform well to make the buy-out a success.

V. QUESTION MARKS OVER MANAGEMENT AND MANAGEMENT STYLE

Despite what has been said above about the encouraging way in which management styles seem to have had positive effects on motivation and performance there are nevertheless certain question marks which are raised concerning the longer-term managerial aspects of the buy-outs. For the most part, the change in role that is required from being a negotiator to being a manager/owner does not seem to have caused problems, especially since it essentially means a continuity of the past. In fact, the major problem was probably the change of role in becoming a negotiator.

However, after an initial period, perhaps up to two years in length, the problems of dealing with a situation of survival tend to be replaced by those relating to success. This problem is likely to manifest itself not least in the form of a change in the degree of motivation experienced from the workforce following the buy-out. Few of the companies in our sample had yet reached this stage. One company that had, see the case of Panache Upholstery in Chapter 8, dealt with the problem by sharply reminding employees of the dangers of returning to the receivership position from which they had escaped. In another company, see the case of Mansfield Shoe in Chapter 8, the continued high growth of the company out of receivership, coupled with an equity stake by a substantial proportion of employees, seems to have kept the momentum going. The rapid growth of DPCE, also a case in Chapter 8, and subsequent flotation on the Stock Exchange also seems to have had a positive effect on motivation and performance. There does seem to be an indication here that for motivation of employees to be maintained in the longer-run some extension of equity participation across all employees may be desirable. On the evidence we have seen concerning management styles to date, this does not imply a move to a workers' cooperative but rather the fostering of a widespread feeling that all employees are working for their own company.

It should also be noted that another problem associated with the rapid growth and success of certain management buy-outs involves the need for senior managers to change from playing a role concerned with detail to one that is more concerned with mapping out the longer-term future of the company. This is not, of course, a problem confined solely to management buy-outs. It applies equally well to all forms of enterprise. However, it does introduce the general problem of succession in the management buy-out team. That is, sooner or later, the buy-out team and more particularly the "leading light" is going to move on or retire. Management buy-outs, as we have noted, are unlikely to suffer from the same succession problems found in more traditional entrepreneurial companies, where refusals to delegate and intolerance of those who are seen to pose potential threats means that there is unlikely to be someone internally who can take on the running of the company.(28) But there seems to be a very real danger that if the "leading light" is removed from the bought-out firms, and if his replacement comes from inside the company, he is likely to be more risk-averse, less innovative, more adept at cost-cutting and improving efficiency but less suited to managing change. The life cycle view of the firm suggests a need for these types of skills at certain stages, particularly when there is relative stability in the firm's environment. However, there is a need for a management presence which can act like this when it is necessary to do so, but which can be more dynamic when increased environmental uncertainty necessitates it. In other words, as was seen in the theoretical discussion, there remains a need for a leader/leaders who can adapt their leadership style to suit the situation to hand. There would thus seem to remain a need for the kind of entrepreneur-manager we have identified as playing a crucial role in the success of management buy-outs to date. This person combines the essential ingredients of an entrepreneur - innovative, risk-taking, and managerial-coordinative abilities - with stress on the importance of the last-named. In a management buy-out all three elements are present but managerial-ordinative ability is particularly important given the prior existence of the enterprise.

VI. CONCLUSIONS

The buy-outs tend to vary in the composition of the team, and with respect to the age and background of personnel. However, the overriding aspect of the management in the companies studied is the existence of true entrepreneurial leadership. In the majority of companies it is possible to identify very clearly the prime mover driving the company forward. Throughout the preceding chapter, in discussion of both the practical and theoretical aspects of management, the intention has been to elevate consideration of management beyond the anecdotal, caricature pen-picture style of much work on such individuals. The management role has been placed in context and managerial changes since buy-out discussed in terms of justification and effect. It is worth emphasising that much of the evidence presented suggests a preference for a small rather than large buy-out team.

The effects of management are often plain to see but it is difficult to identify those specific actions which distinguish good as opposed to indifferent managements. The manager's skill is so often complementary to other features of the company, although the entrepreneur should be pro-active and "make things happen", that it is impossible in discussing other aspects of company performance and behaviour to separate out the independent management roles. Thus the examination of management contained in this chapter should be considered complementary to the discussions of the following two chapters.

NOTES

1. See the case studies in Arnfield, R.V., Chiplin, B., Jarrett, M. and Wright, M.: 'Management Buy-outs: Corporate Trend for the '80's?' IBLO, Nottingham, 1981. See also Lester, T.: 'What the Buy-outs Bring', Management Today, March 1982, and Upton, R.: 'I'm in Personnel', Personnel Management, December 1983.
2. One exception is described in Upton, R. op.cit.
3. See Storey, D.J.: 'Entrepreneurship and the New Firm', Croom-Helm, 1982.
4. See the case study in Chapter 8 on NFC.
5. As reported in Maughan, R.: 'Fashioning a New Image', Financial Times, 5-10-83, p.5.
6. See Deeks, J.: 'Educational and Occupational

Histories of Owner-Managers and Managers', *Journal of Management Studies*, Vol. 9, 1972, pp. 127-149.
7. Ellis, T. and Child, J.: 'Placing Stereotypes of the Manager into Perspective', *Journal of Management Studies*, Vol. 109, 1973, pp. 233-255.
8. See for example, Johnson, P.S. and Cathcart, G.: 'The Founders of New Manufacturing Firms: A Note on the Size of their Incubator Plants', *Journal Industrial Economics*, June 1979 and also Storey, D.J., *op. cit.*, especially Chapter 4.
9. Deeks, J., *op. cit.*
10. Ellis and Child, *op. cit.*
11. Storey, *op. cit.*
12. This view is put forward by Brough, R.: 'Business Failures in England and Wales', *Business Ratios*, 1970, pp. 8-11.
13. Evidence for this proposition is discussed in Soloman, G.T. and Whiting, B.G.: 'Casualties of Ignorance: The Dilemma of Small Business in the USA', Siena Series, No. 16, Acton Society Trust Occasional Paper, London, 1977/9.
14. This point is discussed in detail in Stanworth, J. and Curran, J.: 'Growth and the Small Firm - An Alternative View', *Journal of Management Studies*, Vol. 13, 1976, pp. 95-108.
15. See Churchill, D.: 'Buy-out Proposal Seeks to Tailor Fresh Image For Retail Chains', *Financial Times*, 9.9.83, p. 4.
16. See Davis, K.: *Human Relations at Work*, 3rd Edn, McGraw-Hill, New York, 1967.
17. See for Example Maslow, A.H.: *'Motivation and Personality'*, 2nd Edn, Harper & Row, New York, 1970.
18. This need to restructure suggests clear evidence of the adverse effects of ownership contingencies on the control system. For a fuller discussion see Wright, M., Rhodes, D.J. and Jarrett, M.: 'Growth, Survival and Control in Smaller Manufacturing Systems', *European Journal of Operational Research*, Vol. 14, 1983, pp. 40-55.
19. For a concise review of these studies see for example Buckley, A. and McKenna, E: 'Budgeting, Control and Business Behaviour', *Accounting and Business Research*, Spring 1972.
20. See Marchington, M. and Loveridge, R.: 'Non-Participation: The Management View', *Journal of Management Studies*, Vol. 16, 1979, pp. 171-184 for a detailed summary.
21. Marchington and Loveridge, *op. cit.*

22. Wood, R., Hull, F. and Azumi, K.: 'Evaluating Quality Circles: The American Application', California Management Review, Fall 1983, pp. 37-53.
23. For example see Bradley, K. and Hill, S.: 'After Japan: The Quality Circle Transplant and Productive Efficiency', British Journal of Industrial Relations, Vol. 21, No. 3, November 1983.
24. See Wright, et al., op. cit. and references quoted therein.
25. See for example, Vroom, V.H. and Yetton, P.W., 'Leadership and Decision-Making', Pittsburgh, University of Pittsburgh Press, 1973 and Margerison, C. and Glube, R.: 'Leadership Decision-Making: An Empirical Test of the Vroom and Yetton Model', Journal Management Studies, Vol. 16, Feb. 1979, pp. 45-55.
26. There are numerous studies of this theory in various environments, see for example Rockness, H.O.: 'Expectancy Theory in a Budgetary Setting: An Experimental Examination', Accounting Review, October 1977.
27. For evidence in new companies see Storey, D.J.: 'Entrepreneurship and the New Firm', Croom Helm, 1982; see also Greig, I.D.: 'Basic Motivation and Decision Style in Organisation Management', Omega, Vol. 12, No. 1, 1984.
28. See Kets de Vries, M.F.R.: 'The Entrepreneurial Personality: A Person at the Crossroads', Journal Management Studies, Vol. 14, Feb. 1977, pp. 33-55.

Chapter 6

INDUSTRIAL RELATIONS AND THE BUY-OUT

I. INTRODUCTION

The industrial relations environment which any company experiences will be the outcome of a complex of interrelated factors and it is most unlikely that two identical plants or enterprises could be found. The geographical location, the attitudes and values of the local community, the size of the plant, the size of the company, the extent and type of unionisation, the attitude of management, the sector of industry etc. will all exert independent and complementary pressures on the industrial relations of the company. It is therefore dangerous to over-generalise about industrial relations issues. It is unlikely that broad cross sections of industry under study will fully conform to a broad picture. Despite these difficulties industrial relations is probably subject publicly to more sweeping generalisations than most other parts of British industry. In particular, the complexion of the British industrial relations 'problem' is seemingly 'known' by all - too many strikes, militant unions and low productivity - yet is very often totally misplaced. It is, therefore, important to place the industrial relations aspects of management buy-outs in context, by first looking at the general background of experience in similar circumstances to see if a more accurate picture of the industrial relations experience can be generated despite the complexity.

II. THE BOUGHT-OUT COMPANIES' BACKGROUND

The companies bought-out, which are the subject of this study are for the most part small firms by most

Industrial Relations and the Buy-out

definitions, 70% of them having less than 200 employees, and 46% having less than 100. Only 7% could be regarded as large firms in their own right with more than 500 employees. However, many were previously part of larger groups where the general industrial relations ethos may have been from a big company background. Indeed, 75% had been part of a group prior to buy-out, and had been either divested or purchased following the parent company's receivership. We may expect that the companies would have been affected previously by industrial relations issues generated from outside their subsidiary or division whereas post-buy-out their total concern will be more local and more immediate. There are certainly a number of instances in the sample firms where procedures for negotiation had been determined by group wide agreements, where patterns of union membership and recognition had been a result of group rather than local policy, and where industrial action elsewhere in the group had had its effects on the company bought-out either directly or indirectly.

When the industrial distribution of firms in the study is examined it is evident that it is the traditional manufacturing sector of the economy which is well represented (see Chapter 4). In fact, 78% of the companies are in the Standard Industrial Classification groups 2, 3 and 4 which encompass the UK manufacturing sector. The issues and problems of the companies may therefore be expected to be characteristic of UK manufacturing in general.

Taking these two broad distinctions together it is clear that for industrial relations purposes the experiences against which we should make comparisons are those of small firms in UK manufacturing generally.(1)

III. THE ISSUES

Whatever the size and type of company there are a number of fundamental industrial relations issues which need to be faced and which will be common to most firms. In a highly unionised, generally pluralistic industrial relations system such as operates in the United Kingdom these issues invariably centre around the management-union relationship. In the absence of unions many of the functions now performed by the joint management-union procedures would need to be conducted using alternative machinery because

111

employees, whether through trade unions or not, will generally wish to have their views represented formally to management.
The basic requirements will generally be:

i) a method of formal representation and recognition;

ii) an agreed procedure for negotiation (including an appeals system);

iii) two way channels of communication between workers and management;

All these functions are currently provided by the trade union organisation at the place of work though the way they execute their duties may be a cause for concern to management. The major philosophical difficulty is that unionisation represents a commitment to a body organised horizontally across a large number of firms. As such there is every possibility that issues of no interest, and no concern to an employer can be dragged into a workplace by unions who have divided loyalties. For example, a company may be affected by a national strike-call in support of a minimum wage for the industry even if its local terms are above that minimum. Thus there may be a preference for a local pattern of representation that is company specific to avoid divided loyalties, but it must be recognised that the cost is the replacement of those functions currently performed through procedural agreements with unions by newly created structures.

What we may expect to observe in buy-outs, given that the change of ownership acts as a catalyst that may promote change, is the weighing up of these issues for management to emerge with a pattern which suits their circumstances. Much will depend upon the status quo and recent experience. Thus the existing pattern of representation and recognition, trade union attitudes, disputes experience and restrictive practices must be examined to see if the costs of unionisation are seen to be so great that management actively seek to press through changes.

IV. UNION REPRESENTATION

The wide dispersion of management buy-outs across the whole spectrum of UK manufacturing industry is reflected in the pattern of representation by trade

Industrial Relations and the Buy-out

TABLE 6.1
Representation of Trade Unions

Name of Trade Union	No. of Firms	%	Total Membership of Union in 1981 and rank by size in TUC	
AUEW	33	29.7	1,104,425	(2)
TGWU/ACTSS	19	17.1	1,695,818	(1)
NGA	11	9.9	136,326	(19)
SOGAT 82	11	9.9	136,660	(11)
ASTMS	10	9.0	432,000	(7)
EETPU	9	8.1	395,000	(8)
DATA/TASS	9	8.1	185,690	(16)
GMBATU	8	7.2	865,814	(3)
FTAT	5	4.5	68,598	(24)
NSMM	4	3.6	39,457	(41)
SLADE (part of NGA)	3	2.7		
NUFLAT	2	1.8	50,072	(35)
NUJ	2	1.8	32,637	(45)
NUTGW	2	1.8	81,761	(28)
APEX	1	0.9	122,639	(21)
CATU	1	0.9		
ISTC	1	0.9	100,175	(25)
MATSA (part of GMWU)	1	0.9		
SNBRU	1	0.9	1,100	(89)
UCATT	1	0.9	275,251	(9)

Base for Percentages = 111

unions. As shown in Table 6.1 the three major unions, the Transport and General Workers, the Amalgamated Union of Engineering Workers and the General and Municipal Workers are very much in evidence even though the strength of the two general unions lies in their organisation in large companies. The size of firms in this study, with an average employment of about 170, would tend to place the companies at the lower end of the pattern of trade union organisation such that we might not expect to find much evidence of multi unionism or white collar representation. However, examination of the size of unions in Table 6.1 shows that the white collar independent unions, or white collar sections of the large unions are also in evidence. The most widely represented white collar union was the Association of Scientific, Technical and Managerial Staffs, with representation in ten companies. The ASTMS has been the fastest growing private sector

TABLE 6.2
Management Buy-outs and Multi-Unionism - Pre-Buy-out

Number of Unions Represented	Number	%	
1	29	39.7	
2	21	28.8)	
3	15	20.5)	54.8
4 or more	4	5.5)	
Not Stated	4	5.5	
TOTAL	73	100.0	

white collar union over the past decade and has spread its influence very widely across private manufacturing industry.(2) Organisationally it is very difficult to recruit eligible tiers of management in quite small companies and although ASTMS has been very successful the number of members in each of the firms in this study was quite small.

With respect to multi-unionism, the formal recognition of more than one trade union for negotiating purposes at a place of work, the study also shows that more than one union was recognised in 55% of those companies in which unions were recognised (36% of all companies in the sample) [See Table 6.2.] In the majority of instances the multi unionism was of the 'vertical' type, where different classes of worker are represented by different unions, and the basis of this difference was often the blue collar/manual-white collar/non-manual split. Often the managerial employees that were unionised were in the white collar section of the same union which represented the blue collar workers, a situation not uncommon in smaller to medium-sized firms.

The pattern of representation will reflect, to a great extent the balance of sub-sectors of manufacturing which comprise this study and the patterns of trade union recognition which are found in those sub-sectors. For example, whilst 94% of manual employees in the paper printing and publishing industry are unionised, only 62% are union members in textiles. Thus, all the firms in this study in the printing and related industries had union representation, which is now broadly split on the blue collar side between two unions - The National Graphical Association (NGA 82) and the

Industrial Relations and the Buy-out

Society of Graphical and Allied Trades (SOGAT 82). However, only two of the four firms in the textile industry recognised unions.
The pattern is compounded by the way in which the distribution of companies by size may differ randomly across the industry groups. Unionisation, and the probability of union recognition increases as a function of firm size. Only 59% of establishments with 50-99 employees recognise unions, and the average level of unionisation within those establishments in this size category which do recognise unions is 65%. However, in those establishments with between 500 and 999 employees 92% recognise unions, and the average level of unionisation is 84%.(3) It is not possible to fully evaluate the effect on the figures presented here of the distribution of firms by size across the industrial sub-groups other than to say that part of the variation in recognition may be explained by whether the average size of company bought-out in a particular industry group was at the upper or lower end of the size spectrum.
A more practical aspect of the presence of unions in the sample might be related to the motives of the buy-out team. If unionisation is strong, and its effects inhibiting on the freedom of management to act, then one might expect, a priori, that managers would be less inclined to buy companies in those industries with a tradition of strong and obstructive trade unionism. The high number of printing unions may seem to be out of place given this line of argument particularly after the publicity which the print unions have received in the disputes at The Times Newspapers, and the Stockport Messenger Group. In both instances the unions' resistance to changed working practices and the introduction of new technology would not at first sight seem amenable to the general picture of entrepreneurial owner-managers which characterise this study.(4) In reality, the problems of newspaper printing and the unions on Fleet Street are not characteristic of the rest of the printing industry and the general attitudes to change are quite realistic in most companies. We must observe that buy-outs in the printing group in this study come predominantly from non-newspaper areas where management relationships are generally much better. The experiences provide further support for attention to particular circumstances rather than the general conditions associated with an industry from which the buy-out may come.

115

V. CHANGE IN UNION RECOGNITION

An issue of particular importance is the change in patterns of recognition pre- and post-buy-out. It has been suggested that in so far as management buy-outs represent a reassertion of the entrepreneurial spirit in British industry then there may be a tendency for new owner managers to wish to remove the trade union which may otherwise be a challenge to their freedom of action. Consequently it may be expected that a drastic reduction in the recognition of trade unions would be observed as they are removed on buy-out, possibly with the acquiescence of workforces who were not particularly union conscious in the first place. Particularly where closed shops existed there may have been reluctant trade unionists who would not fight for the union unless it also affected their own mobility.

TABLE 6.3

Trade Union Recognition

	Pre-Buy-out No.	%	After Buy-out No.	%
Recognised	73	65.8	65	58.6
Not Recognised	37	33.3	45	40.5
Not Stated	1	0.9	1	0.9
TOTAL	111	100.0	111	100.0

A second suggestion is that where a buy-out occurs on divestment the parent may be selling off a subsidiary in which a union was strong in the expectation that independence would break the union's monopoly whilst the parent continues to control the subsidiary through contractual relationships in the market. This is an adaptation of the arguments discussed by Ireland and Law with respect to worker cooperatives where it is argued that in the cooperatives case workers are exploited through the capital market as a substitute for exploitation through the labour market.(5) These two suggestions may be examined with reference to the survey results, which are presented in Tables 6.3 and 6.4.

Before the buy-out occurred trade unions were recognised in 73 of the 111 companies (65.8%),

TABLE 6.4

Changes in Trade Union Recognition

Trade Union Recognition	No.	%
Pre- and Post-Buy-out	64	57.7
Pre- but not Post-Buy-out	9	8.1
Not Pre- but Post-Buy-out	1	0.9
No Recognition	35	31.5
Not Stated	2	1.8

whilst after buy-out the number of companies recognising trade unions fell to sixty-five (58.6%). However, this is a net change which needs to be examined in a more disaggregated form as is given in Table 6.4. There were 9 companies that ceased to recognise trade unions after the buy-out and one company which recognised a union after buy-out whereas it had been non-union pre-buy-out. In the latter case the circumstances are a little unusual in that the issue of recognition only arose on the successful acquisition of a new subsidiary by the bought-out company in which a union recognition agreement existed and was continued. Thus in this case the management may be regarded as union-neutral rather than positive in their desire to recognise unions. Overall there were just nine losses of recognition which involved twelve union recognitions (AUEW - 5, TGWU - 3, ASTMS - 2, TASS and SNBRU - 1 each). In sixty-four companies the formal existence and recognition of trade unions carried on much as before. Thus in 88% of all companies recognising trade unions before buy-out the union recognition was not affected on change of ownership.

Looking further at the reasons why recognition ceased in the nine companies, little evidence was found to support the contention that union removal is a definite aim of management. Only in one instance had management made a conscious decision not to recognise trade unions in the new business and had formally drawn up terms and conditions of employment, and established negotiating and representative procedures to specifically preclude unionism. The circumstances of this particular company are quite unusual in several respects, not least because the buy-out team included the former convenor, and two shop stewards from previously militant sections of the union with pre-buy-out recognition. It was through the conduct of negotiations that the leader of the buy-out team had come to recognise their abilities both technical and potentially managerial and which had resolved him to invite them to join him in the buy-out. The reformed company post buy-out was from liquidation, and it restarted with only 5% of its previous employees, although its first year's output was approaching 20% by value of that achieved in the final year before sale. The over-manning and restrictive work practices which had characterised the previous company, and which had particularly been reflected in very strict demarcation lines between the two principal product areas of the company, were to be avoided at all costs in the restart; a point which was appreciated most pertinently by the ex-trade unionists now directors who insisted on the no-union contracts.

Where trade union recognition disappeared in other companies it was for the most part more by inertia than force. The agreements had simply been allowed to lapse and neither the employees nor the local district officials of the union had sought formal recognition. Union membership on an individual basis has continued in all except one instance, where the mass resignation followed dissatisfaction with the union's part in the receivership of the company, despite there being no formal recognition of negotiating rights. There is an awareness amongst management and employees that a union card may be necessary for job mobility and thus employees may be reluctant to give it up altogether.

When the cessation of union recognition is considered with respect to the source of the buy-out it can be seen from Table 6.5 that union recognition disappeared in four cases where receivership was concerned, and five cases where the buy-out was the result of a divestment. In proportionate terms there is therefore more of a tendency for the disappearance of union recognition where receivership is involved.

The use of divestment as a means of removing trade union power does not, therefore, seem to be particularly evident. The refutation of this suggestion is even more complete when one considers the trading relationships between newly bought-out companies and their ex-parents which are discussed in Chapter 7. For the most part there was no trading relationship between parent and subsidiary, and where trading activities did occur they tended to concern only a small part of the bought-out

Industrial Relations and the Buy-out

Table 6.5
Source of Management Buy-outs

Source	No.	%	Union Recognition Pre-Buy-out	Union Recognition Post-Buy-out
Independent company in receivership	5	4.5	5	4
Parent company in receivership	15 ⎫	13.5 ⎫	12	9
Parent company divesting a subsidiary	68 ⎭ 83	61.3 ⎭ 74.8	43	38
Previous owner on retirement	23	20.7	13	14
TOTAL	111	100.0	73	65

company's customer or supplier base. There is also some evidence of consistent efforts to reduce the degree of dependence immediately after buy-out.

On balance the evidence from this survey does not support any suggestion that the buy-out has consciously been used as a means of removing trade union recognition.

Whether trade unions are used to represent workers or not the company will still need some set of procedural arrangements for the conclusion of agreements with the workforce, as a means of communication, and possibly as a focus for consultation and participation. One could argue both from the bald statistics, and from observations made within the companies, that it is because in most companies the existing trade union arrangements are in situ, simple and effective at these tasks that they continue beyond the buy-out. If the union structure did not perform the function then it may be necessary to 'invent' a whole new structure, a task which management would prefer to avoid and get on with more vital tasks unless the situation was critical. Whether or not matters are critical will depend upon the way industrial relations have been conducted in the company prior to buy-out, and may

TABLE 6.6
Strength of Trade Union Representation

Indicator	No.	% of number recognising trade unions
Existence of a closed shop		
- pre-buy-out	29	39.7
- post-buy-out	26	40.0
Recognition of shop stewards		
- pre-buy-out	63	86.3

be expected to be influenced by the existence of recognised shop stewards, the closed shop, and the experience of disputes during the preceding twelve months. A desire to remove may be expected to be positively related to the strength of unionism as measured by these three aspects.

The recognition of shop stewards seemed to go almost without question wherever the trade union representation was more than just a handful of employees. Indeed formal recognition existed in over 86% of those companies which recognised unions although what their duties involved varied enormously across the firms. The acceptance of a closed shop in twenty-nine companies pre-buy-out, and twenty-six companies post-buy-out (see Table 6.6), also indicates a greater degree of stability than might have been expected from a practice which gets a great deal of adverse publicity. The proportions are consistent with the Warwick Survey's major study of industrial relations in UK manufacturing industry.(6) In the Warwick study some 37% of the total full-time non-managerial work-force in manufacturing establishments of more than 50 employees were estimated to be employed under closed shop arrangements. Gennard, Dunn and Wright have estimated the minimum coverage of the closed shop in manufacturing at 39%.(7)

If any strong anti closed shop feeling existed it might have been expected that in the opportunity afforded by the change in ownership management would take steps to remove it. This has not taken place to any great extent and where it has been achieved it has been more at the insistence of the workforce

Industrial Relations and the Buy-out

TABLE 6.7

Industrial Relations Disputes in Twelve Months Prior to Buy-out

Form of Dispute	No.	%	Cause of Dispute	No.	%
Strike	3	2.7	Wages	9	8.1
Overtime Ban	6	5.4	Working Conditions	1	0.9
Other	3	2.7	Manning Levels	3	2.7
			Buy-out	1	0.9
Dispute	100	90.1	No Dispute	100	90.1

Base for percentages = 111; percentages do not sum to 100% because of multiple responses.

than management. Indeed, in our discussions with management more have emphasised the virtues of simplicity in negotiations afforded by the closed shop than have criticised the restrictions. Although the closed shop may give more power to the union controlling it it is seen as a useful procedural device by management when they accept the need to negotiate under some sort of arrangement.(8)

VI. INDUSTRIAL DISPUTES EXPERIENCE

How power, or potential power, translates into action is the important issue for management. It is therefore pertinent to examine the companies' experiences in the face of industrial action during the preceding twelve months. The type and causes of disputes are detailed in Table 6.7 and show that over 90% of the companies were incident free during the twelve months preceding buy-out. In only three companies (2.7%) had there been a strike, in six (5.4%) there had been an overtime ban, and in three others some form of action had been taken. Wages were by far the most important cause of disputes although it is notoriously difficult to give single causes for most incidents and there is a tendency for deeper issues to be disguised by 'monetarisation'. The buy-out itself had been the subject of industrial action in one company where the workers were reacting to the uncertainty which the proposed sale brought about.

These experiences are not atypical of companies throughout UK manufacturing. Even in supposed black spots for industrial relations (e.g. manufacturing on Merseyside) 95% of plants are strike free during an average year.(9) Small companies also tend to be less strike prone than large companies with the probability of a strike rising significantly as plant size increases.(10) Whilst the number of incidents may be lower the number of incidents per 100,000 employees tends to be higher in small firms though the number of working days lost is considerably smaller.(11) The potential exists for frictions to cause problems but the dramatic loss of working days is concentrated in the larger firms such that 0.25% of establishments can account for 80% of days lost.(12)

The sample of management buy-outs therefore seems to produce a pattern of strikes and other industrial action that is no different from the general pattern of industrial action in UK manufacturing. They are neither more nor less strike prone than broadly similar companies. There is no suggestion that managers are only seeking to buy-out companies which have already demonstrated that they have acquiescent workforces, nor that they are buying companies where the 'defeat of the unions' is the short-cut to success.

VII. JOB LOSSES

The 'reasonableness' of trade union attitudes is also exemplified in the experiences of companies which have had to shed labour. Job losses are always an extremely delicate matter to negotiate and to effect and were necessary in forty-nine of the companies at the time of buy-out. In forty-one of these cases the management reported no organised trade union resistance, and of the eight instances of opposition in only two cases was it described as strong. For the most part job losses were achieved through compulsory redundancy (75% of firms), in some places supplemented by voluntary agreements and natural wastage. By no means all of these cases were in management buy-outs from receivership. Overall it would appear that the pattern and manner of job

Industrial Relations and the Buy-out

losses and reactions to them are similar in buy-outs to those experienced in other firms.

There have occasionally been delicate industrial relations issues to resolve surrounding job losses and re-engagements where some compulsory redundancies have been completed before the buy-out and the workers re-engaged almost immediately having picked up their redundancy payments from the previous employer. This may cause some resentment when new workers are taken on, or if, as in one of the companies studied, people from a previous round of redundancies had been re-engaged after a spell of several months' unemployment. The two groups of workers were quite distinct after buy-out, with those having experienced unemployment more moderate in their demands than those taken on immediately on changeover. Where all employees could not be re-engaged the selection of employees has been a crucial factor in the prospects for success of the new company. In every case examined management has been very clear in their desire to employ only 'good' workers and to avoid previous 'trouble-makers'.

It has often been a condition of re-employment that workers either do different jobs, work more flexibly, or be prepared to move between jobs. In this respect, in several instances it is possible to argue that the terms and conditions of employment have changed. For example, at Panache (see Chapter 8) it was agreed that previously non-working foremen would henceforth operate machinery; at a West Midlands manufacturing company machine hands gave support across a number of previously demarcated areas; in a small iron foundry skilled men took less skilled jobs on the understanding that when demand for their particular skill arose they would switch jobs, and then back again. It is worth noting that at the foundry the major variation in the terms and conditions of employment was suffered by management who had to forego their pension rights in the first instance as they were too expensive for the company to bear.

One aspect of the buy-out at Panache worth noting here is that the trade union was opposed to employees injecting any of their redundancy money into the business and at national level the union seemed prepared to let the firm fall rather than concede a point of principle. As a result, in the employees' eyes, the union was cast in the role of 'villain' and the management as 'hero' for restarting the business and continuing employment.

VIII. TRADE UNIONS AND NEGOTIATIONS OF THE DEAL

The role of employee representatives in the negotiation of the buy-out itself is of crucial importance. Where trade unions are recognised in the company this essentially distills to a consideration of the trade union's role and attitude to the buy-out, and can be particularly important if management entertain the idea that employees may wish to participate financially in the new enterprise. The issue of the trade union attitude has been most forcibly brought to public attention in the case of the staff buy-out at the National Freight Consortium (NFC) where the open opposition and campaigning by the TGWU, as an extension of its anti-privatisation campaign, was a feature of the negotiated deal and the share offer.(13) Attitudes at grass roots level have mellowed considerably at NFC helped immeasurably by the impressive post-buy-out performance which has seen significant increases in the value of shares held by those workers who subscribed on buy-out. The change has been so considerable that representations have been made to management for a second share issue to give those workers who did not subscribe the first time (for the most part on union advice) a second chance. An almost parallel share price growth has been experienced at the other staff buy-out at the Victaulic Co.(14) These staff buy-outs are excluded from the main results presented here but serve to illustrate the general union attitude which has been publicised. They are discussed further in Chapter 8.

In the sample under discussion in this study opposition to the buy-out was rare. Twenty-six of the seventy-three (35.6%) firms which recognised trade unions before the buy-out discussed the buy-out in advance with them. The main reason for this apparently low level of consultation, as reported in the companies visited, was the need for secrecy in negotiating the buy-out to avoid possible pre-emptive strikes from other interested parties and the desire to be seen not to prejudice shareholders' interests. In twenty-three of these twenty-six firms the unions offered verbal support for the buy-out whilst one offered financial support. Of the other two, one recommended employees not to support the buy-out financially and only one expressed outright opposition to the buy-out.

It is possible to suggest three principal reasons for this general lack of resistance to the change in ownership. First, in cases of receivership, the buy-out may be the only realistic way of preserving the jobs of at least part of the workforce. The financial institutions and the managers in the buy-outs visited, have suggested that financial support for one alternative often mooted by the unions, a workers' co-operative, would be difficult to obtain. Only three companies in the sample considered forming a workers' co-operative and only six considered a full employee buy-out. The second reason for lack of resistance relates to trade unions preferring the company to be owned and run by the management they know rather than an unknown outsider.

Finally, the fairly small average size of management buy-outs makes them individually relatively insignificant in national terms. As a result, the trade union at the national level may not be aware of the issues, not regard the company as strategic enough and be unwilling to devote resources to supporting any resistance to the buy-out. Evidence of this local emphasis is shown by the levels within the trade unions at which the buy-out was discussed. In only two cases was the national level of the union involved, for the rest the company and district level was involved in roughly equal proportions (nineteen and seventeen companies respectively), though, of course, in most of these discussions took place at both levels.

In the economic climate prevailing during the period covered by this study the rising unemployment levels and the decreasing overall role nationally for the trade unions undoubtedly added to the uncertainty felt by employees at the place of work. Any action which increased uncertainty was likely to be met with suspicion whilst events which emphasised security would generally get local support irrespective of any formal union stance. In this context, it is easy to see that the prevailing management may well be preferred to unknown outside purchasers and although it was very often impossible for local management to give assurances on employment levels and activity the employees tended to be less suspicious of the motives of current management than of outsiders. In instances where the official union line caused a split of loyalties in the workforce there was a tendency for the employees to stick with management and the company rather than to follow the union line.

IX. THE GENERAL INDUSTRIAL RELATIONS ENVIRONMENT POST-BUY-OUT

In all the companies studied in detail for this survey the industrial relations environment in the post-buy-out period has been at worst no different to that prevailing before, and at best there has been a considerable improvement in terms of motivation, morale, and involvement. It is possible to make a distinction between those companies in which the employees have a financial stake (surprisingly few) and those in which they do not. The environment is more likely to be constructive where the employees have invested their money as well as their time in the company.

The over-riding characteristic of the change in workforce attitudes post-buy-out which reflects itself in the company's industrial relations was reported to be the greater awareness of the company in its market, and an enhanced commercial realism from the employees. Formal negotiations, and indeed day-to-day relationships, were conducted against a background of greater involvement by the workers in the fortunes of the company. Thus there was a more even handed approach to negotiations because both sides knew in what general area a reasonable settlement would lie, with neither side having much flexibility or room for manoeuvre. This greater awareness often stemmed from a greater flow of information and communication between management and workforce post-buy-out. Whether the contact was formalised through consultative committees or the production of a company newsletter, or more flexible with reliance placed on a communicative management style at all levels and informal contact, there was generally a higher level of accurate information circulating in the company than beforehand. Undoubtedly, the act of buy-out itself had generated a great deal of information about the company and its prospects that had not fully decayed at the time of the survey.

Some companies had gone to great lengths to ensure that the workforce were fully informed by the use of regular briefing sessions, or as at Mansfield Shoe, a periodic broadcast of company progress over the tannoy. Where a more open style is being pursued the familiar problems of information disclosure have invariably arisen, with the need to balance the benefits of greater employee awareness against the costs should sensitive commercial information extend beyond the factory. In two cases modifications had

Industrial Relations and the Buy-out

to be made to the presentation of written details on company performance when it was learned that they were being sought by competitors.

Very often management have gained a double bonus from the greater involvement of workers, particularly so when the employees have a financial stake also. Perhaps the most distinctive example comes from NFC, which though strictly outside the terms of this study, does share characteristics. On privatisation the management at depot level discovered that the network of delivery drivers was also an extremely efficient information network on the levels of performance being offered, potential new contracts and improvements that could be made in quality of service and scheduling. The changes were most marked in those depots where the take-up rate of share ownership had been highest, and management were able to harness very fruitfully this information and market intelligence provided by the drivers.

At DPCE a company newsletter, and an engineering section employees' newsletter on technical aspects of the job, circulate within the firm and is a vital means by which that geographically diverse organisation maintains a sense of corporate collectivity. At DPCE too, the engineering section at Heathrow have maintained a share prize chart in their workshop since the company went public and employees could subscribe for shares.

A number of other companies were contemplating either or both of the concepts of employees share issue, or a consultative framework to further built upon the good employee relations which had existed since buy-out. A number expressed a desire to have done it before buy-out but claimed that the need for speed and secrecy in negotiations had mitigated against it. In all the companies studied management were fully aware of, and generally appreciative of, the contribution which the employees made to the success of the company. With almost half the companies having less than 100 employees the personal relationships between management and workers were emphasised. It was possible for the senior management staff to know all employees by name and to have a fair idea of each person's abilities within the firm. This point was emphasised in discussion concerning the selection of employees for re-engagement where the buy-out was from receivership and where all employees could not be offered employment.

If there was a single procedural change

post-buy-out which was observed with any frequency it was the increased informality in relationships and negotiations. Whilst the discussions were as serious and earnest as before the buy-out there appeared to be less emphasis on trade union led ritual even where ostensibly the negotiations procedure had not changed. These changes often did not have the support of even the seemingly most militant of union representatives at the place of work. In one company the local shop steward was known affectionately as 'the resident Marxist', and had a totally different view of the world to the managing director of the company, yet he was respected by both employees and management as a realistic and effective contributor to the success of the company. Indeed, he was elected as the employee representative to the employees' trust fund, and led local opposition to the formal union line on buy-out when it put the deal in danger. He saw the more informal procedures as a necessary efficiency gain for the company to progress.

The general environment therefore seems to have been good post-buy-out but it is necessary to add the caveat that all of the companies were 'survivor' buy-outs and most were still in the 'honeymoon' period at the time of survey.

X. CONCLUSIONS

The reaction of employees and their trade unions to the act of buying-out has generally been favourable, with only a few instances of formally organised opposition. For the most part the employees are aware of the fortunes and health of the company and have preferred the continuation of current management to the uncertainty of sale to 'outside' purchasers. This is perfectly in keeping with the usual conservatism and resistance to change that tends to characterise employees at the place of work.

For their part management do not seem to have been unduly influenced by industrial relations aspects in their decision to buy-out although it would undoubtedly have figured in the background. Certainly, there is no evidence that management have consciously used the buy-out to purchase success at the expense of their employees, and to remove formal trade union recognition. In many respects the experience observed is a function of the size of the firms, and the sectors in which they are operating and conforms to the general picture of industrial relations in all such companies over the period in question. The post-buy-out involvement of workers, no doubt boosted by the renewed enthusiasm of many managements means that for companies surveyed for this study it is unlikely that industrial relations problems are going to prove critical.

NOTES

1. For a full description see: Brown, W. (ed.): 'The Changing Contours of British Industrial Relations', Basil Blackwell, Oxford, 1981.
2. Bain, G.S. and Elsheikh, F.H.: 'Unionisation in Britain: An Inter-Establishment Analysis Based on Survey Data', British Journal of Industrial Relations, 18, July 1980.
3. Brown, W. (ed.), op. cit.
4. Gennard, J. and Dunn, S.: 'The Impact of New Technology on the Structure and Organisation of Craft Unions in the Printing Industry', British Journal of Industrial Relations, 21, 1983.
5. Ireland, N. and Law, W.: 'Economics of Labour Managed Firms', Croom-Helm, 1983.
6. Brown, W. (ed.), op. cit., see pp. 54-59.
7. Gennard, J., Dunn, S. and Wright, M.: 'The Extent of Closed Shop Arrangements in British Industry', Employment Gazette, 88, 1980.
8. The connivance of management in preserving closed shops in the face of legislation has been detailed in Weeks, B., Mellish, M., Dickens, L. and Lloyd, J.: 'Industrial Relations and the Limits of the Law', Basil Blackwell, Oxford, 1975.
9. Smith, C.R., Clifton, R., Makeham, P., Creigh, S. and Burn, R.: 'Strikes in Britain', Department of Employment Manpower Paper No. 5, HMSO, 1978.
10. Margison, P.: 'The Distinctive Effects of Plant and Company Size on Workplace Industrial Relations', British Journal of Industrial Relations, 22, 1984.
11. Brown, W. (ed.), op. cit., pp. 91-94.
12. Smith et al., op. cit.
13. See Oakeshott, R.: 'Privatisation and Worker Buy-outs', Public Money, December 1983.
14. Dickson, T.: 'A Buy-out Surges Ahead', The Financial Times, 26 June, 1984.

Chapter 7

PERFORMANCE IN MANAGEMENT BUY-OUTS

I. INTRODUCTION

The theme pursued throughout this book has been the contribution of management buy-outs to the restructuring and regeneration of British industry. The previous two chapters have examined the changes that buy-outs have brought about in terms of management organisation and employee relations. This chapter continues the theme by considering economic and financial aspects of restructuring and their effects on performance.

The under-performance in economic and financial terms that the separation of ownership and control is argued to lead to in companies may be summarised as follows. In general the problem is one of a reduced desire and incentive to adapt optimally to the firm's environment. Essentially, in economic terms this may mean that the employment level in the firm may be inappropriate, the firm's market may be inadequately served, and the level of investment that may be permitted may be insufficient to replace equipment as it wears out. As a result, the firm's ability to compete in the market place is severely restricted. If the remarriage of ownership and control that buy-outs bring is to be beneficial it would be expected that these three problems be substantially reduced if not removed, both through the removal of restrictions imposed by the former parents and the introduction of incentives to encourage the new owner-managers. These economic performance issues are dealt with in the following section.

Financial performance may be considered in terms of profitability and sales growth, liquidity and an appropriate long-term financial structure. These factors are a reflection of the economic problems noted above. Poor performance in the market place has a direct effect on profitability and sales growth. Additionally, the restrictions imposed by the original owners may produce short-term and long-term problems. Short-term problems concern limitations on the ability to control debtors and cash flow (for example, because of pooled banking or credit management arrangements where the bought-out company was formerly part of a group). Whereas long-term problems relate to insufficient funds for investment (for example, because of excessive dividend payments or a former parent 'milking' the subsidiary to provide funds for investment elsewhere in the group). The effects of the buy-out on the resolution of these problems are considered in the third section.

II. ECONOMIC PERFORMANCE

The three main economic performance factors, employment, markets and investment, are considered in their turn in this section.

i) Employment Levels and Changes

A recurrent argument in the debate on the need to restructure British industry has been that inefficiencies have been substantially due to over-manning and that improvements can only be brought about at the cost of widespread job loss. To the extent that buy-outs are part of the movement towards better efficiency in British industry, some shedding of labour may be expected on the change in ownership.

Out of the 111 firms in the sample, 49 (44.1%) reduced their full-time labour force at the time of the change in ownership. In total job terms, this reduction amounted to an 18.1 per cent fall in full-time employment from 18,903 to 15,479.

However, these figures represent only one side of the coin. Against them it is necessary to offset, firstly, those jobs retained which might otherwise have been lost and, secondly, the longer-term employment benefits which may follow the initial reorganisation. Some indication of these benefits is shown in Table 7.1. Overall the post-buy-out level of full-time employment at the time of the survey had risen to 17,517, an 11.3 per cent increase on the employment figure immediately after the company

131

TABLE 7.1

Employment Changes in Management Buy-outs

	Source of Buy-out			
	Receivership		Divestment	Retirement of owner
	Independent	Parent		
Before Buy-out:				
Full-time Employment	953	2704	12,390	2856
Average Firm Size	190.6	180.3	182.2	129.8
After Buy-out: (Time of Survey)				
Full-time Employment	429	2504	11,163	3421
Average Firm Size	85.8	166.9	164.2	155.5
No. of Firms	5	15	68	22

Note: One buy-out on retirement of the owner did not report employment figures.

was acquired by the management. But these overall results mask what is happening in buy-outs from different sources. As might be expected, buy-outs that occur simply on the retirement of the owner came off best in terms of the comparison between pre- and post-change in ownership employment. In buy-outs of independent firms from receivership over half the pre-buy-out jobs were lost with, according to our case studies, some companies continuing to reduce the pay-roll after the change. But if this were not the case, it is likely that all the jobs would have been lost with little prospect of re-employment. As it is, some of the companies in the case studies report the re-employment of a number of those made redundant initially (see the example of Case 1 in Chapter 8).

The figures for buy-outs from parents in receivership are most interesting because they demonstrate that companies which are not viable in a larger form may contain profitable subsidiaries which can be kept as going concerns after the parent has failed.

The remaining category, where parent companies still trading divest unwanted subsidiaries, demonstrates a more intermediate pattern of employment changes.

Table 4.1 has shown that the vast majority of the buy-outs in our sample are less than four years old. This means that many buy-outs are still in the early stages of adjusting to new patterns of ownership and working. It is, therefore, a little premature to draw too many firm conclusions about how employment levels have risen in relation to the number of years which have elapsed since the buy-out. Only one of the firms bought-out prior to 1979 employed more people at the time of the survey than prior to the change in ownership, whereas this increase is true for six out of the fourteen buy-outs which occurred in 1980. For the later buy-outs, a third record increases in employment. In total employment terms, any increases in some firms are more than matched by decreases in others for buy-outs occurring in all years except prior to 1980. So, although there seems to be some slight evidence for an increase in employment levels with age, it is as well not to place too much emphasis on it. A more reliable interpretation would be that employment increases simply reflect differential performance improvements between firms within the year of ownership change. This appears to be true even when acquisition and divestment activity is taken into account. In the sample, fifteen buy-outs had engaged in acquisition activity, two had divested, a further four had undertaken both acquisition and divestment, whilst 87 buy-outs had neither acquired nor divested. (Three companies did not reply to these questions.) A test of the influence of acquisition and divestment activity on employment produced a value of chi-squared of 4.49 which with six degrees of freedom is statistically insignificant. One buy-out, however, did double its size, through the acquisition of another company, to 1,200 employees.

Two important employment questions involving

management buy-outs concern their contribution towards relieving the employment problems in those regions most affected by recession and their part in the small firms debate.

It has been argued that the effects on unemployment rates by the creation of entirely new firms in the depressed regions are likely to be very small, since it takes many new firms to compensate for the closure of one large one. The encouragement of management buy-outs in these regions, particularly in cases of receivership, may be a more fruitful way of alleviating their unemployment problems.(1)

The evidence from the survey reported here indicates that there are marked differences in the changes in buy-out employment levels which appear to be related to the level of unemployment in a region.(2)

The sample sizes in the survey were too small to produce reliable results for the last three named regions in Table 7.2, but it is apparent that West Midlands and Yorkshire/Humberside experienced substantially higher proportionate losses in jobs at the time of the buy-out than either the S. East, S. West or East Midlands. That is, the regions with the

TABLE 7.2

Changes in Employment Levels, By Region

Region	Overall Unemployment Rate (1)	Total Employment Pre-Buy-out(2)	Change in MBOs On Buy-out (3)
	%	%	%
S. East/E. Anglia	10.0	91.2	104.6
S. West	11.2	88.3	101.4
W. Midlands	16.0	81.7	122.5
E. Midlands	11.9	108.0	117.7
Yorks/Humberside	14.5	76.5	106.8
NW/North	17.1	176.5	180.4
Wales	16.5	65.7	85.2
Scotland	15.2	91.2	113.5

Notes: 1. Male Unemployment Rate at July 1983 (time of survey)
2. Post-buy-out employment as percentage of pre-buy-out employment.
3. Post-buy-out employment as percentage of employment following job losses on buy-out.

lowest existing unemployment rates are those in which the buy-outs show the lowest job losses on ownership transfer. However, it is encouraging that West Midlands and Yorkshire/Humberside do experience the greatest percentage increases in employment after the buy-out.

Parallels have been drawn in preceding chapters between management buy-outs and new small firms and it is necessary here to address their comparative effects on employment.

The contribution of entirely new small firms to the creation of employment is difficult to measure. A recent study by Storey suggests that although small firms are increasing employment at a time when large firms are showing reductions their contribution is not as high as has often been claimed and it is unlikely that the employment created by surviving wholly new firms adds more than 1.5 per cent annually to the gross stock of jobs. In addition, the chances are that most of the new firms currently being created will show little if any employment growth with a high probability of going into receivership within a decade of birth. Drawing on information for the Midlands and Cleveland, Storey estimates that the probability of a wholly new firm employing more than one hundred people in a decade is no more than 0.75 per cent.(3)

Management buy-outs include these companies which would be regarded as small (having less than about 200 employees) but not exclusively so, as Table 4.4 has indicated. The effects on employment of different size categories of buy-outs are shown in Table 7.3. The data are presented on the basis of the year in which the buy-out took place in order to emphasise, again, that the full employment effects of the later buy-outs are unlikely to have been realised as yet.

The categories used in Table 7.3 are drawn up to be comparable with those used by Storey.(4) As in the Storey study of new small firms, it is the smaller buy-outs classes which generally display the net increases in employment.(5) But there is another employment aspect of buy-outs which these figures do not reveal. Table 7.1 has already provided an indication of the number of jobs that have been kept in buy-outs from receivership in total. The employment growth arising from new firms compared with the job savings associated with management buy-outs provides an indication of how a few companies saved from receivership can have the same magnitude of effect as many new start-ups. A recent

TABLE 7.3

Employment Changes by Different Size Classes and Year of Buy-out

Year of Buy-out	Employment Change	1-49	50-99	100-249	250-499	500+
1980	Expansions (No.)	+53	+8	–	–	–
	Contractions (No.)	–	-43	-190	-80	-90
	Total (No.)	+53	-35	-190	-80	-90
	% change	+37.9	-15.9	-38.0	-18.6	-16.4
	n	6	3	3	1	1
1981	Expansions (No.)	+109	+164	–	+50	+60
	Contractions (No.)	-58	-45	-600	-260	-670
	Total (No.)	+51	+119	-600	-210	-610
	% change	+10.6	+23.2	-36.9	-13.0	-26.0
	n	13	7	9	5	3
1982	Expansion (No.)	+2	–	+140	+60	+590
	Contractions (No.)	-14	-56	-217	-212	-390
	Total (No.)	-12	-56	-77	-152	+200
	% change	-7.1	-18.7	-2.8	-8.1	+5.5
	n	6	4	17	5	3
1983	Expansions (No.)	+12	+41	–	+30	–
	Contractions (No.)	-7	-23	-208	–	–
	Total (No.)	+5	+18	-208	+30	–
	% change	+3.1	+3.6	-64.6	+3.7	–
	n	4	6	2	2	0

survey of fifty surviving new firms in the Nottingham area (6) showed that 575 jobs were created over a period of five years. In the two buy-outs from receivership in this region included in this study, where the alternative was closure, current employment stands at 484. This compares with 635 pre-buy-out. Though it could be argued that 151 jobs were lost it is perhaps more instructive to regard it as 484 jobs saved, not far off the numbers achieved by fifty surviving new companies. Moreover, given that management have already engaged in a shake-out of surplus labour it would be expected that as these buy-outs grow there is little slack to be taken up and therefore employment levels should increase.

The foregoing discussion of employment has focussed on full-time jobs. Similar effects of the buy-out on part-time employment may also be observed. The total number of part-time jobs in the sample before the buy-out took place was 802. This number fell by some 11.7 per cent to 708 at the time of the survey, spread across sixty-nine (62.1 per cent) companies in the sample.

ii) Markets

The freedom of action in meeting the demands of the market place that the transfer of ownership on buy-out brings concerns both customer/supplier relationships and the product changes.

The uncertainty which surrounds a management buy-out in the initial stages may lead to some loss of customers and suppliers. In the sample as a whole only eight (7.2 per cent) companies lost suppliers and fifteen (13.5 per cent) lost customers as a result of the transfer of ownership. As might be expected, most of these losses occurred in cases of buy-out from receivership, with a quarter of such companies experiencing losses of customers and suppliers. That even this level of loss may be regarded as fairly low may to a large extent be attributable to the efforts made by a number of buy-out teams to maintain payments to key suppliers and deliveries to important customers even when receivership looked unavoidable. For those buy-outs on divestment from parents still trading customer and supplier losses may be minimised if sale to the management is the only transfer of ownership that is acceptable if business links are to be maintained. This strategy has been particularly effective in

TABLE 7.4

Improved Trading Relationships by Percentage of Each Source of Buy-out

	Source			
	Independent		Subsidiary	
	Receivership	Retirement	Receivership	Still Trading
	%	%	%	%
Better Supplier Relationships	40.0	21.7	60.0	38.2
Better Customer Relationships	60.0	26.1	73.3	67.6

buy-outs where the main activity is acting as a distributor for a large manufacturer.

Once the initial losses have been suffered, the indication is that trading relationships will be better than before the buy-out. In only two cases were supplier relationships worse and in only three instances were customer relationships worse than under the previous owners. In Table 7.4 it is clear that improvements are most in evidence in cases of receivership and buy-outs from parent companies. The inference must be for buy-outs from parent companies that restrictive parental policies and lack of incentives inhibited trading relationships which the remarriage of ownership and control was able to substantially rectify. A notable example here is the case of Thermalite, a buy-out from the Laing Group. It has been reported that prior to the buy-out salesmen had "gone to sleep" but subsequently a policy has been introduced which involves giving key builders guaranteed supply, free technical advice, guaranteed prices, rebates for volume sales and the buy-out team's home telephone numbers so that they can be contacted at any time.(7)

For some, however, these improved trading relationships have been obtained at a price, the price being the shortening of trade credit payment periods to suppliers and the need to give large discounts to major customers and suffer slow payment for goods delivered. The cash flow problems that have resulted are examined in more detail below.

TABLE 7.5

Trading Relationships Between Ex-Parent and Bought-out Company Before Buy-out

	Parent as Customer		Parent as Supplier	
Percentage of Sales/ Purchases	No. of Buy-outs	%	No. of Buy-outs	%
0	40	58.8	51	75.0
1-5	15	22.0	7	10.3
6-10	5	7.4	2	2.9
11-20	2	2.9	0	0.0
21-200	5	7.4	7	10.3
Not Stated	1	1.5	1	1.5
TOTAL	68	100.0	68	100.0

The general impression from the anecdotal evidence available prior to this survey was that management buy-outs from parents which were still going concerns did not involve parent-subsidiary trading as the divested unit was peripheral to the parent's main activities.(8) The evidence reported here indicates that some trading relationships do, in fact, exist between parent and subsidiary.

Thirty-two companies had some form of trading relationship with their ex-parent. For sixteen companies the parent was a customer only, for five companies the parent was a supplier only, whilst in eleven companies there was a two-way trading relationship. As may be seen from inspection of Table 7.5, these trading relationships accounted,

TABLE 7.6

Attempts to Reduce Trading Dependence on Parent

Reduce Dependence In Respect of	No.	%
Sales	6	18.8
Supplies	5	15.6
Both	6	18.8
Not Attempted	15	46.8
TOTAL	32	100.0

for the most part, for a very small proportion of the buy-outs' sales or purchases. For some companies the extent of dependence on the parent was substantial and in one case the parent was the sole customer prior to the buy-out.

In the circumstances of a high level of dependence on the former parent it is usual for the financing institutions to insist on a formal agreement that the parent will continue to trade with the subsidiary for a period of up to five years, before they would be prepared to provide funding, (see Chapter 2 for further discussion of this point). Such an agreement allows the subsidiary time to reduce its dependence on the former parent. The attempts by the buy-outs in this sample to reduce dependence are shown in Table 7.6. It is noteworthy that almost half of the companies had not attempted to reduce parental dependence, however, all but one of the companies where the parent accounted for more than ten per cent of supplies or sales had done so. In this company the alternative of going to the supplier direct existed but a preference was expressed in favour of the convenience of buying through the parent.(9)

TABLE 7.7a

The Introduction of New Products in Buy-outs

Form of New Product	Independent Receivership %	Independent Retirement %	Subsidiary Receivership %	Subsidiary Still Trading %
Refinements to Existing Products	20.0	21.7	40.0	47.1
New Product in Same market	40.0	43.5	46.7	58.8
New Products in New Market	40.0	26.1	26.7	30.9
No Change	40.0	34.8	20.0	27.9
Base for %	5	23	15	68

Performance in Management Buy-outs

The developments that have been introduced in the product ranges of buy-outs, the second aspect of market changes, are shown in Table 7.7. These changes relate to both the introduction of new products and the ending of obsolete ones and it is clear that companies have paid more attention to the former than to the latter. The major changes taking place concern the introduction of new products in the same market, with the indication being that buy-outs on divestment from parents still trading have been most active in this respect (Table 7.7a). Overall, buy-outs from parental groups show the most activity in changing their product ranges, which lends support to the hypothesis that it is in these companies that the market restrictions imposed by the former owners were most marked. The evidence on the products which are no longer produced must be more tentative because of the small numbers involved, but the implication from Table 7.7b is that firms have sought mainly to make adjustments in their existing markets rather than to withdraw from them.

TABLE 7.7b

The Ending of Production in Buy-outs

Form of Production Ceased	Independent Receivership	Independent Retirement	Subsidiary Receivership	Subsidiary Still Trading
	%	%	%	%
Replacement by Newer Version	20.0	4.3	-	13.2
Desire to withdraw from Market	40.0	4.3	-	8.8
Rationalisation of Product Range	-	13.0	20.0	17.6
No Change	60.0	78.3	80.0	69.1
Base for %	5	23	15	68

iii) Investment

The extent to which investment expenditure was possible before the transfer of ownership took place depends, clearly, on the resources made available to the company. In buy-outs from receivership the funds available are likely to have been limited by the company's precarious financial state, whereas in buy-outs on retirement of the previous owners excessive dividends may have been removed or the owner may have pursued a quiet life approach and simply not invested effectively. In buy-outs from parents still trading the funds may be limited either because of poor performance in the parent or because the subsidiary was perceived not to fit the main thrust of the group's strategy or because the workings of the internal capital market in the group diverted funds towards those areas which were considered to produce a higher rate of return.(10) A subsidiary may not fit the parent's corporate strategy either because the parent's strategy has shifted and the products produced by the subsidiary are no longer relevant (see for example the case of Dennis and Robinson in Chapter 8 and that of Balding and Mansell reported in the Financial Times),(11) or because the parent has no expertise in managing that product area (see for example the case of Thermalite) (12) or because the subsidiary is below what the parent considers to be the critical size threshold for allocating investment funds (see for example the case of Lanemark in Chapter 8). The workings of the internal capital market may also mean that a subsidiary is starved of investment funds when it is basically a highly profitable entity. Williamson has pointed out that such problems may arise when the parent company goes beyond its optimum point of diversification giving rise to serious control loss that may unduly depress the performance of the subsidiary.(13) In addition, the internal control market may be imperfect to the extent that political processes within the firm are able to exert pressure which diverts funds to those areas which have the greatest influence if not the greatest return on investment.

The evidence from the survey of buy-outs is reported in Table 7.8 and shows that since the buy-out took place only nine per cent of companies had not undertaken investment expenditure. For those engaging in investment expenditure, vehicles and equipment were overwhelmingly the preferred areas. As before, the small numbers problem inhibits the

TABLE 7.8

Investment Behaviour in Management Buy-outs

	Source			
	Independent		Subsidiary	
Investment	Receiver-ship	Retirement	Receiver-ship	Still Trading
	%	%	%	%
Land and Buildings	–	21.7	40.0	19.1
Vehicles	60.0	78.3	80.0	76.5
Equipment	60.0	82.6	73.3	79.4
No Investment	20.0	4.3	6.7	10.3
Base for %	5	23	15	68

drawing of strong conclusions about the behaviour of buy-outs from different sources. There is some slight indication that continued lack of funds has inhibited investment expenditure for independent companies in receivership which were the subject of a buy-out.

III. FINANCIAL PERFORMANCE

The results presented in this section rely primarily on responses to the questionnaire concerning changes in profitability and liquidity. Since buy-outs have only been observed to occur to any great extent during the last five years it was not possible to obtain detailed information on financial performance for many of the respondents. However, in order to gain some insights into buy-out profitability and gearing levels an attempt has been made to report some of the early results for those buy-outs in the sample which were undertaken in 1980 and 1981. These results are discussed in the last sub-section together with some case study evidence on the appropriateness of the long-term finance package that buy-outs have to service.

Performance in Management Buy-outs

i) Sales Growth and Profitability

The buy-out managers' perceptions of the performance of their companies are reported in Tables 7.9 and 7.10. Given the upheaval caused by the change in ownership and its accompanying reorganisation it was thought useful to divide companies into those which

TABLE 7.9

Actual Performance - Buy-outs Two Years Old or More

	Profits		Sales	
	No.	%	No.	%
Substantial Stable Growth	13	38.2	15	44.1
Fluctuating but Some Growth	10	29.4	8	23.6
Slight but Stable Growth	2	5.9	6	17.7
No Change	1	2.9	1	2.9
Decline	8	23.6	4	11.7
TOTAL	34	100.0	34	100.0

TABLE 7.10

Actual Performance Compared with Expected-Buy-outs Less Than Two Years Old

	Profits		Profits	
	No.	%	No.	%
Actual Substantially Better Than Expected	20	26.0	12	15.6
Actual Slightly Better Than Expected	17	22.0	23	29.9
Actual As Expected	11	14.3	20	26.0
Actual Slightly Worse Than Expected	21	27.3	18	23.3
Actual Substantially Worse Than Expected	8	10.4	4	5.2
TOTAL	77	100.0	77	100.0

were bought-out over two years ago, so that a more stable picture may be obtained, and those bought-out within the last two years, which may not as yet have fully completed reorganisation programmes.

The profits and sales performance of the buy-outs greater than two years old (Table 7.9) shows, for the most part, an encouraging picture. About one half of the companies display either substantial or slight stable growth whilst for a quarter to thirty per cent growth has been achieved amidst fluctuating fortunes. For a few companies, however, profits and sales have declined. It is noticeable in Table 7.9 that the performance of sales is better in more companies than it is for profits, indicating that profit margins are being squeezed.

For the recent buy-outs, performance perceptions are more varied (Table 7.10). Although almost one half of these companies have performed better than expected, a substantial proportion have not done so well. Again it is apparent that profit margins are being squeezed, except for those doing substantially better than expected. The handful of companies which had performed substantially worse than expected do not appear to have got the buy-out off the ground. This difficulty may be partially attributable to the continuing depth of the recession. When the sources of the buy-outs are examined it seems that the older

TABLE 7.11

Factors Affecting Profits For the Last Completed Financial Year

Factor	Favourable No.	%	Unfavourable No.	%
Industry/Market	23	20.7	15	13.5
Productivity	19	17.1	–	–
Overheads	18	16.2	–	–
Profit Margins	8	7.2	12	10.8
Purchasing Policies	8	7.2	2	1.8
Development/New Markets	5	4.5	2	1.8
Extraordinary Items	5	4.5	11	9.9
Financing	3	2.7	2	1.8
Currency Variations	2	1.8	2	1.8

Base for Percentages = 111

buy-outs on retirement and on divestment from a parent still trading are the ones suffering a decline in profits and sales, though the successful companies in these categories do perform as well as buy-outs from receivership sources. A similar picture emerges when buy-outs less than two years old are examined by sources, except that some of the buy-outs from receivership also show actual performance slightly worse than expected.

The factors affecting the changes in fortunes of the companies in the sample are shown in Table 7.11. The table illustrates how some items can have a beneficial effect on profits whilst others have the reverse effect. Most notable in this respect are industrial and market factors which have helped improve profits in a fifth of cases, but have contributed to a decline in profits for fifteen of the buy-outs. The increased ability of managers buying-out to control overhead costs and increase productivity is very much in evidence in the table and there is also some support for the suggestion made above that profit margins were being squeezed in a number of instances. The adverse effects on profits of extraordinary items (such as start-up costs, legal fees, reorganisation costs etc.) are also noteworthy.

The factors affecting profits are generally fairly evenly spread between the sources of buy-outs. The most apparent difference is that buy-outs from receivership have benefited by growth in their markets, whilst buy-outs from the other two sources have been just as likely to experience market decline. Buy-outs from parents still trading also appear more susceptible to the adverse effects of extraordinary items in their profit levels.

ii) Cash Flow and Liquidity

Across all firms in our sample, some 46.9% did not experience any cash flow problems and amongst these, those bought out on retirement or as divestments from a parent still trading are disproportionately represented. The 53.1% of companies experiencing cash flow difficulties, was made up of 21.6% who only had problems before the buy-out, 13.5% who had problems only after the buy-out and 18.2% who experienced adverse cash flow both before and after the change in ownership. It is interesting to note two aspects which are evident from Table 7.12. First, four out of the five companies that had been

TABLE 7.12

Sources of Management Buy-outs and Cash Flow Problems

Source	No Cash Flow Problem No.	Cash Flow Problem Pre-buy-out No.	Post-buy-out No.	Pre- and post-buy-out No.	Total No.	%
Independent company in receivership	0	4	0	1	5	4.5
Parent company in receivership	1	12	1	1	15	13.5
Parent company divesting a subsidiary	38	6	10	14	68	61.3
Previous owners on retirement/death	13	2	4	4	23	20.7
TOTAL	52 (46.9%)	24 (21.6%)	15 (13.5%)	20 (18.0%)	111	100.0
		59 (53.1%)				

in receivership before the buy-out had resolved their cash flow problems following the transition to management ownership. Second, there was some tendency for those companies being bought-out from a parent still trading, either not to solve their liquidity problems or to develop cash flow difficulties on becoming independent.

By examining in detail the reasons behind these cash flow problems, some insight into the difficulties facing management buying-out may be obtained. Table 7.13 deals with the causes of pre-buy-out cash flow difficulties and Table 7.14 analyses post-buy-out causes. For most companies,

TABLE 7.13

Cash Flow Problems Before the Buy-out

	All Respondents	
	No.	%
Parent Related Problems	19	43.2
Company's Own Finance Problems	11	25.0
Company's Own Cost Problems	6	13.6
Company's Own Market Problems	8	18.2
Company's Own Management Problems	2	4.5
No Reason Stated	3	6.8

Base No. of Respondents = 44
Note: Totals do not sum to 100% because of multiple responses.

TABLE 7.14

Cash Flow Problems After the Buy-out

	All Respondents	
	No.	%
Not achieving expected profit margins	19	54.3
Debtor Related	14	40.0
Market Related	7	20.0
Interest Payments on Overdraft	9	25.7
Interest Payments on Long-term Loans	9	25.7
Stock Levels	8	22.9
Capital Expenditure	2	5.7
Other	2	5.7

Base number of respondents = 35
Note: Totals do not sum to 100% because of multiple responses.

there were a number of reasons why liquidity was not what it should have been. However, the single most often mentioned cause was parent related (43.2% of respondents). The detailed breakdown of these parent related problems reveals a wide variety of behaviour by the parent which adversely affected the subsidiary. In ten of the nineteen companies the cash flow problem was directly caused by the parent drawing cash from the subsidiary through pooled banking arrangements. The principal other reasons mentioned were, the witholding of long-term finance, the taking of a maximum dividend and the non-payment of trading debts by the parent.

The company's internal pre-buy-out financial problems mainly concern trading at a loss, but there was also some incidence of debtor control problems and over-trading generally. A low level of market penetration was the main market related difficulty, but there was also some evidence that the firms may have benefited from closer scrutiny of the range of goods provided and the spread of customers to whom the goods were supplied. High overheads including excessive stock levels and over-manning in indirect labour areas were the principal cost problems.

The companies displaying post-buy-out cash flow problems are predominantly those divested from parents still trading. As the information in Table 7.14 demonstrates, the principal single cause of post-buy-out liquidity difficulties relates to not achieving expected profit margins, being mentioned by over half of these 35 respondents. Although the high incidence of substantial sales and profits growth for buy-outs in general has been noted in Table 7.9 to 7.11 above, it is clear on closer examination that for those buy-outs experiencing liquidity problems after the buy-out sales increases have often been accompanied by a decline in profits. Amongst all 111 companies, about 55 per cent had made profits and sales greater than expected. For those with post-buy-out problems only 31 per cent reported profit increases greater than expected, though sales were better than expected in 54 per cent of these cases.

This problem may be linked with the difficulties caused by a highly geared financial package, the burden of which on cash flow may only become apparent some time after the deal has been completed.

Direct evidence that this debt burden has in some cases led to difficulties is provided by the quarter of respondents with cash flow problems which were due to the adverse effects of interest payments on loans. But, given the generally high gearing levels in management buy-outs, which have often attracted attention and about which more is said below, it is perhaps surprising that the extent of liquidity problems caused by high interest burdens is not more widespread.

The other important cause of post-buy-out cash flow difficulties is debtor-related problems, which may be divided into two principal sources. First, that which relates to debtors using their greater size or market power to delay payment (and similarly with respect to creditors who demand early payment), and second, that which concerns the efficacy of the debtor control systems in buy-outs. The adverse effects of larger firms' behaviour on the trade credit position of smaller companies has been widely discussed in the economics and accounting literature.(15) For management buy-outs the position may be exacerbated by uncertainty in the minds of suppliers and customers as to the chances of success for the newly independent company, especially if it is a buy-out from receivership. Even where customers and suppliers are attempting to be supportive, a frequent occurrence as has already been noted, problems may arise for the buy-out. These difficulties are well illustrated by the case study from the survey where a buy-out from receivership was both a customer and a supplier to a major electronics company. The buy-out was initially provided with a significant amount of consignment stock and allowed two and a half months' credit. On the other side of the coin, the buy-out was obliged to give big discounts to the subsidiaries of the major company who usually exceeded their trade credit period before making payment. Although in the longer-term this buy-out may be able to become less dependent on this particular company it is for the time being squeezed on both sides of the trade credit equation. The major company as supplier can demand and receive quick payment for the goods it supplies. However, as the department dealing with payments to suppliers of the major company is organisationally separate from that dealing with payments by customers to the company, the buy-out cannot use its intermediate position to obtain alleviation of its cash flow problems.

The efficacy of debtor control systems is of crucial importance to the survival and success of a company. Evidence shows deficiencies in this area to be one of the major causes of small company failure.(16) That only fourteen companies out of the total sample of 111 experience this type of problem is probably a reflection of the emphasis placed by the financing institutions on the existence of a strong credit control system as one of the conditions for supporting a deal.

The importance of good control of debtors was evident from the case studies. Indeed in one of the companies visited, a wholesale textile supplier, the financing institution insisted upon a factoring agreement being taken out before it would extend long-term finance. It is noteworthy that in another, a shoe manufacturer, the management buying-out had very successfully improved on their predecessor's cash control procedures, shortly <u>before</u> the buy-out. This latter company was part of a group which went into receivership. The experience classically illustrates the problem of inadequate central control and the protection of the original management over a number of years from the consequences of their poor debtor control, and lapsed financial management. There had never been any insistence or incentive to radically improve the local position, and the central facility to some extent disguised the poor divisional performance. In another case, a company, making a variety of fasteners and which had reduced its workforce from 220 before the buy-out to 12 afterwards, for a 50% fall in turnover, carried out all its invoicing and credit control using a micro computer - representing a very cost-effective improvement on the previous manual system. That this point needs to be emphasised may be seen from the only buy-out in our sample to have been subsequently acquired. This company experienced a complete reversal of all that has just been said, moving from a localised, micro computer based system to a centralised mainframe credit control procedure. This move has created more needless work, has made debt collection less efficient and has led to the deterioration in customer and supplier relations to such an extent that at least one major customer has taken his business elsewhere.

IV. PERFORMANCE OF TWO COHORTS

As management buy-outs have only been observed to any significant extent since 1980 the number of companies in our sample prior to this date is very limited. At the time of the survey the more recent buy-outs had not had time to deposit their performance returns with Companies' House. It has, therefore, only been possible to compile performance data for those buy-outs in the sample which took place in 1980 and 1981. The data are presented in Table 7.15 and show, for the 1980 cohort, four principal performance indicators for the year of the buy-out and the following year. For the 1981 buy-outs information was only available for all the sample for the year of the buy-out.(17) The four indicators shown in Table 7.15 enable some initial comments to be made about the performance characteristics of this type of company. However, as the samples are fairly small and the number of years

TABLE 7.15

Some Key Performance Statistics

	i) 1980 Cohort			
	Mean	Std dev^n	Minimum	Maximum
Year of Buy-out				
Net Assets (£'000)	113.0	1532.5	148.9	5248.4
Return on Assets (%)	14.9	15.9	(16.0)	39.5
Gearing Ratio (No.)	5.3	24.0	(31.4)	71.0
Finance Service Cost Coverage Ratio (No.)	0.98	2.88	(6.3)	4.8
First Year After Buy-out				
Net Assets (£'000)	1278.2	1801.7	199.1	6173.3
Return on Assets (%)	7.4	11.6	(12.2)	29.2
Gearing Ratio (No.)	(0.9)	7.9	(21.9)	6.6
Finance Service Cost Coverage Ratio (No.)	0.71	1.57	(2.3)	3.3

n = 11

Performance in Management Buy-outs

ii) 1981 Cohort

	Mean	Std dev^n	Minimum	Maximum
Year of Buy-out				
Net Assets (£'000)	1824.3	1074.1	67.1	17,627
Return on Assets (%)	22.3	59.8	(36.7)	303.4
Gearing Ratio (No.)	0.13	7.92	(38.3)	9.0
Finance Service Cost Coverage Ratio	0.92	6.0	(23.5)	9.0

n = 27
Note: Figures in parenthesis are negative.

Definitions:
Net Assets = As below
Return on Net Assets = Profits before interest and tax divided by Fixed Assets plus current assets less current liabilities plus bank overdraft.
Gearing Ratio = Debentures, long term loans plus preference shares divided by ordinary shares plus reserves.
Finance Service Cost Coverage Ratio = Profits before interest and tax divided by debentures, long term loans, preference and ordinary dividends.

information available is limited any appraisal is bound to be indicative only. The performance indicators comprise a size measure (net assets), a measure of profitability from trading activities (return on net assets), a measure of the financial structure (gearing ratio) and a measure of the buy-outs' abilities to service their financial structure (finance coverage ratio).

The main general point which stands out from Table 7.15 is the range and variability of the indicators between bought-out companies. This observation provides further support for the point made throughout this book that buy-outs are a heterogeneous class of company, and is consistent with remarks made by Bougen and Drury (18) in their study of 700 companies in 45 industries throughout the UK. As with their study the performance of the sample of buy-outs reported here contains a number of extreme outliers. However, whilst their study included extremely high performers and companies with high gearing ratios, the buy-outs are also characterised by a number of companies with extremely low levels of the performance indicators. Examining each indicator in detail reveals first of all that the average net assets in these buy-outs was well over one million pounds, though this average hides a wide dispersion of sizes. It is noticeable that the average net assets of the 1981 cohort are substantially greater than that for those buy-outs taking place in 1980. This difference probably reflects the development of the buy-out market-place in the later year, when more institutions became actively involved in funding larger buy-outs (often in syndicates). Previously ICFC, whose major expertise is in lending to the smaller company had virtually had the market to themselves. In comparison with the bulk of ICFC investments the average size of buy-outs taking place in 1980 was a little smaller. ICFC reports that for a sample of 499 of their clients the average net assets size in 1980 was £1.41 million.(19)

The 1980 cohort reports substantially lower profitability in the year of the buy-out than do those buy-outs in 1981. Indeed, the earlier buy-outs show an average profitability fall between their first and second years of independence. These differences may be partly attributable to the larger sample size for the 1981 buy-outs. They may, however, be more to do with the benefits to be derived from experience, which mean that sounder companies, less affected by the general recession, were funded in the later year.

In comparison with ICFC companies, which showed an average return on assets of 15.1 per cent in 1980, the average level of profitability is about the same. This is some way below the average for the larger UK companies covered in the Department of Trade and Industry survey, which recorded an 18.5 per cent return on net assets for 1980.(20)

The problem of high gearing ratios has been alluded to in Chapter 2. The evidence presented in Table 7.15 suggests that high gearing ratios are not a universal feature of management buy-outs. Part of the reason for this is the inclusion of reserves in the denominator of the gearing ratio, which for successful companies bought-out substantially reduces the gearing level. (Note, that high negative gearing ratios mean high borrowing in relation to equity, the negative overall value being the result of negative reserves). The lower gearing ratios in the 1981 cohort reflect the greater profitability of these companies, so inflating reserves, and possibly the effect of institutions entering the market at this time which placed a greater emphasis on providing equity funding than had been the norm previously. The Bougen and Drury study, which by its nature was less influenced by firms raising large amounts of new debt funding, reported an average gearing ratio of 0.6 with a standard deviation of 0.69 and a range from zero to 2.4.(21)

The finance coverage ratio provides a measure of a company's ability to service its capital structure. The companies in the 1980 cohort show a reduced ability on average to service their financing between the first and second year of operating. For some, profits are lower than the total interest and dividend payments required to be paid; for others a healthy safety margin is recorded. High rates of interest at the time the earlier buy-out deals were completed has therefore imposed an added burden on these companies, when they were already having to cope with a recession which turned out to be deeper and more prolonged than anticipated.

The comments made with respect to the two financing ratios have indicated that a number of buy-outs are experiencing difficulties in servicing their capital structure - an issue which provoked a number of comments in the case studies that were carried out.

The financial position of a bought-out company may be influenced by the funding institution at two stages, the negotiation of the deal and some time after the transfer of ownership has taken place. What happens at the time the deal is negotiated clearly directly affects the subsequent position of the company. The extent to which the funding institution is willing and able to be flexible at the later stage can have an important bearing on the success or indeed survival of the independent company.

Whilst negotiations with the vendors conducted on behalf of the management team by the financing institution could be helpful in reducing the price to be paid, subsequent negotiations concerning the form of the financing package could be problematic and store up difficulties for the future. Two major issues became abundantly clear during the interview stage of the study. Managers, whilst appreciative of the requirement for an adequate reward to be earned for the risks taken expressed some concern that the financing institutions appeared to be over-safeguarding themselves in case of failure and taking a substantial reward if the venture were successful. This was achieved through taking charges on the company's assets or requiring personal securities and through the conditions attached to the preferred ordinary shares held by the institution.(22) Quite apart from the burden placed on management, such a policy could seriously reduce the bought-out company's ability to build up retained profits for investment. The effect on investment could be particularly serious where there had been a lack of investment for a number of years prior to the buy-out taking place. It might then be thought that the company was still being 'milked' only the milker has changed! This problem where it exists, may be exacerbated by the conditions attached to the early redemption of the institutions' funds. Those buy-outs wishing to pay-off the institutions early have either been unable to do so because of the conditions attached to the initial agreement or have had to pay a high premium. Hence, those most able to pay are able to extricate themselves from such deals, whilst those less well positioned continue with what many see as an excessive drain on cash resources. This reluctance on the part of institutions to accept early redemption or renegotiation of the package is particularly linked to the possibility of losing income streams, which were fixed when rates of interest were very high, now that rates of interest are relatively low by comparison.

The extent to which the agreed financial package can be a problem is influenced both by the subsequent performance of the buy-out, a fast grower has a better chance of trading out of any difficulties which may arise, and the initial strength of the buy-out team's bargaining position. A team constrained by time and/or one with no alternative employment prospects may be in a much weaker position than one where these conditions are absent. To repeat what has been said earlier, it may be better not to pursue an unfavourable deal rather than agree to terms which make the chances of success remote.

The negotiation stage also produced several other comments from the case studies, to cite four examples: the financial institutions have changed the terms of an agreement at a very late stage when the buy-out team had little alternative but to accept; the institutions usually obtain preferential treatment in relation to other creditors, which may include insistence on excessive insurance levels on premises; the institutions' costs for negotiating the deal can be excessive and the institution also ties in other services besides the basic financial package which have a drain on cash flow.

Although the above problems do exist, and may be serious for some companies, they are by no means the case in every buy-out. Indeed, a number of the buy-outs visited reported very good relations with their financiers. Institutions have been willing to renegotiate the financial package in some cases, or to delay the start of capital repayments where performance is not up to expectations. The objective advice that representatives of the institutions can provide was reported to be most helpful, though if the representative has a large portfolio to oversee the level of detailed advice that can be given may be limited. Finally, the institution may choose not to exercise a right to convert preference shares to ordinary shares and which would effectively wrest control from the management team. This must mean that the institution recognises that the incumbent management is running the company better than the funder could. In such cases one would expect to see further tangible positive support for the team.

V. CONCLUSIONS

So far, it is still too soon to make firm conclusions about the performance of management buy-outs. The evidence presented in this chapter suggests that experiences amongst surviving buy-outs have varied from the highly successful to the barely surviving. It has been clear, however, that a great deal of change has taken place in the firms, in terms of employment levels, cash flow control, markets and products and investment. It is hoped that these changes will form the basis for improved performance in the future. The economic recession is one factor which imposes a general constraint upon performance improvement, but for some buy-outs the form of the financing package is not helpful in this regard. Some buy-outs will grow rapidly so that the financing structure becomes less of a burden. However, as with small firms, many buy-outs whilst being viable businesses are going to display little if any growth. It is in these companies that an onerous financial structure may cause serious problems for the survival of the buy-out as an independent entity, if at all.

NOTES

1. See Storey, D.J.: 'Indigenising a Regional Economy: The Case of Management Buy-outs', Regional Studies, Vol. 18, No. 1, 1984.
2. The Regional Effects of buy-outs are discussed more fully in Wright, M., Coyne, J. and Lockley, H.: 'Regional Aspects of Management Buy-outs', Regional Studies, October 1984.
3. Storey, D.J.: 'Entrepreneurship and the New Firm', London, Croom-Helm, 1982, pp. 20-25.
4. Ibid., p. 23, Table 2.9.
5. The case of the 500+ employment category for 1982 is mainly a result of a large acquisition by one firm.
6. See Binks, M., Vale, P. and Atkin, T.: 'The Nottingham Small Firms Survey', University of Nottingham Small Firms Unit, 1984.
7. Gray, J.: 'Foundations laid for Prosperity', Financial Times, 5.3.84.
8. See for example Arnfield, R.V. et al.: 'Management Buy-outs: Corporate Trend for the 80s?' IBLO, University of Nottingham, 1981.
9. The issues of parent-subsidiary trading are dealt with in more detail in Wright, M.: 'The 'Make-Buy' Decision and Managing Markets: The Case of Management Buy-outs', University of Nottingham, Dept of Industrial Economics, mimeo, 1984.
10. This is the standard M-Form view expounded by Williamson (see e.g. Williamson, O.E.: 'Markets and Hierarchies', New York, Free Press, 1975, pp. 141-81), which argues that the internal capital market is more efficient at allocating resources than resort to the external capital market.
11. Dickson, T.: 'A Classic of its Kind', Financial Times, June 1984.
12. Gray, op. cit.
13. Williamson, O.E.: 'Corporate Control and Business Behaviour', Englewood Cliffs, Prentice-Hall, 1970.
14. Cash flow problems in buy-outs are dealt with more fully in Coyne, J. and Wright, M.: 'Cash Flow: The Reality After the Honeymoon', Accountancy, April 1984.

15. For some case study evidence see for example Wright, M. and Jarrett, M.: 'Will Small Be Beautiful in the 1980s?' Accountancy, April 1981. The quantitative evidence is more ambiguous as to the effect of larger firms on smaller firms' trade credit position, but for a summary of the main studies in this area see e.g. Davies, E.W. and Yeomans, K.A.: Company Finance and the Capital Market, CUP, 1974.
16. See the survey of studies of the causes of small company failure by Berryman, J.: 'Small Business Failure and Bankruptcy: A Survey of the Literature', European Small Business Journal, Vol. 1, No. 4, 1983.
17. It is worth noting that at the time the search of Companies House was made, eight of the 1981 buy-outs in our sample had not filed accounts. Two of these companies were recorded as having gone into receivership since taking part in the survey.
18. Bougen, P.D. and Drury, J.C.: 'UK Statistical Distributions of Financial Ratios, 1975', Journal Business Finance and Accounting, Vol. 7, No. 1, Spring 1980.
19. ICFC: 'The Small Firm Survey', Finance for Industry Ltd, London, February 1983.
20. For details see ibid., p. 13.
21. Op. cit., pp. 45-46.
22. See Chapter 2 for details.

Chapter 8

CASE 1   PANACHE UPHOLSTERY: A MANAGEMENT BUY-OUT
         OF AN INDEPENDENT COMPANY IN RECEIVERSHIP

INTRODUCTION

One of the earlier management buy-outs, Panache Upholstery illustrates clearly the problems and rewards of buying-out an independent company which is in receivership.(1) Of particular interest in this company is the manner in which the receivership and eventual buy-out came about, as the company had been a family business whose succession problem had proved fatal. The general performance of the company after the buy-out is worthy of attention as it is one of the few management buy-outs in our sample where the employees have participated in the financing of the company, even though they went against the advice of their trade union representatives in doing so. The importance of the presence of the type of leader and leadership style that was discussed in Chapter 5 is clearly emphasised in this case study. The managing director played the key role in resurrecting the company, and continues to play the crucial and dominant role in maintaining momentum. Though he is firmly in control, it is recognised that the cooperation of the workforce must be gained for all significant changes, so that any proposals are discussed with them. Two of the essential characteristics for a successful buy-out, that are illustrated in Chapter 2, are present here - the need for management to be clear what business they are in and the need for good customer/supplier relations.

Company Background

The company was originally founded as a family business in 1947 under the name of A. & H.

Case 8.1: Panache Upholstery

Upholstery Limited. The family held 93% of the firm's share capital, the balance being held by the Factory Manager who was also a Director. It was the Factory Manager (together with the former Production Director) who was eventually to buy-out the company.
Up until 1977, the company had made modest profits and had built up healthy financial reserves through the manufacture of three-peice suites for the medium to better end of the UK furniture market. However, it was at this time that problems began to set in stemming largely from the kind of succession difficulties which are well-known in family businesses.(2) The presence of family members in the same business would appear to intensify the usual conflicts that are likely to arise within a family. The existence of such conflict may mean that energy is dissipated in family rivalry rather than being focussed on managing and running the company.(3) The near disaster that may arise when the original family entrepreneur refuses to make changes and hand over control to the next generation has been well documented in a more spectacular vein in the case of the Ford Motor Company.(4) In the case of Ford and many other family companies it is not possible for the rest of the family to remove the patriarch, as it is he who owns the majority of the voting shares. In the case of A. & H., however, the division of the share capital was such that the founder's wife and son were able to out-vote him. This they duly did in 1977. After playing the understudy for many years, the son clearly set out to prove his own entrepreneurial ability and identity. As Managing Director, the son committed the company to a complete change of product range using leather in an attempt to enter new markets, particularly in Europe. The loss of profitability that resulted from these changes illustrates the price of failing to know which business one is in. The change of product range required skills that the existing workforce did not possess and the move to export markets required marketing expertise that the company did not possess. In addition, all attempts by the Factory Manager who had had a great deal of influence in running the factory beforehand, to convince the new Managing Director of the problems caused by the change of direction were ignored. Hence, unlike the Ford Motor Company, where the advent of the new generation saved the company, in this instance the reaction of the new Managing Director to being excluded from influence was to concentrate all power on himself.(5)

161

Case 8.1: Panache Upholstery

The period 1977-1979 saw a continued decline, with the loss of the majority of the UK market and failure in Europe; the technical problems intimated at above being exacerbated by the weakness of sterling and increases in raw material prices. As so often happens in this stage in the life cycle of a company desperate and ill-considered measures were taken in an attempt to regain some of the UK market. For example, the new styles originally developed for the continental market were tried in the UK, but even with substantial discounting of prices the home market was not there. It was at this point that the Factory Manager decided to resign from the company as he was totally frustrated in carrying out his job. However, this move did prompt the Managing Director to reassess the position. As a result he offered the Factory Manager his job back and agreed to accept the policies of the board as a whole. The reversal of the company's policy that resulted and the consequent concentration on the UK market did enable break-even to be achieved on a month-to-month basis by the end of 1979. However, the deepening effect of the recession on retail sales and the depletion of reserves that had occurred over the previous three years meant that the recovery was short-lived. From early 1980 onwards the company's performance fell inexorably so that in July the family resigned their directorships. In August of that year the company went into liquidation and all 83 employees were made redundant.

Negotiation of the Buy-out

The employees initially approached the Factory Manager to ascertain whether it was possible to keep the company going. After some discussion he took the initiative to try and use the employees' redundancy money to form a new company and acquire some of the old company's assets from the liquidator. Given the depressed state of the furniture industry in the local area, and thus little alternative employment available, this option seemed the only possible way of preserving at least some jobs. However, the state of the industry raised a large question mark as to whether such a proposition would attract sufficient external financing to make the company viable.
As the buy-out team of two were both directors of the old company it was necessary to wait for it to enter into voluntary liquidation before negotiations to start the new company could begin. The

Case 8.1: Panache Upholstery

TABLE 8.1.1
Panache Upholstery - Initial Financing

		£
Issued and fully paid share capital		
10,000 Preferred Shares (financial institution)		10,000
20,000 Ordinary Shares (2 Directors)		20,000
		30,000
Loans		
Unsecured 5 year interest free loan - Employees	61,669	
Secured 12 years 17¼% loan - financing institution	180,000	
		241,669
Grant		
Department of Industry		30,000
Total Finance (long term)		301,669
In addition: Clearing Bank Overdraft Facility		£ 60,000

Case 8.1: Panache Upholstery

negotiations began with the former Factory Manager agreeing to finance all accountancy and legal fees himself. After consultation with professional accountants and solicitors a formal proposal was drawn up on the basis of which financial support was to be sought. An overdraft facility was obtained from a clearing bank in return for the normal charge on assets and ICFC very quickly agreed to put up £190,000 in total, broken down as shown in Table 8.1.1.

The balance of the funding was provided by the Department of Industry under the provisions of the Industry Act 1972. This Act provides for the payment of sums of money which are necessary to bridge the gap between the purchase price of a company and the finance which can be raised from more conventional sources. Though a grant was obtained, payable in two instalments (£23,000 initially and the balance of £7,000 six months later) it was reported to us that the procedures and paperwork for obtaining the grant appeared to be unnecessarily complicated and required information concerning future performance which could at best be described as somewhat speculative. It was also reported that at the time there seemed to be a certain lack of awareness within the Department about what funding was available. Given the greater amount of activity since this date in this area this lack of awareness may be less of a problem now. But given the plethora of schemes that are available it may be difficult to identify which are the more appropriate to particular needs.

The role and form of employee financial participation in the company is an important aspect of the setting-up of the buy-out and its subsequent performance. The choice of the appropriate company form lay between a workers' co-operative, a company owned solely by one or two people or a company incorporating worker equity or loan participation. The workforce were in favour of a management buy-out with worker participation in funding. In this form the employees felt more secure. First, by investing their redundancy money in the form of loan finance they would be able to receive some return if the company did not succeed. Second, as management had also invested heavily in the firm they would be less likely to leave and more likely to fight harder to secure its future. However, there was resistance from the union to employees putting their money into the company if the company were to take any form but a workers' co-operative. The union was also

Case 8.1: Panache Upholstery

sensitive to the fact that the previous company had gone into receivership and recognised the difficulties they, as a union, may have subsequently in calling out the employees to support national issues. Despite the union sending an Assistant General Secretary to try to change their minds, the workforce decided to commit their redundancy money to the new company. It was reported to us by employees that we spoke to that they recognised that the cause of the previous company's demise did not lie with the buy-out team and that they were prepared to let the management do what they were good at, managing, and leave them to concentrate on their skills - making furniture.

The re-formation of the company was with a reduced workforce of 60, management seeing the need and taking the opportunity to make certain alterations to working practices, to which we return below. The employees' financial participation was to be administered by a trust fund comprising two employees selected by the workforce, an accountant and a solicitor. Employees will be able, if they wish, to convert their loans into shares at the end of the five-year period. The employees are also able to vote a non-executive director onto the Board.

With the prompt payment of employees' redundancy money the new company was able to commence trading on 1 October 1980 after a two month period of negotiations. The final initial position is shown in Table 1.

The Company After the Buy-out

Events after the buy-out focus on two main areas. First, the re-establishment of a more profitable market position. Second, the changes which have occurred in management style and employee motivation.

<u>Performance</u>. Following the disastrous attempts to penetrate European markets with an unsuitable product efforts after the buy-out were concentrated on re-establishing the company's position in the UK furniture market. One important aspect of this change was the decision to diversify into the less competitive, although expanding markets, of printed-material suites for the middle to upper price range and the loose-cover sector. Part of this approach has involved a more positive marketing effort whereby a mobile showroom tours the

Case 8.1: Panache Upholstery

independent and small chain stores. This enables customer reaction to new designs to be tested quickly, as well as enabling the more traditional designs to be displayed. Substantial goodwill from customers and suppliers during the buy-out negotiations, and subsequently, has contributed to a steady growth in sales coupled with fluctuating fortunes in terms of profits. The company pursues a tight debtor management policy but has experienced cash flow difficulties due to two incidents of arson and a flood in part of the factory which mave meant a loss of 5 per cent of production in each of the last two years. The commencement of capital repayments on the loan during the last financial year, coming on top of these set-backs, has required renegotiation of the overdraft facility and a change to another clearing bank prepared to provide a sufficient amount.

Despite some dissatisfaction with the clearing bank's willingness to extend the overdraft facility, relations with the institution providing long-term finance were reported as good esepcially as they had agreed to delays in the repayment of the loan.

Organisation and Management. The company re-employed 57 of the original workforce of 83, and of these about forty invested their redundancy payments. During the past three years, ten additional employees have been taken on and management report no problems in their integration with workers who had participated in financing the company. Any 'US and THEM' problem appears to be minimal. There are no separate arrangements concerning information on the performance of the company for employees who have invested their money. This question may not arise so much here anyway since funds are in the way of loans rather than equity.

Although management retains the same kind of authority as existed before the buy-out, the change in ownership has involved a number of changes. For management it has increased the freedom of decision-making and their equity stake has added an incentive to perform well. The increased motivation on the part of management has been matched by a similar improvement in workforce motivation. The finance element engenders a feeling that employees are working for their own company, a feeling that was emphasised by the employees we interviewed. The workforce had a real feeling that the buy-out team had saved their jobs. This increased motivation is enhanced by the introduction of an element of

Case 8.1: Panache Upholstery

employee participation in decision-making, which was entirely absent in the old company. Communication with the employees is via the works noticeboard, regular meetings with employee representatives, employees as a whole, and the Trust Fund Committee; and by the management being seen on the shop floor. The meetings between shopfloor employees and management allows issues to be discussed in an open and informal way and for disagreements on management's decisions to be raised. For the most part, these meetings involve the management and departmental spokesmen chosen by the employees themselves. Though shopfloor employees as a whole do not participate in decisions concerning strategic and operating policies they do vote on issues such as the dates of the annual holidays and other minor issues. This direct communication with the employees has further reduced the role of the trade union, which was weakened initially by its approach to the employees' financial participation in the company. Though a full union shop still exists the committee of two shop stewards currently have little influence. It is noteworthy that when the employees elected their departmental spokesmen they preferred someone else to the person who had been their shop steward. As a result of these changes, the company no longer experiences the kind of disputes which used to arise during national pay negotiations. Pay issues are now dealt with initially through the departmental spokesmen before being discussed collectively and have been limited to periods when there has been growth in sales.

The introduction of departmental spokesmen has been accompanied by the removal of non-working foremen, primarily as a part of post-buy-out rationalisation but also as a means of shortening the chain of command.

For about two years after the buy-out, the euphoria surrounding the saving of jobs, the financial stake in the enterprise and the introduction of some element of employee participation exerted beneficial effects upon motivation, performance and employee relations. However, management report that this honeymoon period began to wear off after this time with some slack creeping into piece-work operations and employee behaviour generally. The company has not returned to the pre-buy-out position since management have made clear to employees the ultimate consequences of such action. Our impression from talking to a cross-section of the employees was very

167

Case 8.1: Panache Upholstery

much one of the existence of a strong positive motivation towards the success of the company and confidence in the buy-out team. Whether this confidence will manifest itself in the conversion of loans to equity shares by employees in two years' time remains to be seen.

Conclusions

At the time of writing the company, as reformed after the buy-out, has been trading for three and a half years. Though profits have been very modest, they appear to have done well in re-establishing themselves in the market-place, particularly in view of the substantial loss of production in circumstances outside their control. They have suffered some cash flow difficulties and will be looking for a significant upward movement in profitable sales to overcome them.

The circumstances surrounding the transfer of ownership, the buy-out itself and the changes that have followed do seem to have produced increased motivation by employees to perform well for 'their' company. But, in common with the other case studies, the substantial disappearance of the dichotomy between management and employees does not by any means imply the sacrifice of management control. Rather, the success of the venture depends crucially upon the ability of the leading member of the buy-out team to act as both entrepreneur and manager and to motivate the rest of the workforce.

NOTES

1. The management team's side of the buy-out story is told in R.V. Arnfield, B. Chiplin, M. Jarrett and M. Wright: 'Management Buy-Outs: Corporate Trend for the 80s', IBLO, Nottingham University, 1981, Ch. 5.
2. See for example H. Levison: 'Conflicts that Plague Family Businesses', Harvard Business Review, Vol. 49, No. 2, March-April.
3. To some extent this problem was also present in certain departments in the case study of Mansfield Shoe Co.
4. See A. Jardin: 'The First Henry Ford: A Study in Personality and Business Leadership', Cambridge, Mass. MIT Press, 1970.
5. M.F.R. Kets de Vries: 'The Entrepreneurial

Case 8.1: Panache Upholstery

    Personality: A Person at the Crossroads', *Journal of Management Studies*, Vol. 14, Feb. 1977, pp. 33-55.
6. See J. Argenti: 'Corporate-Collapse: Causes and Symptoms', London, McGraw-Hill, 1971.

CASE 2   MANSFIELD SHOE CO (1981) LTD: A MANAGEMENT
          BUY-OUT FROM A PARENT IN RECEIVERSHIP

INTRODUCTION

This case study demonstrates three main points. First, how a company in receivership may contain parts which can be viable independently of the parent. Second, how a market which may generally be considered to be in a recession and adversely affected by cheap imports can contain profitable elements. Third, it demonstrates how equity participation by employees outside the central management team can be crucial to effecting a buy-out and to its success thereafter.

BACKGROUND TO THE BUY-OUT

In order to fully appreciate the circumstances leading up to the change in ownership it is necessary to examine both the company eventually bought-out and its erstwhile parent.

THE BOUGHT-OUT COMPANY

The company was formed at the turn of the century, supplying ladies' sandals, shoes and boots aimed at the middle price range of the market. During the 1930s it was acquired by the parent and remained a wholly owned subsidiary until the time of the buy-out. Throughout its period as a subsidiary a separate identity was maintained with control and all management functions, except finances, left with the subsidiary. The behaviour of the parent in the latter years of its life caused serious financial problems for the subsidiary, as will be seen in the next section.

Case 8.2: Mansfield Shoe Co. (1981) Ltd.

One crucial problem facing any manufacturer in this industry is that the shoe market is highly fragmented, and highly competitive, both in terms of types of retailers and types of shoes. The company sells its shoes through the following main types of outlets:

- independent retailers (25% of pairs sold);
- multiples and chain stores (45% of pairs sold);
- mail order (15% of pairs sold);
- sport (2.5% of pairs sold);
- direct from the factory (12.5% of pairs sold).

The higher fashion shoes produced by the company are mainly sold via independent retailers. The rest of the outlets deal with a wide range of more 'basic' shoes varying from boots to leisure shoes.
The market segment into which the company sells is affected by changes in fashion and the outlets through which shoes are brought to the market have changed considerably over the past two decades which have witnessed major rationalisation of the structure of retailing. In particular, there has been a substantial decline in independent retailers from holding 40 per cent of the ladies shoes market in 1960 to 18 per cent in 1982. Correspondingly multiple stores have grown steadily and account for half of the market, whilst chain stores have grown from having 3 per cent of the market in 1960 to a market share of 15 per cent in 1982. Mail order now accounts for 11 per cent of the market as against 5 per cent twenty years ago. Annual consumption of footwear per head has also increased over this period from four pairs to five pairs per head per year. With the recent increase in imports, especially for unbranded footwear, it is evident that a shoe manufacturer needs to be able to adapt readily to a complex series of changes in order to succeed. Two important aspects of this need to adapt are firstly to minimise direct competition with cheaper imports and, secondly, to achieve a balance of sales to the different types of outlets. This last requirement has important implications for maintaining cash flow. The pattern of export and mail order trading helps smooth out seasonal peaks whilst multiples and chain stores tend to be consistent and predictable payers. In 1980, the last full year before the buy-out, the twelve largest customers accounted for 44.5 per cent of turnover. Of these six were multiples or chain stores, three were mail order and the rest were independents.

Case 8.2: Mansfield Shoe Co. (1981) Ltd.

TABLE 8.2.1

Mansfield Shoe Performance in the Period Leading up to the Buy-out

	1978	1979	1980
Production (pairs of shoes)	747,588	695,492	406,666
Sales (pairs of shoes)	742,900	721,235	434,414
Sales (£)	4,638,410	5,337,685	3,303,459
Gross profit (£/% on sales)	1,185,215 (25.6%)	1,502,196 (28.1%)	546,762 (16.5%)
Net profit (loss) (£)	70,665	126,143	(722,246)
Quick Asset Ratio	0.66	0.57	0.39
Debt/Sales (days)	32	39	38
Creditors/Purchasers (days)	92	126	165
Overdraft (£)	152,950	250,000	335,574
Group interest charges (£)	72,474	111,395	170,000

Case 8.2: Mansfield Shoe Co. (1981) Ltd.

The company had been reasonably successful in adapting to market changes until the late 1970s. But from then on, its markets proved to be highly vulnerable. In export markets, previously valuable contracts with the USSR ceased whilst the profitability of new markets in West Europe was severely affected by the rise in the value of sterling in 1978 and 1979. Performance in the home market was affected by a number of factors. The general decline in demand made it difficult to maintain sales to those retail outlets which were themselves subsidiaries of another manufacturer. Sales to mail order outlets were adversely affected by the increasing rise of credit cards and credit accounts by the multiple stores. The high quality range to independent retailers was affected by their long-term decline and by a failure by the company to adjust its marketing strategy accordingly. In addition, the company's ability to retain customers was badly affected by deteriorating performances in delivery and quality of finish, due to managerial deficiencies, to which we return below.

The deteriorating performance of the company in the three years leading up to the buy-out are vividly shown in Table 8.2.1. Sales both by volume and by value fell substantially between 1978 and 1980 with a consequent depression of profits. Although the company was clearly pursuing a satisfactory debtor collection policy as shown by the debtor/sales ratio the remaining indicators of liquidity all deteriorated sharply. The significant increase in group interest charges also adversely affected the company's liquidity position.

The effect of the general recession on these results is, of course, substantial. But by the end of 1979 it was recognised that there were serious weaknesses in the existing management structure, which had particularly contributed to low order book level, high stocks and high overheads, particularly with respect to the ratio of non-productive staff to production employees (see Table 8.2.2). The company's current managing director was appointed in May 1980 and set about a major rationalisation programme. This programme involved a reduction in weekly production by 40 per cent to 9,000 pairs of shoes, the introduction and tightening of management control systems, and a substantial number of redundancies which helped return the ratio of staff to production to more realistic levels (Table 8.2.2). The reduction in manpower was achieved gradually in such a way as to avoid the statutory requirements on

Case 8.2: Mansfield Shoe Co. (1981) Ltd.

TABLE 8.2.2

Mansfield Shoe Employees

	Production (1)	Staff (2)	(1)/(2)	Total
July 1979	562	148	3.80	710
Jan 1980	535	137	3.91	672
July 1980	412	83	4.96	495
Jan 1981	310	67	4.63	377
July 1981	282	55	5.13	337
Aug 1981	242	48	5.04	290

notification of impending redundancies. Greater effort was also put into marketing which resulted in significant orders from the larger multiple stores. As a result, although cash flow was still adversely affected by redundancy payments, trading results improved so that by mid-way through 1981 the company was making a profit. However, whilst this turnround put the company in a favourable position for when the buy-out eventually took place, the position of the parent company was such that the group as a whole could not avoid receivership, as will be shown in the next section. Paradoxically, the receivership was a positive contributory factor to the eventual setting-up of the buy-out since it is unlikely that the management team could have afforded to buy it as a going concern.

THE PARENT COMPANY

The life cycle of the parent company demonstrates very clearly Argenti's (1972 pp. 160-164) type 3 trajectory to failure - a mature company which has been trading successfully for a number of years begins to develop certain managerial weaknesses such that product profitability, product investment requirements and general financial considerations are neglected. The company's management realise eventually what is happening and indulge in ill-thought-out action to remedy the position (e.g. launching of new products, diversification, rationalisation etc.). But, as the management has lost touch with the market, the chances of success are slight. Couple this with cripplingly high gearing ratios brought about through taking out excessive finance to fund new products and ventures, and it is hard to avoid failure. In this company

Case 8.2: Mansfield Shoe Co. (1981) Ltd.

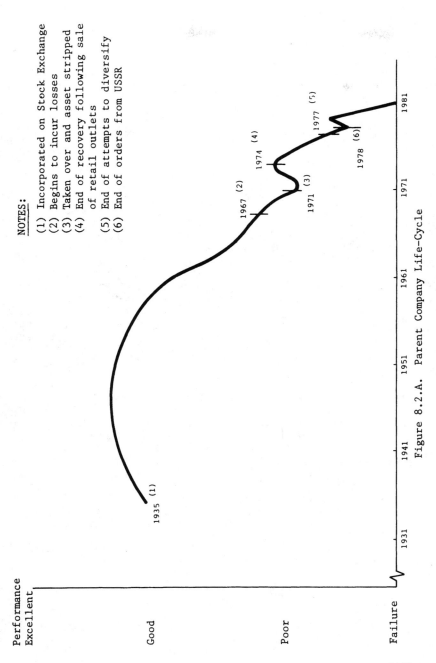

Figure 8.2.A. Parent Company Life-Cycle

NOTES:
(1) Incorporated on Stock Exchange
(2) Begins to incur losses
(3) Taken over and asset stripped
(4) End of recovery following sale of retail outlets
(5) End of attempts to diversify
(6) End of orders from USSR

Case 8.2: Mansfield Shoe Co. (1981) Ltd.

this process was further exacerbated by the general conditions of the recession.

The parent was originally incorporated in 1935 and was quoted on the London Stock Exchange until 1971.(2) Although a public company, the management style was very much that of a family business. During this period the company first expanded steadily and profitably to become a market leader. It had substantial overseas interests in South Africa and Australia, factories in four separate UK locations and 143 retail outlets. However, from 1967 to 1971 it incurred pre-tax losses in four out of the five years which amounted to a total net loss over the period of £583,000.

The parent was acquired in late 1971 by an investment company, and became subjected to the then fashionable process of 'asset-stripping'. Within seven months, it was considered that it was not worthwhile keeping the overseas assets and the shops. The retail outlets were sold for £2.9 million to a large high street chain with an agreement that they would continue to purchase footwear for three years. The reorganised company was then refloated on the Stock Exchange in the middle of 1972. Pre-tax Profits for 1972 and 1973 improved to over three quarters of a million pounds but by 1974 had fallen considerably to less than £100,000 following the closure of the former retail outlets as the acquirer was itself taken over.

At this point the strategic choice which presented itself was either to develop the shoe business or to diversify. It was decided that the best prospects for growth lay outside the company and from 1975 to 1977 a number of share purchases were made in prospective acquisition targets. A bid for an electro-plating company failed and together with write-downs on the other share purchases, provisions for the fall in market value of quoted investments were made of £360,000 and £260,000 in 1975 and 1976 respectively. Strategy was focussed again on shoe manufacturing accompanied by a change in the directors.

During this period both the parent and subsidiary were heavily dependent on contracts with the USSR to top up their domestic business. With the ending of this work, which in any event had been erratic, it was necessary to seek new markets.

It was from this time onwards that the decline began in earnest. The need to find new markets was matched by declining resources with which to carry out such a policy. The low value of sterling and a

176

Case 8.2: Mansfield Shoe Co. (1981) Ltd.

short-lived increase in demand in 1979 enabled new markets to be opened up in Europe and for overspill production to be taken from other UK based shoe manufacturers. Pre-tax Profits which had fallen from £257,000 in 1976 to £115,000 in 1978 recovered slightly to £143,900 in 1979 on sales of £16 million, but at the expense of increases in stocks and bank borrowing.

From the beginning of 1980 the group embarked upon a major rationalisation programme. Smaller production and warehouse units were closed in the East Midlands, the men's shoes factory was closed in June and the ladies' shoes factory in August. As noted earlier, the company that was eventually bought also announced a large number of redundancies. In all, these closures resulted in a reduction of 900 jobs from a peak at the beginning of the year of 2,000 employees. The parent company was now essentially left producing children's shoes. Concurrent with this rationalisation process the parent company also began to experience severe cash flow problems. The substantial fall in demand had reduced revenue and necessitated the closures. But the need to make redundancy payments, averaging between £3,000 and £5,000 per employee, and totalling £1.5 million plus reorganisation expenses of £3 million exacerbated the cash flow position.(3) These expenses could not be financed out of operating revenue and consequently bank borrowing increased to £2.9 million. Despite these measures the company recorded a pre-tax loss for 1980 of £1.8 million on a turnover that had fallen by £3.7 million in one year to £12.3 million. Interest charges of £518,700 contributed to the size of this loss.

The beginning of 1980 saw a further large fall in the demand for children's shoes and a fall in export demand generally. In order to be able to produce stock for the Easter peak further borrowing of £750,000 was required. This sum was apparently only obtained following representations from local members of Parliament, the bank seemingly unwilling to rely on revaluations of properties and positive cash flow projections as sufficient evidence of viability.(4) It was reported by the chairman that adverse publicity over the negotiations for extra finance had not helped the company (5) and with demand for children's shoes continuing to fall, and the accounts for 1980 being issued in June 1981 with an auditor's going concern qualification the receiver was called in on 1 July. In its last six

Case 8.2: Mansfield Shoe Co. (1981) Ltd.

months trading a £0.4 million pre-tax loss was reported, with net worth of £1.3 million against total borrowings of £4 million and a debt-equity ratio of over 200 per cent. The company was operating at only 45 per cent of capacity on receivership, producing some 9,000 pairs of shoes per week.

The compulsory winding-up order was issued on 8 October 1981. Another manufacturer purchased £1.1 million of children's shoes and took over part of the market, whilst the remainder was the subject of the buy-out discussed here.

THE TRANSFER OF OWNERSHIP

All staff and production employees were made redundant by the receiver and although the reorganisation that had been effected had virtually returned the subsidiary to profitability, its resurrection as a management buy-out was by no means automatic. Enquiries for financial support were made of three financial institutions and of local companies, with a deal eventually being achieved with the support of a financial institution administering a Pension Scheme.

At the time of the buy-out there were four members of the management team, covering the areas of managing director, sales, production and design. The financial director joined shortly after the buy-out, the finance function previously having been dealt with at head office. The average age of these five directors at the time of the buy-out was forty-one years, with the oldest having at least a decade to go before retirement. The team was thus fairly young, enabling it to take a long-run perspective from the beginning.

Moreover, the team apart from the financial director had worked together before the buy-out successfully improving the product range, introducing a formal marketing, planning and control system and removing the company's image of poor quality, poor customer service and slow paying of suppliers. The changes that had been effected before the buy-out which had involved the promotion of the sales and production directors and the acquisition of the design director also enabled a good second tier of management to be installed. In a company of this size, a formal organisation structure below the director level is necessary to co-ordinate activities, and helps to avoid the risks inherent in

Case 8.2: Mansfield Shoe Co. (1981) Ltd.

depending upon one person or a small group.

The redundancies which had occurred before the buy-out had enabled some reorganisation in the workforce to be carried out and this was completed in the process of recruiting employees to join the new company. There had been no disputes of note with the fully unionised production workers, and following the contraction in the local coalmines labour turnover, which had always been small, was virtually non-existent.

Costs levels had been substantially reduced through the programme of events leading up to the buy-out and were further improved by the removal of the parental service charge following the move to independence. Wage costs were also to be reduced through offering different work contracts when employees were re-employed. Nobody was offered more money and the senior staff were offered up to ten per cent less than they had been earning before. However, a profit bonus was to be introduced, which in the first year of trading actually amounted to an extra week's pay. Employee shareholders received the same amount in addition as dividend.

Due to these cost changes and the recovery from receivership the company forecast a pre-interest profit of £217,000 by year three.

The price to be negotiated for the assets of the company concerned the acquisition of raw materials, work-in-progress and certain machinery. The buildings were leased as was most of the machinery. It was agreed with the receiver that unwanted machinery was to be returned to the lessor, so reducing annual outgoings, and finished goods were to be sold on a commission basis on his behalf.

The finance required for the purchase of this package of assets also included a substantial amount of working capital that the cash flow forecasts had identified would be needed to deal with initial seasonal fluctuations. In addition to the above approaches to financial institutions, employees were asked to pledge their redundancy money. This request was made on the understanding that pledging money did not guarantee a job, since some employees would not receive any redundancy money.

All management employees were strongly urged to pledge money in order to demonstrate their commitment to the project and encourage the rest of the employees. In the event, eighty out of the three hundred and thirty employed at the time of the buy-out bought ordinary shares in the company amounting in total to £30,000. Some difference

Case 8.2: Mansfield Shoe Co. (1981) Ltd.

between the attitudes of the unions representing the 270 production employees (NUFLAT) and 60 staff (ASTMS) to the buy-out was noticeable. Maximum cooperation was considered to be received from NUFLAT, whereas ASTMS were not so helpful. As a result the management team approached staff members directly in order to gain their support. Some resistance from this union continued up until the second day of the restart as attempts were made to negotiate a procedural agreement.

The strong position held by the company in respect of all the above areas enabled sufficient finance to be raised, so that it restarted in August 1981 with the following (simplified) Balance Sheet:

	£
Fixed Assets	80,000
Working Capital	330,000
	410,000

Represented by:

Ordinary Shares	133,000
Loans	202,000
Overdraft	75,000
	410,000

PERFORMANCE SINCE THE BUY-OUT

An explanation of changes in performance following the buy-out essentially requires an examination of management styles, industrial relations, and financial and economic performance.

The management structure which had been developed prior to the buy-out provided for clear lines of responsibility and authority which had previously been lacking. Within this structure the buy-out team strive to minimise any feeling of 'US and THEM', in terms of either shareholders and non-shareholders or management and non-management employees. Regular meetings are held between management and representatives from the unions to discuss progress. In addition, the managing director broadcasts over the tannoy the latest progress on orders, profits etc. The minutes of the meetings between unions and

Case 8.2: Mansfield Shoe Co. (1981) Ltd.

management are circulated to employees and access is available to monthly progress reports. Initially these reports were circulated to all union representatives but this practice was discontinued as they were often left lying around the factory. Management learned a lesson on the issue of disclosure of information and commercial secrecy. Whilst they wanted workers to be fully informed about the true trading position of the company they needed to ensure that information did not get into competitors' hands. Wide discussion on certain issues is encouraged, but matters relating to trading policies are decided on by the management team. The views of employees as shareholders are dealt with through the employee-shareholder director, who is appointed by them and has full director's power. In addition, special meetings are held with employee shareholders in order to explain and discuss transactions with which they are not familiar. The buy-out team report that the existence of employee-shareholdings has had a positive general effect on motivation towards the success of the company, and that this positive attitude is greatest in the department where all employees are shareholders.

Generally, industrial relations are good. However, the company may still be experiencing a honeymoon period, especially as performance has been better than expected and employee-shareholders are seeing a good return on their investment. Whether this pattern of events will continue into the longer term, especially if profits turn down, is open to question. Whilst the production employees remain happy with the new arrangements there has been some recent pressure from the staff union for an interim pay increase on the grounds that current profits are far higher than expected. This problem of success is accompanied by another one. The growth that the company has experienced means that it is now trying to recruit further skilled footwear workers, but without much success. It is therefore in the process of training new employees to fill this gap.

The profitability of the company in the first quarter of the second year of trading after the buy-out was far higher than that budgeted for. Trading Profit was twice that budgeted for and Sales were 28 per cent greater than expected, mainly due to greater volume in the UK market. The actual profit to turnover ratio was running 7.2 per cent against a budgeted level of 2.8 per cent. Improved credit and stock control has contributed to a

Case 8.2: Mansfield Shoe Co. (1981) Ltd.

positive cash balance as against a budgeted overdraft.

The rapid improvement in the company's financial position has had two results. First, the financial institution's share of funding has been bought out, using the provisions of the 1981 Companies Act.

From the management's point of view this action has the benefits of increasing their control and removing any potential cash flow problems from interest and dividend payments if performance begins to turn down. The second action taken has involved the acquisition of another local shoe company that had entered into receivership. Although the acquired company had been under review for some time as it was a competitor which was undercutting prices, the initial approach about making an acquisition came from the area official of the union, who had witnessed the turnround in the original buy-out. If anything, it would appear that the negotiation of this acquisition was more traumatic than the original buy-out. An accountant's report on the acquiree was 'not-too-favourable' and there was resistance from some of the acquirer's directors, who feared that its failure would drag down the parent company. As far as the acquirer was concerned, the acquisition could not take place without local authority support. However, the County Council considered the venture too risky to extend loan finance and was not prepared to grant rate relief. After a delay of some weeks during which production was stopped, a grant of £22,000 was obtained. This delay did enable the price to be reduced by a substantial amount, so that the deal became feasible with the local authority grant, £80,000 from the Department of Industry, the acquirers' own funds and £10,000 from the employees of the company being acquired. Subsequent to the acquisition all money put in by the acquirer has been recouped and the subsidiary is now generating sufficient funds to pay a dividend to the parent. In terms of employment, the subsidiary, which restarted with 180 people compared with 300 before receivership, now employs 220. Overall benefits are received through cross-fertilisation of markets and experience.

Following continued progress the company has also recently acquired three small companies in receivership in the south-west of England.

182

Case 8.2: Mansfield Shoe Co. (1981) Ltd.

CONCLUSIONS

This company which is one of the most successful buy-outs that we have encountered, particularly amongst those resurrected from receivership, demonstrates the whole spectrum of required ingredients for success. It also forcefully shows that ailing parent companies may contain viable units which, if required changes are accepted and made, can make a more positive effect on employment than mere job preservation.

NOTES

1. J. Argenti (1972), 'Corporate Collapse: Causes and Symptoms', London, McGraw-Hill, 1971.
2. C. Muir, 'Management and Staff Buying-Out Mansfield Shoe for §0.35 m', Financial Times, 25.8.81.
3. Ibid.
4. Ibid.
5. Ibid.

CASE 8.3: LANEMARK THERMAL SYSTEMS - A MANAGEMENT BUY-OUT FROM A PARENT STILL TRADING BUT NEEDING TO REORGANISE

INTRODUCTION

In general, a company which perceives an inability to achieve the financial targets that it sets for itself with its current product mix should engage in strategic search for ways of closing this performance-gap.(1) This case study illustrates how a parent company attempted to diversify from its initial product base over a long period of time, through both acquisition activity and through the setting-up of new product divisions which were eventually intended to make significant contributions to sales and profits. However, a greater than expected decline in demand for the base product and slower growth than expected in some of the new, more diverse, areas meant that this initial strategy had to be revised. The parent subsequently focussed on the selective investments likely to make a significant contribution to profitability. It was the reorganisation that this change in policy required which presented the opportunity for the very small division, which is the subject of this case study, to be bought-out by its management.
The bought-out company itself, which is one of the smallest we have interviewed, illustrates a number of other interesting issues concerning changes in management and employee relations. In particular, the company ended formal recognition of the trade union for bargaining purposes, and had to establish an independent image as it was prevented from retaining the parent's distinctive name after the buy-out. In order to become independent, it was necessary to buy patents from the parent company. Finally, the company, as in so many cases, found the

Case 8.3: Lanemark Thermal Systems

need to examine very carefully the whole aspect of cash flow management.

PARENT COMPANY HISTORY AND BACKGROUND TO THE BUY-OUT

The parent company provides an interesting case of a firm whose fortunes were initially founded upon one product, the manufacture of tyres, but who attempted to broaden its base and reduce its vulnerability over a long period of time. The main stages in this process may be described as firstly, a move towards vertical integration in tyre production; secondly, a move towards horizontal integration/narrow spectrum diversification in the production of other rubber-based products; thirdly, the development of non-rubber based activities and, finally, an attempt to abandon tyre production altogether.

The Dunlop Company was formed in 1889 and was initially concerned with the production of pneumatic tyres for cycles. The rapid growth experienced in sales of cycle tyres was supplemented in 1900 by the commencement of car tyre production. Share capital was increased several times in the next twenty years in order to finance expansion and the strengthening of the company's position through vertical integration. The expansion process principally involved the acquisition of a wheel manufacturing company, the acquisition of rubber estates in the Far East and the purchases of a cotton mill and a steel rolling mill. By 1920, the company had wholly-owned subsidiary manufacturing and selling operations throughout the world.

However, a slump in rubber and cotton prices in 1921, which nearly bankrupted the company, and intensifying competition in both home and overseas markets throughout the 1920s forced the company to widen its field of production by including such rubber-based products as footwear, clothing, belting and rubber hose through the acquisition of the Charles Macintosh Group in 1925. This horizontal development was continued through the 1930s with the introduction of further latex-based products plus further expansion of the tyres side of the business through acquisitions at home, setting-up new factories abroad and through reciprocal selling arrangements with Goodyear. Following the hiatus caused by the Second World War, expansion was resumed after 1945 with capital investment of £15 million being made in the period up to 1952, followed by further growth which paralleled the huge

Case 8.3: Lanemark Thermal Systems

increase in car production during the 1950s and early 1960s.(2) Throughout this period the company was the largest tyre manufacturer in the UK with half of the company's productive capacity being devoted to tyres.

The 1960s saw two major strategic objectives being followed. First, the company invested in further tyre producing capacity to meet an expected continued substantial growth in demand. Second, attempts were made to diversify further from tyres and rubber-based products through a number of acquisitions, such as those of the George Angus Hose Co. for £29 million in 1968, USI Engineering in 1966 (an oil-seal manufacturer) and Aerospreen in 1977 (flexible foam products). The first objective was to lead to serious problems for the company as demand did not increase in the 1970s because of the 1973 oil crisis and its consequences and the advent of the radial tyre which substantially increased the replacement interval for tyres. The problem was further exacerbated by the world-wide excess capacity caused by other producers making the same mistakes. In an attempt to overcome these difficulties in the tyre market an agreement was entered into in 1971 with the Pirelli Company of Italy whereby Dunlop acquired a 49% interest in Pirelli's operations in exchange for the transfer to Pirelli of equivalent interests in Dunlop. However, this early attempt at European industrial co-operation did not succeed because of failures by the management to agree on strategy and the financial difficulties faced by Pirelli which placed a further burden on Dunlop. The agreement was dissolved in 1981. As may be seen from Figure 1, the performance of the tyre division during this ten year period follows a continually downward trend, due both to poor market demand and delays in responding to the new radial tyre and to slow improvements in productivity. However, the other three major divisions of the company displayed healthy performance figures, at least until the late 1970s.

The main corporate strategy at this time, as expounded in the Chairman's annual statement for 1978 was one of 'steadily modernising tyre facilities while concentrating on the development of non-tyre activities'. In addition, certain parts of the business were chosen as part of a selective investment policy for priority in expansion and development, for example cables, engineering, industrial products and fire protection. This policy

Case 8.3: Lanemark Thermal Systems

5.

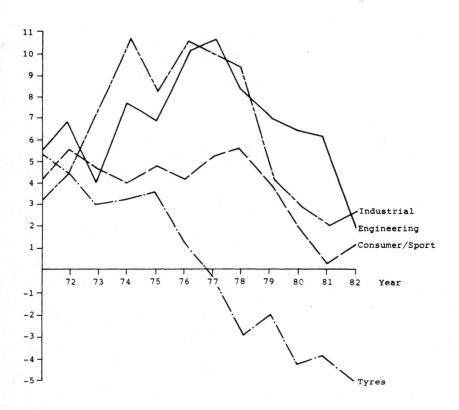

Figure 8.3A: Dunlop Holdings Divisional Return on Turnover

Case 8.3: Lanemark Thermal Systems

of developing away from tyre and rubber related activities was further strengthened in 1971 and 1978 by the acquisition of three small companies which it was hoped would grow rapidly. Singlehurst Holdings was bought for £0.6 millions as a supplier of hydraulic assemblies, Soil-less Cultivation Systems was acquired for £30,000 as a pioneer in nutrient film technique hydrophobics and Rice Trailers was acquired for an undisclosed sum. It was at this time also that the division that was to become Lanemark was formed to exploit new developments in methods for heating liquid in tanks.

However, the company's ability to exploit fully the non-tyre activities was severely limited by the continued downward trend in the tyre market which produced large trading losses and required a programme of severe rationalisation to reduce costs and capacity; a process which was expensive to finance. Poor overall profitability meant that the funding had to come from two non-trading sources. First, through the disposal of assets, in particular £119 million from the sale of Malaysian interests in 1982 and a further £20.5 million from the sale of Angus Fire Armour in 1980. Second, through increased long-term borrowing, so that for 1982 annual financing costs had risen to £56 million for the group as a whole with a debt-equity ratio of 94 per cent. Despite such injections in finance and a reduction in the UK tyre divisions employment from 11,500 to 3,500 from 1978 to 1983 it became unavoidable that the company would have to dispose entirely of its tyre making activities. In September 1983 it was announced that these were to be acquired by the Japanese company Sumitomo.

During the period that rationalisation in the tyre division was occurring, similar moves were being made in the other divisions whose profitability had taken a downward turn since 1978 (see Figure 1). Lanemark, at the time operating as Dunlop Energy Engineering Division, was being slowly developed from a Research and Development activity into a commercially viable unit with a target turnover of £3m per annum by 1981 (which would still make it very small in comparison with other Dunlop divisions.) But by 1981, although the division was certainly viable its turnover had only reached £1m per annum. This perceived disappointing level of performance by more senior managers in the group resulted in a reorganisation of the larger division of which Lanemark was a part with a proposal that Lanemark itself would move to the site of another

Case 8.3: Lanemark Thermal Systems

subsidiary. Disagreement with this proposal led to the proposition from the then general manager of the division, and now managing director of Lanemark, to buy-out the company. After some reluctance on the part of some less senior superiors to take-up the proposal, more senior management agreed to discuss the proposal seriously with the view that there were advantages to be had on both sides. Negotiations were carried out using professional advisors on the purchaser's side. After some initial inability to decide on an appropriate price a deal was eventually agreed for a consideration made-up as follows:

Buy-out Team	£	£
£1 Ordinary Shares	11,700	
12% £1 Cum Redeemable Pref Shares	33,000	
		45,000
Financial Institution		
10% Cum Conv Partic. Pref. Ord £1 shares	5,000	
12% £1 Cum Red. Pref. shares	20,000	
Loans	100,000	
		125,000
Total Finance		170,000

There were four members in the buy-out team all of whom were aged under fifty at the time of the deal. It is noteworthy that £50,000 of the loans were from the parent company in the form of delayed payments covering a period of five years. A significant part of the assets purchased were patents, trademarks and copyrights costing £50,000 which are being written off in equal instalments over ten years.

THE COMPANY AFTER THE BUY-OUT

Despite being the management buy-out of an existing business, Lanemark displays certain of the characteristics of a new start-up. First, being unable to use the parent's name, which in itself was only just penetrating process heating markets the

Case 8.3: Lanemark Thermal Systems

company has to effectively enter markets anew and establish a new name. Second, this penetration of the market has involved substantial supportive expenditure on marketing literature. Third, the products themselves were also fairly new. Fourth, the company had to move to new premises and incur associated set-up costs.

The company now has three main product areas - liquid heaters, rapid steam generators and petrochemical and chemical burners. Liquid heating forms the major part of the business, having been substantially developed under the ex-parent. Gas burners are fired into a heat exchanger immersed in the liquid. The system can be used to heat most liquids in a wide range of industries. Average order value is around £3,500 with contribution levels around 60 per cent.

The other two product areas are still being developed. The Rapid Steam Generators market is essentially a factoring exercise for Lanemark which is considered to hold potential for substantial growth as many companies are forced to replace large central boilers for reasons of economy. The company has recently begun to trade with Dunlop in this area for the first time. The Petrochemical and chemical burner applications market appears to offer good prospects for growth in a worldwide context. The company now has experience of, and a foothold in, the market which should enable it to develop sales further. These developments are aimed at effecting a substantial improvement in the £20,000 loss in the first year of trading on a net asset base of £130,000.

The changes that have occurred since the buy-out primarily concern the ability of management to attack these markets in ways which they were prevented from pursuing because of the restrictions imposed by Dunlop. Given the high technology of the products and the small workforce, all the management team need to be technically competent and are heavily involved at the operational level in meeting and satisfying customers'' needs. The removal of the restrictions on management's freedom of action that breaking away from the parent has brought enables each manager to take overall responsibility for a particular product and to exercise his entrepreneurial skills in its development. As part of the parent company presentations had to be made to group management to justify action and although a business plan was prepared by the company's management the final decision on what could be done

Case 8.3: Lanemark Thermal Systems

was always taken at a higher level. Given the difficulties which were being faced by the parent company, as we have already noted, the decisions were taken with respect to Dunlop's global difficulties and often perceived at the subsidiary level as being detrimental to Lanemark's ability to penetrate the market. In particular, the pooled banking arrangements that existed before the buy-out meant there was no control of their own cash flow nor direct access to it. Following the buy-out, Lanemark now has control over its cash flow. Prior to the buy-out, the company did insist on control of its debtor and creditor management because of the need for personal contact in keeping customers and suppliers satisfied. This approach is particularly important given the staged nature of payment for orders (part with order, part prior to dispatch and the balance within 30 days). Since the buy-out the company follows a strict policy of chasing payment if an invoice is not paid within 30 days. The company report that all sizes of customers try to lean on them to delay payment. The largest customers tend to be less of a problem as long as the invoice is presented to the right place to be processed by the computer by the appropriate date. Smaller companies which can pay but who decide to delay payment are reported to be the major concern. Indeed, the managing director takes an important personal role in credit chasing and in some cases High Court action has been threatened. Factoring has been considered but rejected partly because of the cost but also because staged payments ease cash flow sufficiently. Although the company has had very few bad debts it is currently examining the case for using credit insurance.

The move away from being part of a parent company has affected the management-employee relations, making them considerably less formal. A fairly open book policy on information is maintained, except insofar as salaries are concerned. Regular meetings are held with all employees to keep them informed of developments and monthly financial information is made available. Employees in the workshop visit customers as a matter of course on installation work which provides them with a knowledge of customers and the management with feedback on customer satisfaction. In addition to the move away from the parent as such the reduction in the workforce from twenty-seven to twelve through redundancy at the time of the buy-out has made an informal approach more appropriate and has required greater

191

Case 8.3: Lanemark Thermal Systems

flexibility on the part of those remaining. Although the parent handled the redundancies there was initially some resentment from those not asked to join the new company towards those who had. Two of the management team of six were also not asked to join the new company as it was felt it could not carry more than four, but they remained in other positions within the parent. However, contact was maintained with the two left out in case some arrangement could be worked out in the future. The removal of the formal wages structure has also contributed to the more informal hierarchy. Under the previous ownership there was an agreement to have only one negotiating body, the AUEW. Even when there were twenty-seven employees this did not seem necessary and now that there are only a dozen it appears even less so. The formal system of leading hands has been replaced by an informal arrangement. Though this approach seems appropriate in these circumstances, if the company were to grow more formal arrangements may become preferable again, a fact which the management team recognises.

Since the buy-out, one employee has left the company because of his reluctance to fit in with the more flexible approach demanded if the company is to succeed and has been replaced by someone who initially lost his job on the buy-out.

CONCLUSION

The company seems to have successfully made the transition from being a very small part of a large and troubled parent group to independence, particularly in establishing itself in the market place. The move to a more informal organisation appears appropriate given the size of the company, but it also reflects the attempts that we have noted in other buy-outs which is to reduce any 'US and THEM' notions between management and other employees. The introduction of a permanent health insurance scheme and a death-in-service scheme for all employees, which did not exist under the ex-parent, helps to reinforce this approach.

However, although the company has so far broken-even before the payment of interest on loans it is still looking for the kind of volume growth that would be required to meet these and the capital repayments which are scheduled to begin in the next financial year.

Case 8.3: Lanemark Thermal Systems

NOTES

1. See e.g. Porter, M.: 'Corporate Strategy'. For an excellent review of the issues see Chiplin, B.: 'Corporate Strategy', Ch. 11 in Bates, J. and Parkinson, J.E. (eds): Business Economics, 3rd edition, Basil Blackwell, Oxford, 1982.
2. For further details on the earlier history of Dunlop see e.g. Monopolies and Mergers Commission, Report on the Supply of Pneumatic Tyres, 1955/56.

CASE 8.4: DENNIS AND ROBINSON LIMITED (TRADING AS "MANHATTAN FURNITURE"), A MANAGEMENT BUY-OUT FROM A PARENT STILL TRADING

INTRODUCTION

Dennis and Robinson Ltd, were bought out from Smiths Industries in October 1982, a date which places them at the more recent end of our buy-out sample. However, the seeds of purchase were sown in 1975, some two years after the present chief executive was promoted, and pursued in earnest from 1979 onwards. The entire period was not dominated by active attempts to purchase the company but the desire to sell, in the right circumstances, and a desire to buy on behalf of the managing director, at the right price, existed throughout the period.

This case illustrates admirably the coincidence of circumstances necessary for a buy-out to proceed, and then be successful, not least the existence of an able, forceful and entrepreneurial chief executive, as has been argued in Chapter 5. The case is also of interest because it demonstrates how the initial reason for owning a subsidiary (vertical integration) may become obsolete as changes in corporate strategy and the market lead both the parent and its subsidiary into unrelated areas.

THE COMPANY AND THE PARENT

Dennis and Robinson had been part of Smiths Industries since the early 1950s and had been acquired as part of that group's desire to vertically integrate wherever possible in its principal product lines. As suppliers of clock cases to Smiths, Dennis and Robinson were an obvious target. The company at that time was serving most of Smiths needs, and had sound investments in woodworking technology which gave it flexibility and adaptability in making

Case 8.4: Dennis and Robinson Limited

related products. This product adaptability was certainly required, for very soon after the acquisition the market for wooden cased clocks began to diminish, and with it the ready market at Smiths. As a reasonably independent entity, with Smiths only exercising arm's length involvement the company began to look for new products using the existing equipment. It was but a short step to enter the furniture market specialising initially in fully assembled kitchen units. By the mid-1970s, the balance of the business had completely changed, and the company was primarily a kitchen furniture producer with a secondary, and very minor business of clock case manufacture which netted less than £20,000 per annum. The clock case business disappeared entirely after 1976 as Smiths moved out of the market altogether leaving two principal development activities, which were ready assembled kitchen and bedroom furniture.

As the balance of the business moved progressively away from mainstream Smiths Industries business, so the parent company's interest and involvement with Dennis and Robinson diminished. Concern switched from seeing it as an integrated part of a vertically organised operation serving an end market over which Smiths had direct control, to regarding it as an anomolous but profitable cash contributor. There is little doubt that throughout the 1960s and into the 1970s the company was a valued part of the group as it consistently made profits which Smiths took out for reinvestment almost exclusively in the rest of the group. In particular, the funds generated by Dennis and Robinson contributed towards the parent company's shift into aerospace, electronics components and medical products. Whilst ever the company was profitable, and had a positive cash flow, the Smiths involvement was limited to the approval of five year plans, and the annual budget. The major managerial grumble about Smiths, despite the general goodwill, was the negotiation of funds for reinvestment; funds which were hardly ever forthcoming. The problem was particularly intense during the early 1970s because the one instance when the Smiths board had sanctioned a major re-investment the subsequent local management of the programme almost brought the company down. The investment had begun in 1969 and by late 1970 the company was already beginning to experience difficulties in finding market growth.

It was during this period that the current chief executive, and major shareholder, joined the

195

Case 8.4: Dennis and Robinson Limited

company, initially as contract sales manager, though he very soon became a director and general manager. The specific attributes which enabled him to get the top position were, in his own words, because he was 'cheap, young and available'. From 1973 onwards, with the current Managing Director at the helm, the company progressed quite quickly, and cash generation was very strong. The recovery was so good, in fact, that in 1975 Smiths saw the company as a very saleable asset and put it on the market. Having used it as a 'cash cow' they were looking to take all their investment out in one piece to reinvest elsewhere in the group. A number of potential buyers reviewed the company but although Smiths received two serious offers, neither matched their valuation and the company remained unsold. It was the experience of having turned the company round only to see it offered for sale that first alerted the managing director to the frailty of his position and first sowed the seeds that he wanted a stake in the business; either to buy it outright or at the very least to take a substantial shareholding in it.

The company continued to progress, but no reinvestment was taking place. The changes in the product and the market were beginning to become sufficiently severe for the company's future position to be placed seriously in jeopardy if the money was not forthcoming. In 1979 the managing director of Dennis and Robinson wrote to Smiths Industries in support of reinvestment and asking to become a shareholder in the company. There was no question of a separation of risk, responsibility and return; the managing director was perfectly prepared to take a personal stake in the business to support his investment plans. Nothing came of the move at this stage, and in the following year a further request was submitted for £750,000 of new investment. At this point Smiths Industries, through their chairman, offered the company to the managing director if he could put together a financial package that could meet their price. So, in March 1981, the managing director set about trying to arrange a package that would enable him to purchase the company, and he was coming to the end of a road which had begun some six years earlier.

During the intervening years the continuing success of Dennis and Robinson had become increasingly bound up in the performance of its chief executive. He had made himself, through his actions and effective management of the company, an

Case 8.4: Dennis and Robinson Limited

almost indispensible asset. There was a widening gap between the value of the company with him at the helm and the value of the company should it be sold to an outside purchaser and he decide to leave. The management buy-out, if the parent were to sell the company, was the best prospect of realising a good price. To remove the existing managing director, and continue to own Dennis and Robinson would have committed Smiths to management time and effort, as well as the essential reinvestment which would have reversed the accepted flow of funds associated with the subsidiary. A disaffected managing director could easily have put paid to attempts to sell to an outside party, especially as he had the support of the key personnel within the subsidiary. Thus, we see a not atypical example of the preconditions for a successful management buy-out as discussed in Chapter 2, the two parties' aspirations reasonably complementary, and the management team in a strong position to influence the terms of the eventual outcome.

NEGOTIATING THE DEAL

The company was offered to the managing director in March 1981 with no other prospective purchasers involved. There was no real urgency at this stage though a general desire to proceed as quickly as possible lest something go wrong undoubtedly existed in the managing director's mind. Although in all cases there is a tendency to talk about the buy-out 'team' it must be emphasised again that the successful buy-outs invariably involve one person leading the team - an individual of entrepreneurial foresight who makes things happen for the rest. The Dennis and Robinson experience is a classic illustration, it was one man's vision that he now had to translate into reality and the first question he had to answer was 'Do I need a team?', and if so 'Who should be on it?'. The task of choosing a team, and raising finance are inextricably related. The team will be expected to put up money of their own, and the prospects of attracting loan finance depends critically upon the lenders' assessment of the capabilities which the team members contain. The buy-out team in this case was one of the largest in our total sample containing nine members (see Chapter 5). As has been noted earlier, there are three basic arguments for spreading the team widely, first it increases the probability of a substantial

Case 8.4: Dennis and Robinson Limited

equity investment being forthcoming; second, it broadens and deepens the degree of commitment and incentives for the company to do well, and finally, it probably ensures that all 'key' functions in the company are led by people with a financial stake in it. The disadvantages are that it may make decision-making and consensus seeking more difficult, and that those who are not invited to join the team may take it all the harder when it is quite a large number of people that are involved. There were undoubtedly some difficult decisions to be made at the margin but the team which was formed has ensured that the primary functions in the company are led by director/owners (the finance representation has changed following the untimely death of the Chief Accountant with his successor becoming a shareholder).

One interesting aspect of this team is the inclusion of the consultant designer who works on a contract basis. In a market which is very dependent on fashion and good design it was regarded as essential to have the designer's returns so closely linked to the company's fortunes.

Having his team, and being assured of their contribution the prospective deal could be taken to the City in search of finance. The first stop was Warburg's Merchant Bank with the assistance of Smiths Industries, and in July 1981 Warburg's referred them to ICFC who had already established a reputation as the major lenders to buy-outs. Their investigations began in late 1981, and in conjunction with the company's accountants a package was assembled which, it was felt, would be acceptable to all sides. However, the ICFC funding involved was at a level which was outside the authority of a local office to sanction and, consequently, the deal was referred 'upstairs' for a decision. It came as something of a surprise when ICFC's higher authority turned down the deal, in no small part due to their general reluctance to finance within the kitchen furniture industry which was attracting attention primarily because of the difficulties which some companies were in. So, although the basic preparation, and all background work had been done the company found themselves without finance in April 1982. A whole year had elapsed and they seemed no further on. In April a meeting was held at which Smiths were going to withdraw the offer for sale - the offer was eventually reinstated with a three months deadline.

Negotiations continued throughout the summer

Case 8.4: Dennis and Robinson Limited

which resulted in two significant changes, notably a reduction in the anticipated purchase price, and a restructuring of the financial package to reduce ICFC's exposure. The final purchase price was agreed at £356,000 made up as follows:

Buy-out Team	£ 50,000 equity £ 50,000 loan	£100,000
ICFC	£ 9,000 equity £141,000 loan	£150,000
Coutts & Co	£106,000 loan	£106,000
		£356,000

Equity Distribution:
  Managing Director - 30%
  ICFC   - 15%
  Other directors   - 55% (7% each)

In addition, Coutts & Co, made available an overdraft facility of £100,000 for which the company paid a fee of £500 per annum. (The facility has not been used.) The general body of the workforce were not invited to put up money for the buy-out and no formal negotiation with them took place. However, in full recognition of the contribution that they would make to the eventual success of the company the managing director kept the employees briefed on proceedings. When the transfer was completed, groups of about 15 at a time were assembled for the deal to be explained to them. The union was not formally consulted or involved in the process prior to completion because the management wanted to safeguard the commercial secrecy of the impending deal.

The buy-out was completed in October 1982 after a hectic 18 months of negotiations during which time the management needs of the company also had to be met. Many buy-out managers describe the act of management after completion as something of an anticlimax after the excitement of the chase. Although there was no need to fight off alternative purchasers in this instance it is undoubtedly one of the longest negotiations, and was not without its trials and tribulations.

Case 8.4: Dennis and Robinson Limited

THE COMPANY AFTER THE BUY-OUT

The Market and the Product

The company trades as Manhattan Furniture and sells fitted kitchen and bedroom furniture into a potential market currently worth about £600m per annum. The industry has been a growth area on three fronts - the replacement kitchen market, the new builder direct supply and the general fitted bedroom market. However, there have been a number of difficulties experienced by companies in this area because of the highly competitive nature of the business, the need to keep up with design changes and the presence of continential imports. In this respect, the industry is regarded as anything but a blue chip invetment area and there have been some spectacular difficulties which have caught the public attention. Notable amongst these has been the substantial fall from favour of the long standing manufacturers Eastham, Grovewood and Wrighton all of whom have experienced declining turnover; in Eastham's case because they did not respond to the market's move towards real wood. Bankruptcies among building firms have produced difficulties for certain firms in this industry, and the purchase by MFI of the Hygena brand name has created a high degree of concentration in the CKD, home assembly market.

The kitchen and bedroom furniture market is therefore concentrated, volatile, and fashion orientated. Nevertheless, there are market niches, on a regional basis, or in particular segments that can be successfully exploited and it is this path that Manhattan have successfully pursued. Their turnover of approaching £6m places them in the mid rank of companies by size, but they sell extremely well into the South East of England for the ready assembled market. Their major customers are builders who demand a good quality, competitively priced, ready assembled kitchen offering prompt and reliable delivery onto site generally within eight weeks. The tendency for builders to allow customers for new houses to specify design from the catalogue generally dictates the period within which final completion must be done prior to the customer moving in. Reducing lead times in order to offer a reliable four week delivery is currently a marketing priority of the company.

Approximately £4m of turnover goes to builders in

Case 8.4: Dennis and Robinson Limited

the UK with the top 10 clients accounting for 60%, and another 240 live accounts taking the remainder. Some of the company's products are sold through their own shops in Croydon, Guildford, Lancing and Worthing and these direct sales account for £800,000 of turnover. The final £1m worth of business comes from exports which are for CKD kits which are sold mainly through agents and for which they have been particularly successful in the Middle East. Export sales, with the possibility of new products is an area that the company is seeking to develop.

In the main UK business the operation can be summed up as intermediate technology, high fashion, high coordination. Because of the ultimate customer satisfaction coming from the installed product the installation procedure is a vital element. Turnover has grown since the buy-out and forward planning is for continued growth in turnover, profits, and employment.

Performance

The company had performed well for a number of years preceding the sale but the improvement since the change of ownership has nevertheless been marked. The lack of investment prior to the sale meant that with fixed assets in machinery 67% depreciated the company needed to re-equip in key areas of the business in order to produce long-term results. When evaluating the price paid for the company there is little doubt that it was very attractively priced if the intention had been to engage in short-term surgery and 'window dressing' to sell the company on, but on a longer term basis a substantial sum was required to be retained in the business if it were to achieve the growth envisaged by the management. This reinvestment has begun in earnest and been paid for out of retained earnings. In addition, the company has not had to use its overdraft facility and the interest earned on deposits has met approaching one third of the finance charges on the outstanding loans. Trading profit tripled between 1982 and 1983, with investments in new assets totalling £112,000. Including extraordinary profits the total profit before tax increased from about £100,000 to over £400,000 and has enabled management to plan for new capital investment of £300,000 to £350,000 in 1983/4. This increased profitability has been the result of a very tight control of all aspects of the business from production, through

Case 8.4: Dennis and Robinson Limited

finance to marketing. A more efficient plant layout with more flexible jigs and some purpose built company designed equipment has helped contain production costs and improve quality. A very close scrutiny of cash flow, and tight debtor control has ensured that funds flow has remained strong and that positive cash balances have been maintained. The marketing of the products, as befits a company whose managing director is an ex Procter and Gamble marketing executive, has not been neglected and the direct selling operation has been reorganised with the closure of unprofitable shops and the opening of new outlets. There is no single reason for the surge in performance other than to observe that the management team fully recognise that all aspects of the business must be tightly controlled and contribute to overall performance, and that at board level all have a personal incentive to ensure that the company succeeds, especially given the aim to bring the company to the market at the earliest opportunity.

The progress of consolidation will meet with some problems in the near future when difficult decisions will have to be made. The momentum of the company will have to be maintained at all levels for new volume to be produced. The company operates from 100,000 sq. ft on a 5 acre site literally within one mile of the sea on the south coast. There is ample room for expansion on the site which is currently leasehold with a rent review in 1986. Effective tax planning will become important over the next two years and the removal of 100% capital allowances in the 1984 Budget will not make the process any easier.

On the industrial relations front, with a product which requires a lot of handling, and high quality it is essential that the workforce are fully involved and receptive to the objectives of the company. Communications are generally good in the company with shop stewards of the Furniture Timber and Allied Trades Union meeting weekly with management, and a works committee sitting every two months. Management are currently reviewing the introduction of quality circles into production areas to emphasise, and ensure, the high quality standards required.

Organisation

Effective Management organisation is fundamental to

Case 8.4: Dennis and Robinson Limited

good performance, yet is so often overlooked, or given low priority by small and medium sized companies. Dennis and Robinson are unusual, and therefore worthy of study, in our experience because of their sophistication in thinking about the organisational requirements of their business. The managing director is clearly a conceptual thinker as well as an accomplished practitioner and has given close attention to putting together a structure which is flexible enough to adapt to the market needs and ensures clear lines of accountability for performance.

In his view there were three tasks of paramount importance. First, to fully comprehend the extent of the managerial talent at his disposal so that each individual's capabilities were used to the full. Second, to establish a company information system which would enable both prompt action to be taken to maintain managerial control over profit, and allow forecasting and sensitivity analysis for forward planning. Finally, and all important, to draw a clear organisation chart which ensured complementarity in skills and provided the maximum utilisation of managerial manpower from minimum numbers.

The first of these tasks has been completed with the aid of a management consultancy firm which has conducted a management audit for the company; the second is in progress with the introduction of a financial package for a micro computer which will be used purely as a managerial tool, and the organisation chart has been redrawn. The changes, effective from Octover 1982 can be seen by comparison of Figures 8.4A and 8.4B. The former design director's role has been widened into a fuller deputy managing director range of tasks but retaining responsibility for new product design in association with the consultant designer. Elsewhere, a regrouping of functions has put together complementary talents into five broad functional areas - Personnel, Finance, Manufacturing, Export and Marketing. The Personnel role has been combined with that of company secretary to produce a more complete individual portfolio, and the Finance department has been strengthened by the inclusion of a Systems section.

It is currently too early to form a judgement on the effectiveness of this new structure but the managing director has great faith in it. The final outcome was decided following a 'think tank' session which has been introduced into the company. The

Case 8.4: Dennis and Robinson Limited

DENNIS AND ROBINSON LIMITED
SENIOR AND MIDDLE MANAGEMENT ORGANISATION CHART

FIGURE 8.4A Before

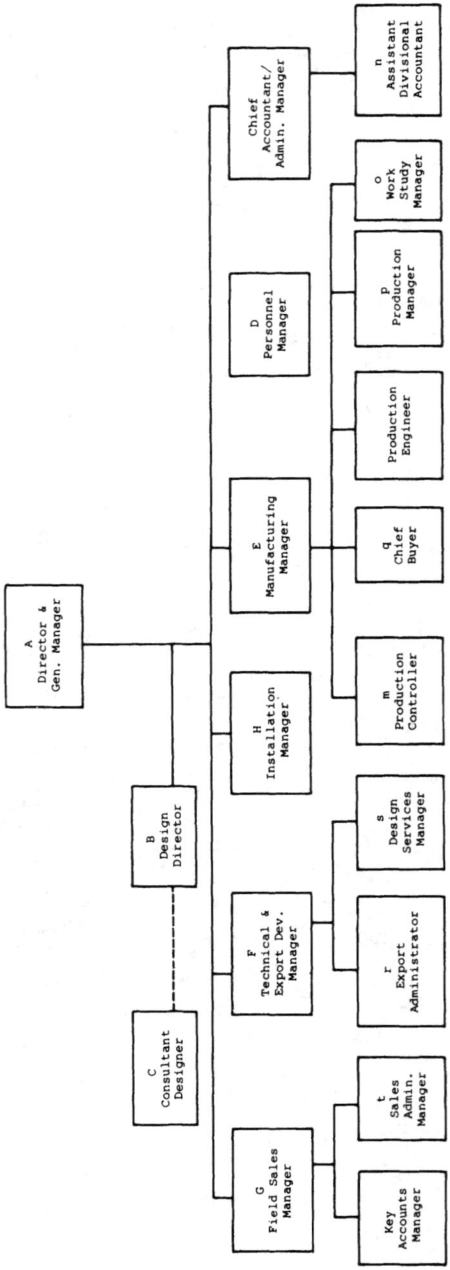

```
                                    A
                              Director &
                              Gen. Manager
                                    │
   ┌────────────┬────────────┬──────┼──────┬────────────┬────────────┐
   │            │            │      │      │            │            │
   C            B            F      H      E            D            Chief
Consultant   Design     Technical & Installation Manufacturing Personnel Accountant/
 Designer    Director   Export Dev.  Manager    Manager      Manager   Admin. Manager
             (dashed    Manager
             to C)
   │            │            │             │                          │
   G            │       ┌────┴────┐    ┌───┬┴──┬─────┬────┐            n
Field Sales    │       r         s    m   q   Production  o        Assistant
 Manager       │    Export    Design  Prod. Chief Engineer Work    Divisional
   │           │  Administrator Services Cont- Buyer    p  Study   Accountant
┌──┴──┐        │              Manager  roller       Production Manager
Key   t                                              Manager
Accounts Sales
Manager Admin.
        Manager
```

NOTE: Letters cross-reference personnel in Figure 8.4B.

204

Case 8.4: Dennis and Robinson Limited

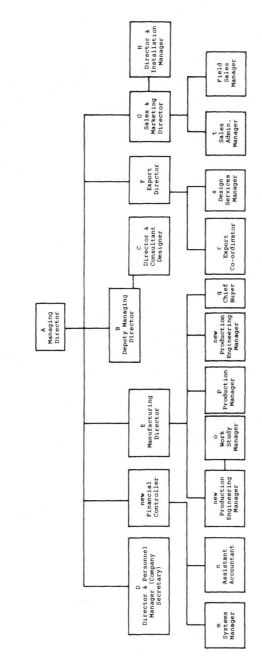

DENNIS AND ROBINSON LIMITED
SENIOR AND MIDDLE MANAGEMENT ORGANISATION CHART

FIGURE 8.4B After

NOTE: 1. Letters cross-reference personnel in Figure 8.4A.
2. The company also appointed one non-executive director.

Case 8.4: Dennis and Robinson Limited

senior executives have a 3-day break in a hotel to produce an annual review of the business and decisions are made on which future development will be based.

Managing the company has undoubtedly been helped by the existence, over a long period, of a stable workforce in an attractive non-militant location. Although there had been a dispute in 1979, with the workforce on strike for 8 days over the laying-off of workers during the slack season, the company has been relatively incident free. The buy-out was concluded without any redundancies and total employment has climbed from 188 employees pre-buy-out (178 full time + 10 part time) to 223 at the time of writing (203 full time + 13 part time). Much of the increase in labour requirement has been fulfilled through the use of temporary workers who are engaged as the season demands on short contracts. If the level of business will sustain a person in full-time employment into the medium term then management can select from the ranks of the temporary staff the person to whom they would wish to offer full-time employment. The risks associated with new engagements are thus diminished, and the pool from which seasonal fluctuations are taken is known and understood with minimum disruption to full-time employees.

Whilst the management style could be described as one of firm managerial authority there is nevertheless, an acknowledgement of the desire for, and merits of, participation from the workforce. In the longer term it is hoped that a share participation scheme can be introduced to give workers a financial stake in the business but at present relationships are on a 'conventional' collective bargaining basis.

CONCLUSIONS

The Dennis and Robinson buy-out is a good example of the purchase of a business on divestment from a parent company, where the transfer is of a substantial, and profitable going concern. In operation the company has exemplified the importance of the entrepreneurial managing director, where in this instance we observe also a level of thinking about the company on a conceptual level which has enabled good organisational consolidation to take place. Growth of turnover, employment and not least profits, augurs well for continued success,

Case 8.4: Dennis and Robinson Limited

specifically because the new investment in technology has been funded from retained earnings. The company is well on target for its projected growth, and an early stock market quotation, although much will depend upon how well it copes with the major decisions ahead.

CASE 8.5: DPCE HOLDINGS PLC - A MANAGEMENT BUY-OUT FROM A FOREIGN PARENT STILL TRADING

INTRODUCTION

DPCE is one of the best performers in our survey of management buy-outs, a distinction which it merits not least for being the first to come to the Stock Exchange with a full listing. Its growth in turnover, and profits during its very short life also commend it, although it had a good start in so far as it has always been profitable and had a good sound contracts base. The company is judged in terms of its observation and exploitation of new market opportunity rather than on the management of a turn-round, as was the case with Mansfield Shoe Company.

The past three years have seen very rapid change at DPCE, a company which began 1981 as the UK subsidiary of a listed Australian company, was bought out in April 1981, and came with a full listing to the Stock Exchange only two years later in July 1983. The experiences of DPCE exhibit the importance of identifying a market and of having the entrepreneurial management flair to exploit it to the full. In many respects although the buy-out sparked off the company's surge in performance its progress began in 1979 with the arrival of a new managing director and his role in leading the company, and in organising the buy-out has been crucial. Current experiences and future managerial dealings owe less to the fact that it is a bought out company than to the specific attributes of the market it is in, and the speed at which the company has had to adapt.

Case 8.5: DPCE Holdings Plc

THE COMPANY AND THE MARKET

The business began in Australia in 1971 as Data Processing Customer Engineering Pty Ltd ('DPCE Pty'). The founders were three engineers who had previously worked for UNIVAC, and who had become personally disillusioned at the role of the engineer in large organisations. Philosophically they wanted to form an engineering company, run by engineers, selling an engineering service of high quality to multi-product computer users. They had the foresight to recognise the market but insufficient backing or business acumen to develop it fully at that time. In 1972, the company was acquired by an Australian leasing company, Dier Computer Corporation Limited, which was itself taken over by Datronics Corporation Ltd in 1977. DPCE was thus owned, for most of its life by Australian leasing companies whose initial interest in DPCE, ironically, may have been as a tax loss.

DPCE Pty obtained its first major contract in 1973 with an Australian airline, Ansett, to maintain its computer terminal network. This was the first such contract in the airline industry and has had a major impact on the company which has continued to win airline business. In 1974, it gained the contract to maintain the Qantas central site, and was able to use this award as a testimoney to its abilities, and to give wider credibility. Other large Australian contracts followed.(1)

It was the Qantas connection which first introduced DPCE Pty to the UK. A senior member of British Airways operations staff was alerted to the third party computer maintenance service which Qantas were getting, and which they regarded as extremely cost effective. It was prompted to offer DPCE Pty a contract to do a full hardware audit at Heathrow and to tender for the maintenance contract at both Heathrow and the West London Air Terminal. This contract was won in 1976, and a UK division was set up to handle the business. British Airways were instrumental in bringing DPCE Pty to the UK not only by the award of the contract but because they also had been sufficiently impressed by DPCE to make a loan (at commercial rates) to help them to get started. DPCE (UK) was effectively a one contract operation, and in 1978 of the £859,000 turnover some 90% was attributable to British Airways.

When the new managing director joined in 1979 the company had less than ten contracts, and a turnover of les than £1m. However, from that point onwards

209

Case 8.5: DPCE Holdings Plc

contracts, profits and turnover have all seen a fivefold increase.

The principal activity of the company remains third party computer maintenance; that is the provision of a maintenance service, under contract to users of computer equipment. The service covers all aspects of computer use and all types of equipment. The advantage which a contract of this kind gives to the end user is that equipment from all manufacturers can be covered under the same contract thus ensuring that the company has the minimum number of maintenance contracts, an engineer to hand whenever the need arises, and no vested interest in trying to persuade them to upgrade or replace equipment. The separation of sales and service, and the projection of an independent service has been a feature of DPCE's approach to the market. DPCE will act in a consulting capacity and conduct hardware audits in addition to its mainstream business but these 'peripheral' activities count for less than 10% of turnover.

DPCE believes itself to be the largest independent computer servicing group outside North America, and is therefore a clear market leader in the UK. The competition to the company comes mainly from equipment suppliers who may offer maintenance contracts as part of the initial sales package. Where this occurs it is often on advantageous terms for the warranty period and for major systems DPCE would look to pick up this business at the expiry of the manufacturer's contract. So, although DPCE are market leaders in their field they nevertheless have to price competitively and win business from the major equipment manufacturers. In winning this business they are sometimes at a disadvantage when the original manufacturer will not release detailed specifications to them on new equipment, and will not disclose servicing schedules. The company is currently engaged in discussion with the Office of Fair Trading over some such disputes, but in the meantime has had to invest heavily in analysis and training to develop its own schedules. Some schedules have been purchased recently from IBM, and the background of many of their service engineers in the major manufacturing companies means that this disadvantage has not adversely affected growth.

The overall market is currently estimated to be worth in excess of £300m per annum of which DPCE took just over £5m in 1983 and is looking for £7m in 1984. The market offers scope for expansion which DPCE feel confident they can exploit. The

Case 8.5: DPCE Holdings Plc

developments in the computer industry provide a complex set of pressures on DPCE, some to their disadvantage, others to their advantage. On balance it is felt that the wider choice of equipment available and the development of many brands of plug compatible equipment for use with major manufacturers' mainframe equipment will ensure a growing market for their broad based service agreements.

NEGOTIATING THE DEAL

The growing market opportunities were very much in mind when the original proposal to purchase DPCE from its Australian parent were mooted. Soon after the arrival of the new managing director in 1979 DPCE (UK) began to investigate means by which they could break away from their Australian parent. The new managing director was concerned that the UK division's profits were greater than profits for the entire group, and that all money was simply transferred to Australia. If the Australian parent got into trouble then the UK end could be a major casualty in the collapse and the existing management team could find the company sold over them. Managerial control from Australia had always been very remote and limited to 3 or 4 visits per year from the Australian owners in addition to cmmunication by telephone and telex. The UK end had outstripped the Australian end in growth of turnover and profits so it had developed into a very independent entity more suited to local ownership and control.

Formal investigation of a possible purchase began in 1980 when it became apparent that the parent may sell. Datronics' own trading position in Australia, where it had invested heavily in new equipment ahead of an anticipated sales boom, gave the UK management confidence that the UK subsidiary may now be seen as peripheral to Datronics major concern. The essential elements - a desire to buy and a willingness to sell - had coincided very fortuitously and an opportunity to translate a remote division into hard cash was very appealing to Datronics. In late 1980, an offer of £1.7m was accepted by Datronics based on a price set by Candover and Thompson Clive Instruments, a venture capital company specialising in high technology companies in the UK and USA, who were to be leaders of a consortium financing the deal. Valuing a company like DPCE was not easy and account

211

Case 8.5: DPCE Holdings Plc

TABLE 8.5.1

DPCE Initial Finance Arrangements

Share Capital		£	
Management Team:	350,000 20p "A" Ordinary	70,000	
Institutions:	700,000 25p "B" Ordinary	175,000	
	750,000 £1, 11% convertible cumulative redeemable preference shares*(1)	750,000	
		975,000	975,000
Loan Stock			
Institutions:	£750,000(2)		750,000
			£1,725,000

*Notes: (1) Redeemable at 113p per share.
(2) Unsecured, redeemable at £105 per cent before 31 December 1985 and at par after 31 December 1985, and before 31 December 1988.

Source: Company Accounts, Offer for Sale.

Case 8.5: DPCE Holdings Plc

had to be taken of two very significant factors - it still had high exposure to one contract, at British Airways, which in 1980 accounted for something like 60% of turnover, and the important assets of the company were in its staff. If the BA contract were lost, or its staff poached away in large numbers the company could very quickly find itself in difficulties. In any event, the price was deemed fair, and subsequent events have proved the abovementioned problems to be much reduced. (The BA contract now counts for less than 30% of turnover, and staff are now being trained internally on direct post-high education recruitment.)

The financial package was put together by fund managers Thompson Clive and involved the buy-out team of 6, 11 financial institutions, and money invested by some of the senior management grade.

At the time the press comment on announcement of the deal tended to concentrate on the role of the financial institutions rather than the concept of a buy-out. The 'Financial Times' on 19 February 1981 announced the impending deal under the headline: 'Institutions Join DPCE UK in Datronics Deal', and the only intimation that the deal was actually a management buy-out came in the statement that: 'The UK management will have a substantial minority stake in the operation ...'.(2)

PERFORMANCE

DPCE quickly began to justify the faith which the management team had in the company by continuing to grow. The financial performance for 1979-1983 is given in Table 2 where it can be seen that in 1981 DPCE had 19 maintenance contracts on buy-out. These increased to 30 in 1982, the extra 11 new contracts adding £1.1m to turnover, and by flotation in 1983 the position had improved further to 47 contracts and a total turnover of £5.47m.

There are strong indications that when the 1984 figures are published they will again show significant improvement on the previous year. Profit margins have been healthy throughout the period 1980-1983 inclusive, and consistently over 20%. Entirely new contracts have been added and old contracts, up for renegotiation have been maintained often with increased business, although the margin available for profit is being squeezed rather more at the present time. Since 1980, and particularly since the buy-out the company has sought to extend

Case 8.5: DPCE Holdings Plc

its operations overseas again building from an airline base. In 1980, it was awarded the maintenance contract for KLM Royal Dutch Airlines NV which is the mainstay of its Dutch business but during 1983 two further major contracts were added in other sectors which could lead to the same kind of contract extension and development that the company has seen in the UK.

Much of the increased business may be attributed to the company's ability to win contracts in a new market which is still developing an awareness of the third party maintenance concept. Undoubtedly being the first in the market in the UK has been a tremendous help, especially when backed with the prestige of the BA contract. However, the entire company is geared internally to a closer profit control concept with a pattern of incentives throughout the company which gives the maximum benefit to those bringing in their contracts under budget. The company rewards employees well when compared with the rest of the market, and pays significantly more than large organisations would pay for maintenance personnel employed internally. Nevertheless, contracts managers can earn significant bonuses ranging from hundreds to thousands of pounds, paid on a quarterly basis, for managing projects within budgets. The structure is so designed that effective management could ensure that all sites earn the bonus, although at present some 90% do achieve the targets allowing the company to concentrate higher managerial time, on a management by exception basis, in the remaining 10%.

Two aspects of the business which are important to performance are worth mentioning. First, the minimum contract price for work which they look is about £3,000 per month; only at this level is it worth putting a man 'on site' - a vital part of the service they offer. Smaller contracts do exist, usually where they have excess capacity in an adjacent location which can be used to cover a second contract. The company therefore has a clear threshold above which they actively seek business thus limiting the number of prospects on which they would do market intelligence and prospect for business. As a consequence of this pattern of business, the employees work from the customer's premises (the customer provides space as a term of the contract) and there is thus a great reliance on the people in the field representing the company adequately. Secondly, the small number of large contracts, the nature of the equipment on which the

Case 8.5: DPCE Holdings Plc

TABLE 8.5.2
Financial Performance of DPCE 1978-1983

	1978 £'000	1979 £'000	1980 £'000	1981 £'000	1982 £'000	1983 £'000
Turnover	859	1089	1574	2537	3636	5469
Profit before loan stock interest	209	158	341	550	756	1315
Profit before Taxation	209	158	341	522	636	1195
Retained profit for the period	131	88	207	263	346	849
Number of contracts	5	8	15	19	30	47
Pre-interest profit to turnover ratio	24.3%	14.5%	21.7%	21.7%	20.8%	24.0%
% change in turnover on previous year	–	+26.7%	+44.5%	+61.2%	+43.3%	+50.4%
% change in Profit for the period on previous year	–	−32.8%	+135%	+27.0%	+31.5%	+145%

Case 8.5: DPCE Holdings Plc

service contract is given, and the terms of payment (one month in advance) means that DPCE has very little problem with respect to cash flow. Each of the contracts brings in a regular and predictable sum, and all credit control is comfortably handled by one person.

On buy-out the management team had a very clear idea of where they wanted to take the company and how. It was always their intention to seek a full Stock Exchange listing and they intended to seek one as soon as gross profits were over £1m and sustainable. They anticipated that this could be reached in 3 to 5 years. In the event, after only two years they had made sufficient progress to take the company to the Stock Exchange and were thus able to complete their major transition from UK subsidiary of Australia Co to full UK listing.

THE FLOTATION

DPCE came to the Stock Exchange in July 1983 as an 'Offer for Sale by Tender', at a minimum tender price of 170p. There were 3,869,000 ordinary shares of 5p each for sale and the proceeds were to be used to remove the unsecured loan stock (£750,000 at 16%) and the 11 per cent cumulative redeemable preference shares of £1 each (£750,000) at 113p per share.

The issue was three and a half times over-subscribed at the minimum tender price and a striking price of 200p was established. The 6 members of the buy-out team each sold some shares on issue. With the exception of ICFC, who sold a large part of their holding, the rest of the financial institutions kept their stakes in the company substantially intact. Prior to flotation the management team had 28% of the equity but only 13% afterwards. On flotation the largest shareholder was Thompson Clive and Partners, who had put together the package for the buy-out two years earlier. After full listing they held approximately 22% of the equity.

In order to ensure the greatest involvement of the workforce in the company, and to reinforce attitudes supportive of the company a share was given to each of the employees, and all were encouraged to purchase shares on flotation. Approximately 105 bought shares but some employees sold very quickly afterwards having successfully 'stagged' the issue. By the November following flotation 90 employees, about 60% of the total

Case 8.5: DPCE Holdings Plc

payroll, were on the share register but their total holding represented only a small proportion of the equity. The shareholding of the company remains dominated by the original supporters of the buy-out. In total some 64.5% of shares are held by the original funders of the buy-out. A small number of significant holdings (100,000 shares) have been taken by new groups, and this enhanced body owns 72% of shares in the company.

Since flotation the share price has risen considerably to a 1984 peak of 4.25p. The share price movements have been carefully monitored by those members of staff that acquired shares, and indeed the maintenance team on site at British Airways keep a chart in their office which keeps them in close touch with its progress, emphasising the motivational impact of their shareholdings.

THE ISSUES

There are a number of interesting aspects of this particular case, not all of which are related to its status as a buy-out per se. In many respects the transformation of the company is linked to the entrepreneurship displayed by the Managing Director who joined the company in 1979. He provided the impetus which led to the buy-out, and gained the confidence of his senior managers who joined with him in taking the risks associated with buy-out. The senior managers, who had met weekly for two years prior to buy-out constituted the team which the M.D. led in approaching financial institutions for the necessary funding. His influence has been vital to the growth of the company. This is not to say that the other members of the team were not very good - they were excellent in their own area of expertise and formed a complementary team - but they were well led by the entrepreneurial spirit of the new M.D. He brought qualities to the company that had been lacking before and commanded management respect. But he too was aware of the vital contribution that the potential within the management group held.

Since the buy-out there have been middle management changes and there will be others as the company grows still further. Some of these changes are a function of the larger turnover, and greater number of contracts, but all is overlain by the considerations that the manager/owners are now moving to assume a more strategic role in the overall group. The changes are being compressed into

Case 8.5: DPCE Holdings Plc

a short period of time as a function of the speed of growth of the company. In an early article in the Harvard Business Review, Greiner characterises growth through periods of 'evolution', and 'revolution' where periodic major changes take place. In his analysis the first major 'crisis' faced by a growing firm is a 'crisis of leadership', which requires the change from an 'individualistic and entrepreneurial' through a 'directive' to a 'delegative' management style.(3) The company DPCE Holdings Plc has two operating subsidiaries, one in the UK, and one in the Netherlands. Whilst most of the owner/managers are still in operational positions in the UK subsidiary, and hold main holding company positions in an almost titular capacity, they are now looking to develop full-time holding company roles to release more of their time for the forward strategy the company now requires.

This change will require the emergence of senior managers from within the subsidiaries and managerial changes have been made to add in another tier of management to strengthen the line control and to provide promotion positions and development opportunities as the company grows. This is seen as an essential change if progress is to be maintained. The company is young, its staff are young (27-35) for the most part, and further opportunities will have to be offered for people as they, and the company, develop.

As can be seen from Figure 8.5A (p. 218) the new tier has been introduced just below engineering director level to release more of his time, and to provide a broader base for new contract management. The structure is geared for growth in the number of live contracts. A promotion slot is produced for site managers to aim for, and there is the opportunity which exists in the short-term, for one of the engineering managers to 'grow' into the engineering director's job.

In introducing the extra tier, and creating an added level by which managers can broaden their expertise the comany is avoiding, in its engineering section, a succession problem. Because of the active involvement of management buy-out teams and the operational motives which often prompted them to buy their company, there is often a problem of succession, especially when all members of the team are approximately the same age and cover all major functions in the company. There is less freedom and flexibility in changing top personnel as a company grows when these managers are also part owners.

Case 8.5: DPCE Holdings Plc

FIGURE 8.5A: Illustrative Management Structure DPCE 1984

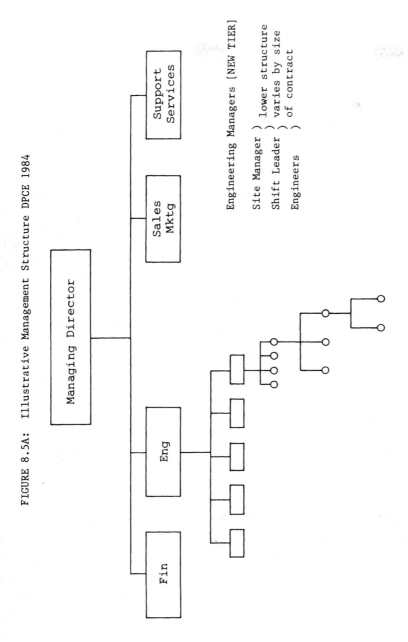

NOTE: 90% of Staff are in the Engineering Section

219

Case 8.5: DPCE Holdings Plc

There may be a need to redefine owner/manager roles to ensure the most productive contribution. Such considerations are not, as yet, critical in most of the companies in our survey, but at DPCE it is likely to become a question that will have to be dealt with very quickly. The buy-out team will have to devote more time to strategic issues and less time to operational ones, and decide whether they have the skills to do it and whether there are personnel in the company that can take operational responsibility. If not, it may be necessary to try and graft on somebody from outside who would effectively be working at the same level as some of the owner/managers who have a great deal of recently acquired personal wealth in the company. These issues are recognised by management and they are giving serious thought to how best they can solve the succession problem. If they do not manage to adjust their organisational structure and personnel sufficiently then they risk losing momentum in the company.

Two aspects of the company's image and credibility in the market place are worth mentioning. As soon as the company became independent it received a market boost. It suddenly found that as a UK company it could talk to some customers that had previously not been interested in discussing a contract with an Australian owned subsidiary. However, after buy-out the company was still small compared to the customers it had, and the new clients that it sought. The second boost came with flotation which firmly established its credibility, not least because of the well publicised and successful issue. The effect on buy-out we have seen in a number of cases; there still appears to be some admiration and support for managers striking out on their own from the rest of industry and they are given a 'fair break' by their customers. This was exaggerated in DPCE's case by the removal of the overseas parent.

The flotation has proved to be something of a double edged event. Whilst giving credibility it has also laid bare the company's commercial base, and the offer for sale document must have made fascinating reading to all those companies who had contracts with DPCE. As a public company all its customers have ready access to its accounts, and can see the progress of its shares. The company reports tougher negotiations on the price of new contracts now than it did before flotation, especially when it is the renegotiation of an existing contract.

Case 8.5: DPCE Holdings Plc

Thus, the company is having to face a whole series of challenges at the present time, most of which stem from the act of buying-out but not all of which can be simply ascribed to the act alone. The company's problems are more a product of its own success and are therefore welcomed by a management which is seeking solutions with some relish.

CONCLUSIONS

DPCE has been one of the fastest growers in a modern technological market. Its early history was as a remote subsidiary of an Australian leasing company but it has received a new vitality since buy-out. The act of putting ownership and control firmly together in a wholly independent UK operation has provided the platform from which it has become not only one of the star performers in our portfolio of buy-outs but also one of the Stock Exchange's high fliers.

NOTES

1. See: 'Offer for Sale by Tender' document for history and background.
2. Financial Times, February 19th 1981, p. 25.
3. Greiner, Larry E.: 'Evolution and Revolution as Organisations Grow', Harvard Business Review, July/August, 1972.

CASE 8.6: A MANAGEMENT BUY-OUT ON RETIREMENT OF THE PREVIOUS OWNERS, WHICH WAS EVENTUALLY ACQUIRED BY ANOTHER COMPANY

INTRODUCTION

This case study illustrates the unusual event of a management buy-out subsequently being acquired. It is of interest because, following acquisition, many of the beneficial effects in terms of management, industrial relations and trading relations that the buy-out had brought were reversed. The necessity for the acquisition in saving the company from bankruptcy emphasised the need to get the price and financing package correct, especially when trading activities do not develop as fast as expected. Owing to undertakings of confidentiality this case study, though of an actual company, is presented anonymously.

BACKGROUND HISTORY

In 1974, the current Managing Director was the Financial Director of a Company, which was taken over. New management were brought in, which led to conflict between the new and the old staff. Thus on 1 January 1975, a new company was set up by the Managing Director, financed by an ex-colleague from the original company. The firm consisted of one holding company and two subsidiaries, located in the Midlands and the North, with a sales outlet in London run by one sales representative.

THE BUY-OUT AND AFTER (DECEMBER 1980-DECEMBER 1981)

Owing to the needs of the other shareholders it was necessary for the new company to cease operating in its present form and to change its equity holding.

Case 8.6: A Management Buy-out on Owner's Retirement

This was achieved through a Management Buy-out, with the Managing Director as the sole purchaser. The total cost of purchasing the company was in the £100,000-£250,000 range and was funded by a single financial institution. A finance package of £220,000 was raised which included a 33 per cent equity stake. In addition, overdraft facilities were also negotiated with a clearing bank. There was a capital repayment holiday of two years and the firm was relatively free of cash-flow problems.

In 1979, prior to the Buy-out, the company had made a net profit of £100,000 and prospects looked encouraging, but the company soon ran into financial difficulties and incurred losses in both 1980 and in 1981. The losses were mainly attributed to three major causes. Firstly, it had suffered as a result of the recession and thus sales and profit figures fell. Secondly, the company had moved to larger premises (from a 10,000 sq. ft warehouse into a 25,000 sq. ft one), and hence rent and rates increased three-fold to between £35,000-£40,000. Finally, there were the interest payments on the £220,000 loan finance to be met. Hence with falling revenue and increasing expenses the company was heading towards bankruptcy, although they were not experiencing cash-flow problems in the sense that firms were refusing to pay. The major difficulty was pressure from the bank, as the company had no reserves.

The company's 1,400 customers are mainly small firms with an average order size of approximately £160. The firm operated an efficient credit control system with customer credit limits in theory of approximately 45 days, although due to severe competition from two particular firms in the industry, in practice the limit was normally 80 days. Trade Credit given was thus being used as a form of non-price competition. If there was any difficulty with payment after this period the company would stop further supplies until payment was made. As a final solution customers would be taken to the Small Claims Court, although usually the threat of this action would secure quick payment. Suppliers were usually paid after 80 days, or when they needed to be. Paper work was kept to a minimum and the Credit Control System operated efficiently.

Being such a small firm the workforce was kept informed of the progress and financial position of the firm and in profitable years were given six-monthly bonuses. Naturally when losses began to

223

Case 8.6: A Management Buy-out on Owner's Retirement

occur bonuses were stopped but the workforce was still well-informed about the state of the company.
 The financial difficulties forced the Managing Director into talks with a potential acquirer, who had been interested in the company at the time of the Buy-out, and a takeover deal was arranged. The Managing Director remained with the company as General Manager but has no authority on the new parent's main Board.

THE TAKEOVER

In January 1982, the company was acquired by a parent operating in similar market areas, and who has an annual turnover of between £15-£18 million. Although the takeover has averted the possibility of bankruptcy it has not been without its costs. These costs concern the effects on both the short-term and long-term management of the company and the motivation of the employees. The main short-term effect has been on the credit control function. When the company was independent a mini-computer was used to deal with all purchase and sales ledger control and provided useful reports on overdue payments of invoices. The ability to maintain a tight grip on credit control that this provided and which has already been described, was of crucial importance to the company in maintaining cash flow whilst losses were being incurred. Since the buy-out these benefits from close control of the debtor profile have been lost with the enforced computerisation of sales and purchase ledgers on the parent company's computer. This change has entailed a dramatic increase in the amount of paper work involved, as the parent requires all the purchase return slips, etc. The number of customers has not really been affected by the takeover, although the introduction of new types of product at the main site has meant an increase in that sector of the business. The supplier side of the company is now controlled by the parent, who because of its size is able to enforce a certain degree of purchasing power over supplies. This centralisation does however cause problems for the company as a subsidiary and which is linked to the change in the credit control system. For example, on one occasion a firm would not supply the subsidiary as the parent had not met the previous payment. This was due solely to a statement being mislaid and hence no record of the supply was known at Head Office. The general

Case 8.6: A Management Buy-out on Owner's Retirement

disruption caused by the change has affected the company's ability to trade on the quality of the service it provided. Indeed, it has led to the recent loss of one major customer.

The long-term and motivational effects stem from the lack of a formal management organisation structure in the parent. The highly unitarised management style which results means a complete absence of formalised budgetary control and corporate planning procedures, and is an important contribution to the large fluctuations in profits observed in the parent (from £500,000 loss some years to a £200,000 operating profit in others). There is no participation by the general manager of the former buy-out in the setting of his budget targets, quite unrealistic ones being handed down from Head Office. For example, in the year just completed a fifty per cent target increase in sales was set. Although after some discussion this was reduced to 25 per cent the adverse effects on managerial motivation in a market severaly affected by the recession are obvious. In such a market, accurate pricing policy plays an important part in surviving against strong competition. However, as the company now obtains all its supplies through the parent the room for flexibility and fine-tuning in pricing is severely limited.

The main cause of the problem is that the parent does not inform the subsidiary of the real cost of individual items and imposes a handling surcharge on goods supplied. The adverse effects at the managerial level are fed through to the other employees. They too have little idea of the direction of the company and experience the adverse effects of the new approach to credit control through having to deal with customer and supplier complaints. A particularly severe adverse influence on motivation is exerted since great store was previously set on the quality of service offered. Although there is recognition of the fact that the acquisition contributed greatly to the safeguarding of jobs, there are limits to the willingness of all employees and management to exert a great deal of effort under such conditions. Since the takeover there has been one redundancy, and one person has been transferred to another division of the parent.

THE FUTURE

The opportunity for a re-buy-out remains an

Case 8.6: A Management Buy-out on Owner's Retirement

impossibility as the parent needs the subsidiary as part of its national network because of its location, thus there is little likelihood of its selling the division. Even despite the rather difficult position that the ex-Managing Director now finds himself in, the five year contract that he has does not give him much incentive to consider a re-buy-out.

CONCLUSION

Although this buy-out's existence as an independent company was short-lived, there is some indication that the closeness of ownership and control had beneficial effects on management/employee relations. However, the over-riding problem was an inability to generate sufficient cash to service the financial package because of the unexpectedly severe effects of the recession. The transfer of ownership to a new parent company appears to have set in reverse the beneficial effects that the buy-out had brought.

CASE 8.7: NATIONAL FREIGHT AND VICTAULIC: SOME
         EARLY EXPERIENCES IN TWO STAFF BUY-OUTS
         FROM NATIONALISED INDUSTRIES

INTRODUCTION

Employee buy-outs from Nationalised Industries, particularly that at National Freight have attracted a great deal of attention (1,2) and have been welcomed by some commentators as a more acceptable form of privatisation than conventional sale via the Stock Exchange.(3) Since the National Freight buy-out has been described in detail from the company's point of view elsewhere (4) this case study will focus on issues that have so far tended to be ignored. In particular, the problem of how management deals with employees in their new, dual role as both employees and as shareholders.

Although NFC is something of a special case, about eleven per cent of straightforward management buy-outs do have some employee finance element according to our survey. The way in which NFC has handled these problems may therefore highlight important lessons for buy-outs in general and those with equity participation in particular.(5) The principal issues concern how NFC has handled the new form of ownership, in terms of internal communications, industrial relations and participation in decision-making and how any resulting change in motivation has fed through to performance. Evidence on these issues for NFC is presented below, followed by some points as to how the problems may have to be tackled in a different kind of company such as in the Victaulic Co. employee buy-out from British Steel, which in many respects is closer to a more conventional buy-out. What follows is based on personal interviews by the authors with representatives from both NFC and Victaulic.

Case 8.7: National Freight and Victaulic

COMMUNICATIONS

Within any company, satisfactory communications are important to ensure that decisions are carried out and that employees know what roles they are supposed to perform. Communication becomes a particularly crucial aspect of a staff buy-out since it helps to strengthen the feelings held by employees that it is their company and enables increased motivation and attitude changes to exert a positive effect on performance. In the development of communications in NFC after the buy-out it is important to note the role played by the public relations department. Formerly concerned with presenting the company's image to external parties, this department now has had to look inwards and become the centre for disseminating information about the progress of the buy-out to employees. In a company like NFC with about 730 widely dispersed operating units, such a communication function is seen as fundamental to motivating employees toward the company as a whole.

In the communications process within NFC there is a need to balance a desire not to divide shareholders and non-shareholders against the danger of accepting financial contributions from employees without letting them have any increased influence in the running of the company.

In its communications to the 37.5 per cent of its 24,000 employees who are shareholders, NFC employs three main channels - the annual general meeting, quarterly regional meetings (with a director being present) and a quarterly newsletter. The regional meetings in particular, which are reported to attract between 50 and 100 employees and pensioners at a time, illustrate the problems of a multi-site company. They provide important two-way channels of communication. The feedback from employees as to their views on the strategy and aims of the company as well as more detailed issues are fully minuted and form the basis for discussions at Board level. The newsletter is used as a means of answering technical questions on aspects of shareholdings, and on the performance and direction of the company generally.

Communication to employees as employees at a general level involves the dissemination of a number of specially prepared employee information sheets and progress reports. This information, whilst distinct from that received by shareholders, does keep non-shareholders informed of the progress of the company, the change in value of shares and the

Case 8.7: National Freight and Victaulic

opportunities to purchase shares, amongst other things. Some of the major operating units of the company produce their own staff newsletter whilst managers receive a monthly company information bulletin. In general, an important balance needs to be struck when only a proportion of total employees are shareholders to ensure that the full rights of shareholders <u>as shareholders</u> are met without generating a <u>harmful division</u> in the workforce. It is vital to avoid an 'US and THEM' mentality.

INDUSTRIAL RELATIONS

The exchange of information in consultation and bargaining exercises at local branch and company level between trade unions and management provides another dimension to communication. However, in addition, the views of trade unions towards privatisation through an employee buy-out rather than a worker co-operative have implications for post-buy-out industrial relations. Privatisation is a policy to which trade unions are collectively opposed and it has been declared often that they will press for re-nationalisation of those activities removed from public ownership. The high political profile of NFC, coupled with the fact that one of the unions involved (TGWU) is one of those most strongly opposed to privatisation, led to resistance to the buy-out in those parts of the company where TGWU membership was strongest. As a result, the company report a marked unevenness in the spread of share ownership across depots, being lowest in the TGWU dominated depots. Since the buy-out, NFC report an improvement generally in workplace relations with union negotiations being no different. The exception is some lingering resistance by TGWU.

There are clear problems here for the success of the employee buy-out as non-shareholding depots may not be as highly motivated as those departments where a large proportion hold shares. NFC senior management has shown itself to be aware of this problem and is making positive attempts to widen the spread of share ownership on the quarterly dealing days, to which we return below.

PARTICIPATION IN MANAGEMENT

One of the key features of a worker co-operative is

Case 8.7: National Freight and Victaulic

a very high degree of membership participation in decision-making and management. This factor may limit the size at which co-operatives can operate. In an enterprise the size of NFC the level of participation that would be required for it to be considered as a workers' co-operative is simply not possible. But, there is scope for some participation in and decentralisation of managerial functions which helps make feasible an employee buy-out and which the form of ownership itself helps to promote. Each manager in NFC participates in agreeing his budget target with his superior, with control focussing on numerous profit centres. This approach is not new to the buy-out and has been developed in the company in the past twenty years. The operation involves incentive schemes down to junior management, clerical and manual staff levels, with an emphasis on team performance rather than simply that of the individual. It is recognised that one important reason for the emphasis on participation is that the nature of much of the work in NFC allows a great deal of scope for individual effort. One possible development which could have been made was for individual depots to operate, where possible, as co-operatives in terms of their decision taking, but within the ambit of a federated whole. A necessary constraining factor on individual depots would be that decisions taken would need to be consistent with the overall objectives of NFC. However, NFC has presently chosen a more conventional form of management.

The attempts at decentralisation have also extended to wage negotiations, so that they are now conducted on an operating division as well as a company-wide basis. In this way, NFC aims to achieve salary and conditions packages which relate more specifically to the different circumstances prevailing in each division.

IMPACT ON PERFORMANCE

The positive impact on performance that should be looked for may be observed in two principal ways. First, performance may increase in a qualitative sense through improved motivation that the change in ownership, communications and participation may bring. Second, the quantitative aspects of

Case 8.7: National Freight and Victaulic

performance may be observed through increased profits and the value of shares.

Changes in performance following from improved motivation may be seen in the following ways. The company reports a noticeable change in individual employee's concern that the customers they deliver to are receiving satisfactory service. In addition, marketing personnel and tactical management levels are able to benefit from an increased informal feedback of market intelligence from employees at the many depots.

Aside from market-related factors an interesting aspect of shareholder participation at meetings has been their attitude towards redundancies. The overwhelming consensus amongst employee shareholders has been the recognition of commercial realities and to agree to redundancies when the need has arisen.

Many redundancies were effected during the reorganisation which occurred in the period leading up to the buy-out, but the company does report a net reduction in total employees by about 500 to 23,500 by July 1983. An unspecified proportion of these were shareholders. This observation reinforces the point that share ownership does not guarantee the employee long-term job security though the management would seek very hard to find an alternative position for someone so affected. The interests of those who bought shares for capital gain may thus at present seem to be prevailing over those seeking job security. But clearly in the final analysis the key to overall job security lies in NFC, as a now independent company, maintaining its profitability.

Although the company does not report comparable figures for the period prior to the buy-out, the £13.9m pre-tax profits reported for the first 56 weeks of the new arrangement do represent a marked improvement as reflected by the increase in the value of individual shares. The shares which initially cost one pound are revalued for each quarterly dealing day. For the June 1982 dealing day shares were valued at £1.65; for October 1982 this had risen to £2.00 and by March 1983 the shares were valued at £3.20 each (though a one-for-one rights issue reduced this to £1.60 each but with a doubling of the number of shares held). The total dividend per £1 share declared in this period was 22p - a rate of return substantially greater than the cost at which many employees were borrowing money to finance their shareholdings.

The continuing high level of interest in the

Case 8.7: National Freight and Victaulic

buy-out amongst the workforce can be gauged by the demand for shares on the quarterly dealing days. On the May 1983 dealing day, 169,000 shares were offered for sale, whilst 350,000 were applied for. The order of priorities in meeting share requests is to meet new employees and existing employees with no shares first and existing shareholders last. The contrast between the May dealing day and previous ones when few shares were offered or demanded, reflects the improvement in performance of NFC which has been much greater than expected. As a result, existing employees have wished to become beneficiaries and existing shareholders have often realised some of their holding at a profit to pay off the £200 interest-free twelve-month loan taken out initially to buy the shares. In total fewer than one per cent of shareholders have liquidated their holdings completely. (A proportion of these will be those leaving the company through redundancy or retirement.) This picture is in marked contrast to that found in those nationalised industries privatised via the Stock Exchange. For example, in British Aerospace, the initial 158,000 shareholdings fell to only 27,000 within the first year of privatisation and in Amersham International the number fell from 65,000 to 10,000 in only ten weeks. Hence, whilst the motive to make a capital gain may still be strong in NFC the internal worker/ownership pattern does appear to encourage shareholders to take a longer-term view.

The evidence we have presented for NFC shows how the important issues relating to the buy-out have been dealt with there in a very positive manner. However, it is necessary to recognise that each emnployee buy-out will be different and will need to tackle the issues in its own way. The Victaulic Co., which is a recent employee buy-out from British Steel, illustrates the point.

THE VICTAULIC CO.

In contrast to NFC, the Victaulic Co. operates from only two sites, producing pipe couplings and fittings on the one and polythene pipes, rubber rings and pipe joints on the other. It is the leading manufacturer in Europe for these products. Overall, some ten per cent of sales are to British Steel and its subsidiaries, though for certain products this rises to fifty per cent. The company is a conventional manufacturing set-up with each

Case 8.7: National Freight and Victaulic

department offering less scope for individual initiative. The communication issues which were raised in NFC become less of a problem because of the much lower number of sites and the lower number of employees and employee shareholders, as may be seen in Table 8.7. However, the problem of communication under the new ownership arrangements needs to be addressed. As yet, it is still early days in Victaulic but the company is developing a process of involving management and other employees more in the decision-making process, working from the top down. In addition, the company utilises employee newsletters as a means of disseminating information about its performance. But the question of how to deal with certain specific obligations to and rights of employees as shareholders remains to be tackled. The approach of NFC, suitably adapted for the fewer number of sites, may provide a model here.

The view of trade unions towards the buy-out can affect the way in which certain areas may be managed, the motivation of employees and the ultimate success of the company. At the time of the buy-out, the main concern in Victaulic was to avoid the adverse consequences for industrial relations that had been caused in another subsidiary of BSC when a possible staff buy-out had been prevented by its sale to a competitor. The remoteness of Victaulic from steel industry bargaining generally, and its relative insignificance nationally meant that only the local trade unions were involved in negotiations. In contrast to NFC all unions represented at Victaulic were generally supportive of the buy-out with a resultant more even spread of ownership amongst both employees and trade union representatives. Since the buy-out the main industrial relations questions have involved negotiating changes to BSC agreements which were no longer considered appropriate, especially profit-related bonuses (from the union side) and the pension and redundancy schemes (from the management side).

The much higher proportion of employees who are shareholders in Victaulic (see Table 8.7, page 234) will possibly assist the minimisation of the 'US versus THEM' feeling between shareholders and non-shareholders and have some positive effect on the state of employee relations.

A final important point of comparison between NFC and Victaulic concerns the consequences of Victaulic being a subsidiary company and its ability to effect

233

Case 8.7: National Freight and Victaulic

TABLE 8.7

The National Freight and Victaulic Staff Buy-outs in Summary

	NFC	Victaulic
Price paid (gross) (£m)	53.5	15.5
Number in central buying-out team	14	9
Number of employees (at time of sale)	24,000	880
Number of employee shareholders	9,000	562
Percentage employee ownership rate (%)	37.5	63.9
Equity stake held by all participants (%)	82.5	40
Number of times shares over-subscribed	1.14	1.40

Financial Package:		
Financial Institutions' Loans (£m)	51.0	6.0
Employee Equity (£m)	6.2	0.8
Parent Co/Financial Institution Equity (£m) (Ordinary & Preference shares)	1.3	4.7
	53.5	11.5

Note: Financial Package for Victaulic does not equal price paid as Victaulic retained debtors and creditors as part of the ownership change.

restructuring before the buy-out. Having been a subsidiary company has clear implications for future control, particularly as in this case BSC retained a thirty per cent equity stake in Victaulic. The desire of BSC to maintain the close trading relationship which had prevailed, resulted in its continued ownership interest and also helps explain why the company was privatised in the form of a buy-out. The possible control problems which may arise relate to, firstly the influence which BSC may seek to have on the general management of the company and, secondly to the vulnerability to outside control if the Stanton-Staveley division of BSC, through which its stake is held, were to be divested. The transfer of ownership agreements with BSC provide that whilst BSC owns at least twenty per cent of the equity it will not compete with Victaulic. A further safeguard, from the viewpoint of Victaulic, is the existence of five-year contracts to supply to and buy from BSC.

In the event of Stanton-Staveley being divested,

Case 8.7: National Freight and Victaulic

the shares must be transferred to BSC or to some other person approved by Victaulic (which could include remaining with Stanton-Staveley). The retained link with the ex-parent is thus seen by the company as crucial to prevent control-loss and to protecting certain markets where Stanton-Staveley is by far its major customer. Prior to the buy-out in any case there was little managerial interference from the parent as Victaulic was a healthy but very small subsidiary in relation to the whole of BSC. However, sales ledger and cash collection administration and research and development functions were handled by the parent prior to the buy-out. These are now handled in-house and provide some increase in control, though Victaulic did not experience the same restrictions on cash flow as other parts of BSC in any case.

CONCLUSIONS

The evidence presented shows that the mode of ownership as such is not the only important factor affecting the success of a buy-out. It is most important for buy-outs to address the issues of communication, industrial relations and participation and the impact that these can have on performance. As we have seen from the contrasts between NFC and Victaulic these factors themselves will be influenced by the views of trade unions, the number of sites on which the company operates, the proportion of employees who are shareholders and the extent to which management restructuring was necessary and had been carried out successfully before the buy-out. On the evidence so far available from NFC and Victaulic, an important positive effect on motivation and performance can be obtained within the essentially capitalist framework of the buy-outs.

The need to safeguard the control of Victaulic in the event of Stanton-Staveley being divested from BSC is worth noting as it portrays another dimension of the important problem of ownership dilution. If further employee buy-outs are to take place, many will probably arise from the divestment of subsidiaries of the major nationalised industries. Where some significant parent-subsidiary trading occurs, provision must be made to safeguard employee interests as shareholders.

Case 8.7: National Freight and Victaulic

NOTES

1. Oakeshott, R., 'Privatisation and Worker Buy-outs', Public Money, December 1983.
2. Lester, T.: 'What the Buy-outs Bring', Management Today, March 1982.
3. Coyne, J. and Wright, M.: 'Staff Buy-outs and the Privatisation of Nationalised Industries', University of Nottingham, Dept of Industrial Economics Discussion Paper, May 1982.
4. McLachlan, S.: 'The NFC Staff Buy-out: The Inside Story', Basingstoke, MacMillan, 1983.
5. Whilst some would liken these to a workers' cooperative we would not, for reasons that have been set out elsewhere, see Coyne, J. and Wright, M.: 'Employee Buy-outs and Worker Cooperatives', Public Money, April 1984. For a contrary view see Oakeshott, R.: 'Privatisation and Worker Buy-outs', Public Money, December 1983.

Chapter 9

CONCLUDING REMARKS

I   THE SIGNIFICANCE OF MANAGEMENT BUY-OUTS

The management buy-out has been shown to be one of the most important commercial phenomena to have arrived on the United Kingdom business scene over the past decade. Though the act itself, has probably had some part in company ownership transfers whilst ever there have been companies, its significance has increased dramatically with the annual number of transfers multiplying tenfold in the past six years. The management buy-out has become a very fashionable part of the business world, an interest which is best illustrated by the number of lending bodies who now advertise themselves as having funds available for financing management buy-outs.(1) The growth of lenders has followed closely the growth of buy-outs and has extended from its original domain of specialist venture capital houses to pension funds, commercial banks, insurance companies, enterprise boards, local authorities, and Business Expansion funds. The manager wishing to purchase his company in 1985 will undoubtedly get a more attentive hearing than people in a similar position would have received ten years ago, and will certainly have a much wider choice of finance available.

Overall, in terms of the total value of assets employed in British industry and the total stock of companies the buy-outs so far completed have done little more than scratch the surface. Over the past decade, in broad terms, they may have accounted for less than 1,000 individual company creations, and the transfer of less than £1 billion worth of assets. Nevertheless, the annual number of deals completed now match the number of 'conventional' sales of subsidiaries between parents groups. There is some evidence that the number of deals completed is

Concluding Remarks

beginning to decline but every expectation that it will continue to be an important part of company transfers adding an extra option to the range available to corporate planners. The rise of the buyout has added an extra dimension to the corporate strategy debate within companies and raises many issues. The companies studied in the research reported here demonstrate an admirable record of success during a difficult trading period and have arisen in a wide variety of circumstances. Some measure of the complex pattern of backgrounds from which the buy-out may arise has been demonstrated in the case studies presented in Chapter 8. In those from divestment the sale by management buyout can be seen to have been an entirely rational and logical decision for the ex-parent to have made in terms of its own corporate strategy.(2)

The significance of the buy-out has been seen to extend beyond the purely numerical considerations of their size and growth (see ch. 4). The experiences of the companies studied have emphasised the importance of the exercise of the full range of managerial skills for the creation of a successful business.

II WHAT HAS BEEN LEARNED?

One of the over-riding impressions to emerge from the study as a whole is the vital role that entrepreneurship has to play in the success of a company. All the entrepreneurial attributes of administration, alertness, and risk taking, as developed in Chapter 3 have been seen to be essential for the creation and development of the companies under study. In almost every instance these skills were represented in one individual who could be genuinely identified as the prime mover. Nevertheless, the selection and creation of an appropriate management team, comprising the necessary balance of skills and with an equity stake in the business, has been seen to be the crucial decision which the leader has to take as has been shown in Chapters 2 and 5. Crucial not only because of the need to gather the expertise to run the company but also because of the need to convince outside lenders to put up the necessary capital to effect the purchase.

The general pattern of buy-out teams is for them to be comprised of able executives in mid-career for whom the buy-out is their first venture into company

Concluding Remarks

ownership. As the analysis in Chapter 5 spells out, they tend to be well established in the company which they buy and the majority have worked for them at least 10 years with an average length of service of about 12 years. The financial executives tend to be the youngest on average and to have been with the company the least number of years.

The great challenge to the majority of these individuals was freedom; freedom to act in their own interests, to make decisions and take risks on their own account. The incentive which guided their actions was the knowledge that they would get a direct benefit, through their ownership stake, from the success of the company; and a few might become extremely rich!

Managers on buy-out have exercised their freedom. They have had the ability and the will to make decisions and they have done just that; they have managed in the true sense of the word. For some, the challenges of management were possibly mundane after the even greater challenge of the act of buy-out itself but for most the skills and perception they showed in mounting a change as fundamental as the buy-out have served them well in managing the economic, organisational and financial changes during the early life of their new companies. The new wave of owners have not been afraid to face difficult decisions and make necessary improvements, often requiring more compact organisational structures and flexible attitudes.

One area in which management have not flexed their muscles as much as might have been expected 'a priori' has been on the industrial relations front. In dealings with the trade unions it is clear from Chapter 6 that relationships have generally been quite harmonious and there has been little opposition either to the buy-out itself or the necessary changes in working practices under the new owners. This degree of cooperation must be evaluated against the background of economic recession, high unemployment and uncertainty amongst employees. Experience also varies depending upon the previous attitudes in the company and its performance pre-buy-out but even in those instances where the change has necessitated job losses there has been little prolonged or organised obstruction from the employees. Unpleasant as job cuts are there has been a general sense of necessity in those instances where they have been effected. There has certainly been no evidence to suggest that the success of the buy-outs has been achieved at the expense of

239

Concluding Remarks

employees or that the simple solution of industrial relations issues has been a short cut to success. The buy-out has been of mutual benefit to both employers and employees in most cases.

There has been a general acceptance of the valuable contribution which employees make to the success of the companies. Management have generally been seen to encourage a greater involvement by employees in the company after the buy-out, and have often formally introduced means by which information may be better communicated to the entire workforce. In general the companies have tried to reduce any notion of 'us and them' which may divide the company.

Successful organisation, and the cooperation of employees have undoubtedly played a great part in the overall trading performance of the companies. The Economic and Financial aspects have been examined in some detail in Chapter 7 concentrating on employment changes, trading relationships with ex-parents, the level of new investment, the growth of the market and profits for the company, and its overall financial management. Two cohorts have been looked at more closely to quantify the pre- and post-buy-out performance as judged simply from information gained from company accounts.

The buy-outs as a group have been net re-employers of labour after their initial 'shake out' on ownership transfer. Though the job losses suffered have not been made up in the relatively short period since buy-out there is strong evidence of real and sustained employment growth in the sector as a whole. It is important to emphasise that jobs so created are 'real' jobs, in the sense that they come about without the assistance of government aid schemes or grants but purely as a result of a straightforward commercial decision on the viability and sustainability of increased employment. This growth has come about notwithstanding the natural reluctance of many managements to refrain from irreversible commitments to higher overheads when already faced with the need to meet interest payments on their loan finance.

Most companies have endeavoured to develop and enhance their independence by reducing any trading relationships they may have had with their ex-parent. The majority of companies report that the trading relationships at all levels, with suppliers and customers tend to have been better since the buy-out. These relationships have been translated into better profits and sales Performance. If those

Concluding Remarks

buy-outs more than two years old for whom reliable pre- and post-buy-out performance figures can be sustained, (34 companies) almost 75% report profits growth, with 38% describing it as substantial. Almost 86% reported sales growth, 44% reporting it as substantial. The company performance is certainly impressive after buy-out but it must be remembered that the evidence in this study concentrates on those companies that have survived. That the overall performance is good is perhaps best confirmed by the reports from financiers where ICFC report failure rates of only 1 in 8, and other financial institutions have not yet had a failure in their portfolio! That they continue to look for more buyout business harder than for other classes of comparable lending is indication enough of the value lenders place on buy-out business.

The financial side of the buy-out is possibly the most crucial because of the high gearing the purchase package generally required. The management of cash flow, as in companies in general, has been seen to be the vital element in the financial management of the company. Good debtor control and tighter internal cost control had made significant contributions to the success of the companies and is clearly demonstrated in the case studies presented in Chapter 8.

The high gearing levels mean that tight control of cash flow and an efficient management of funds will continue to be a prime area of concern in the future. In those companies which concluded deals at the height of UK interest rates, and are left with fixed interest rate charges well ahead of the current rates, financial control will remain a priority. Financiers are obviously not eager to renegotiate terms in these instances because the returns to them are rather better than alternative investments at current interest rates. Where rates are variable, an unusual occurrence, the company will have to be quick to adapt to the vagaries of international events which affect UK rates.

The volume of cash required to service the loans places some limits on funds available for reinvestment and the long term development of the companies may be hampered in the initial years in such a way that future earnings potential may also be reduced.

When considering the overall sample, it is necessary to remember the wide range of experience that is encompassed within it. All buy-outs are different and although many will share some aspects

241

Concluding Remarks

of performance, each will be affected differently by certain other facets. Just as within the small firms sector as a whole there are those companies that are merely surviving and others which truly justify the 'high flyer' label, so it is with management buy-outs. The very successful, such as DPCE and Mansfield Shoe, whose experiences are related in the case studies in Chapter 8, are quite different to many of the less dynamic companies which are not making significant advances but nevertheless continue to trade satisfactorily. The employment growth is thus disproportionately due to a few high flyers rather than to all buy-outs adding a few new employees each. Whilst the average return on assets is 14.9% in the year of buy-out the range is from -16.0 to +39.5. It is therefore unwise to think of all buy-outs in the same terms. As a phenomenon its exponents are going to experience differing degrees of success and failure, but it is true to say that in a considerable number of cases the act of buying out itself has been the trigger that has sparked off a remarkable transformation in the fortunes of a company.

Thus, the buy-out is an entrepreneurial activity that within the broad range of experience has been seen to produce a heartening level of success for the companies so bought out and in so doing has brought some benefit to the economy as a whole, and has certainly paved the way for a significant appraisal of performance and opportunity across a broad range of British industry.

III HOW MIGHT THE PHENOMENON DEVELOP?

The management buyout is firmly established conceptually within the UK business scene and will undoubtedly figure large in considerations of strategy within companies. It is also reasonably well developed technically in the way in which the transaction can be concluded and the facilities made available to ease the transfer. The market for advisory services is quite well developed, the legal position is well understood and has attracted specialist practitioners and there is a growing group of financial institutions ready and willing to commit funds for buy-outs. The future growth of the phenomenon may be in two directions - the continued growth in the number of companies subject to a buy-out each year, and the growth of support services, professional and financial that will offer

Concluding Remarks

advice, funding and consultancy services as the market place becomes more sophisticated. These developments and their future potential may be considered in two distinct ways: first the natural, unaided development of the concept, and second the development which may take place should it attract policy support from government.

(i) Natural Development

There is still plenty of scope for further buy-outs to take place within the framework of opportunity as exemplified by this study namely: reorganisation of companies, receiverships and retirements. The deconglomerisation of industry still contains plenty of scope for further opportunities to arise as a result of rationalisation wherein particular subsidiaries may become peripheral to a parent company's contemporary needs and development. Similarly, the continuing recession in the United Kingdom, with continuing high levels of bankruptcy being reported by Dun and Bradstreet, and Trade Indemnity, will produce casualties which may be resurrected in some form or another, in whole or in part, as management buy-outs. The total number of opportunities will be limited by the state of the economy with the expectation that the longer the recession continues the greater the number of opportunities. In the conventional reorganisations the economic recession may be expected to exert greater pressures on groups of companies which may lead them to more critically appraise their composition in terms of products and organisation. Nevertheless, whatever the state of the economy one would expect a number of opportunities to arise as companies prepare corporate plans and look to their long term strategic futures. The process of change in the economy through acquisition and divestment by large companies is part of the fundamental dynamic of enterprise. In this respect the management buy-out, having been added to the range of options through which change may be brought about can be expected to continue prominently on the scene. There need be no change in accepted commercial criteria surrounding divestment, it is simply that one can expect occasions to continue to arise when it is in the parent's interest to sell the company, and where a sale to its existing management is the most efficacious way to bring about the transfer of ownership. The advantages may be financial, because

243

Concluding Remarks

a sale can be concluded speedily, or because it can be concluded quietly. Whatever the reason the opportunity for sale is expected to arise. But what of the desire to buy? There is no reason to believe that the desire to take an ownership stake in a new business bought out from an ex-parent, and the acceptance of the entrepreneurial role that that requires is a purely temporary phenomenon. Whilst it has burst to the fore only over the past six years, and was heralded by the re-emergence of small scale independent business only over the past ten or twelve years, the prominence which the successful entrepeneurial manager has received will have raised the threshold of consciousness sufficiently high for the aspirations to endure. There seems to be no reason why people should not continue to want to own and manage their own enterprise, and there should be opportunities for people to do so. Whether these will coincide, and whether the financial market will continue to have funds and view them favourably depends upon a whole range of extraneous factors, many international in character, which will affect their portfolio of alternative opportunities. If there is no coincidence of management and opportunity then we may see a development of leveraged buy-outs where a management team buys out a related company, with some internal management assistance. The financial market will only impose a constraint on the marginal projects - there always appears to be funds available from somewhere for the 'best buys'. In any event all the evidence so far points to a growth and development of the UK venture capital market at least into the medium term (5-7 years).

One aspect of the financing of industry is the extent to which finance is extremely mobile internationally. With the majority of the world's leading Banks having a wide international network they are able to switch funds to where they perceive the best opportunities. If the opportunities in other countries develop much better than in the UK then we may expect some of the available capital being sucked out of the UK. The development of leveraged buy-outs in the USA where $4-5 billion was committed to buy-outs in 1983 alone, (3) has begun to mature and there is some indication that venture capital may find itself into the UK to support similar ventures. By the same token if opportunities arise in Europe we may expect to see flows of venture capital from the UK.

Thus the natural development of the market will

Concluding Remarks

depend upon the extent to which the current recession continues, the alternative investment opportunities available at home and abroad, and the constraint which the availability of funds may impose. Nevertheless, it is not too imprudent to predict that the number of buy-outs per annum should not fall significantly in the immediate future.

(ii) Policy Enhanced Development

The picture could look quite different if the buy-out became either the subject of policy support from government, or alternatively if barriers were introduced to prevent them. The encouragement of private enterprise and the pro-entrepreneurial philosophy of the government during the period since 1979 has undoubtedly done a great deal to provide the philosophical underpinning and encouragement of the phenomenon. If that general support was translated into specific encouragement then the numbers could increase substantially. There are a number of reasons why buy-outs might be singled out for central support. They have shown that they can produce efficiently, they generally demonstrate good insutrial relations, they have shown real employment growth after the initial 'shake out', and they are distributed across industry and regions. Politically, a phenomenon which spreads its benefits so widely, and can specifically point to employment growth and market growth must be very attractive.

However, the buy-out also has characteristics which make it an uneasy target for government attention. It is essentially a product of the free market embarked upon by independent commercial spirits for whom government involvement and government interference are not to be welcomed. That is not to say that they would turn down any financial help that was to be given to them but they would certainly be wary of any 'strings' that may be attached or of any greater demands made upon them as a consequence. The individuals that take part in buy-outs tend to be doers rather than talkers and loners rather than joiners. Any policy would have to ensure that it gave genuine support where it was needed but not encourage the 'wrong' people to take on the onerous responsibility which comes from being an owner manager. That could be a recipe for disaster.

Thus the kinds of policy that would aid the development of the buy-out would be those which took

Concluding Remarks

government away from companies and which simply made it easier to conclude the transaction, and provided some benefit to compensate those owner managers who accept a major part of the risk.

In the former case some advances have already been made, as has been discussed in Chapter 2, which make the transaction easier. The law could still be eased a little to encourage employees to participate financially, and to remove the burden of redundancy payment obligations when the buy-out starts up as a new entity. It would be advantageous if means were found to encourage the boards of large groups to think more readily, and more quickly about the advantages of a management buy-out, possibly by giving some form of tax credit to the parent to offset against any tax liability which might arise on the sale of a subsidiary. In this way the creation of smaller, more independent, and hopefully more efficient units would be assured with potential benefits for the economy. Care would need to be taken to avoid abuse and to safeguard against the kind of 'filialisation' which has been undertaken by Citroen in France, possibly as a means to more easily close plants.

With respect to the buy-out team themselves they generally have a substantial personal stake in the company which they buy on which they will have had to pledge substantial security. Yet the money they invest in their own company will have been accumulated after tax, and on which they could have received additional tax benefit had they invested it through a BES Fund in somebody else's business. There seems to be a good case for examining this aspect of the buy-out carefully to see whether a tax benefit could be carried against the income tax of the individual or corporation tax of his company for the first few years after investment.

Both measures, if they were adopted, might be expected to accelerate the deconglomerisation of British industry and to encourage managers to consider investing in their own future by putting money into their own company.

It is therefore possible to encourage the growth of buy-outs beyond the level which they might attain through their natural impetus, and the ordinary appearance of buy-out opportunities. To do this would require appropriate non-interference politics, but may attract a serious debate of the role and rights of shareholders. Any support that was given should be regarded as assisting the market to operate more efficiently in producing more easily

Concluding Remarks

the end which the market forces are producing anyway.

IV A KEY ISSUE

One argument which would mitigate against a management buy-out and which a tax-credit scheme may allay is that surrounding the legal rights and obligations of the management to the shareholders of the company. It could be argued that as soon as management decide they wish to 'buy-out' - their interests are immediately at variance with those of the shareholders because management's incentive must be to purchase the assets as cheaply as possible. Where sales have been conducted by large groups in the UK at a substantial discount on net asset value, one ought not to be surprised when shareholders begin to express their disquiet. This has not been an issue so far in the UK but has been very important in the USA where the companies must be open to counter bids from third parties. In the field of leveraged buy-outs in the USA experience is littered with managers who have had purchase attempts thwarted by third party bids.(4) There is a very clear regulatory framework in the USA to ensure that a 'fair price' is determined so that the shareholders' interests are not set aside. It is evident that many of the buy-outs conducted in the UK would either have been impossible in the USA, or contested vigorously by third parties. The element of secrecy which has been stressed at various stages in this study is not possible for similar transactions in the USA.

As the management buy-out group grows in the UK there will inevitably be some conflict between shareholders and a buy-out group at some stage, either in the private or the public sector, and the question of an appropriate regulatory framework for the UK will undoubtedly be raised. If, in the short term, buyouts are to be encouraged, then this would need to be set aside, and some tax advantage may offset any discount and assure shareholders of a 'fair price'.

V CONCLUSIONS

It is necessary to reiterate that the buy-outs are a natural evolutionary development which have arisen in the economy and are different simply in terms of

Concluding Remarks

their purchaser's origin. In every other respect they are conventional capitalist companies, operating and making decisions in the standard framework of enterprise. That they are making them successfully, and meriting attention for their achievements, is a bonus for the economy. That management also seem to be aware of the contribution made by employees to their success and are encouraging the removal of 'us and them' attitudes also bodes well for a longer term benefit. The lessons to be learned from the success of the buy-outs, and the essential principles and characteristics which they embody are worthy of attention by owners of all companies.

NOTES

1. Investors Chronicle, 'Finance and the Small Business' An Investors Chronicle Survey, February 1984.
2. See Coyne, J. and Wright, M. (eds), 'Divestment and Structural Change: Concepts and Cases', Philip Allan/Barnes and Noble, 1985 (forthcoming).
3. Waters, C.R., 'Banking on the Entrepreneur: The Leveraged Buyout Boom', Inc., September 1983.
4. Lederman, L., Citron, R. and Macris, R.N., 'Leverage Buyouts - An Update'.

INDEX

A and H Upholstery Ltd 160
accountants 198
accountant's report 182
acquisition 15, 43, 133, 182, 222, 243
Addison, J.T. 62
advisory services 242
Aerospreen 186
Akerlof, G 56, 62
Alchian, A. 51, 61
Amalgamated Union of Engineering Workers (AUEW) 113, 117, 192
Amersham International 232
Angus Fire Armour 188
Ansett 209
Anslow, M. 10
Argenti, J. 169, 174, 183
Arnfield, R.V. 39, 40, 107, 158, 168
assessment criteria 13
asset purchase 179, 189
Association of Scientific, Technical and Managerial Staffs (ASTMS) 113, 117, 180
asymmetric information 14, 56
Atkin, T. 158
'Austrian' school 46, 59
Aylen, J. 39
Azumi, K. 109

Bain, G.S. 129
Balding and Mansell 142
bankruptcy 96, 222
Bannock, G. 59, 60
Barclays development capital 7, 32
bargaining 13
Barnett, A.H. 62
Baronchelli, A. 58
Bates, J. 59, 193
Beed, C. 51, 61
Berle, A. 50, 60
Berryman, J. 159
Binks, M. 59, 158
BL-Austin-Rover 12, 33
Blackstone, L.R. 39
Bohm Bawerk, O. 59
bonuses 214, 233
Bougen, P.D. 153-154, 155, 159
Bradley, K. 109
British Aerospace 232
British Airways 12, 39, 209, 213, 217
British Gas central pension schemes 32
British Rail 8, 12, 39
British Shipbuilders: see Tyne Ship repairers
British Steel Corporation 12, 233
British Transport Hotels 12, 13
Brough, R. 108
Brown, M. 40, 81

249

Index

Brown, W. 129
Bruce, A. 39
Buck, T.W. 62
Buckley, A. 108
budgets 214
Burn, R. 129
Burton, J. 62
business expansion scheme 4, 32, 35, 36, 237, 246
buy outs:
 age distribution 64, 66-67, 136
 arrangements of 30
 characteristics of 64
 growth of 67, 99
 marketplace 7, 37
 number of 4-5
 performance of 17
 practical aspects of 11-39
 sites 73
 size of 74-76, 125, 136
 source of 67-69, 118-119

calibre 89
Candover Investments 32, 38, 211
Cantillon, R. 59
capital gains tax 51
'cash cow' 196
cash flow 139, 146-151, 191, 195, 202, 216, 223-224
cash flow:
 factors affecting 148
Casson, M.R. 59, 60
Cathcart, D.G. 60, 108
Caves, R. 62
centralisation 224
Charles Macintosh Group cheap imports 170
Child, J. 94-95, 108
Chiplin, B. 39, 59, 63, 81, 107, 168, 193
Churchill, D. 40, 108
CIN 31, 32, 38
Citibank, 43
Citicorp 7, 32

Citron, R. 248
clearing banks 24, 33, 223
Clifton, R. 129
closed shop 116, 120-121, 167
Coase, R.H. 54, 55, 62
cohorts 151-156
collective agreements 111
collective bargaining 101
commitment 21
communication 103-104, 112, 167, 228-229, 233
Companies Act 1948 31
Companies Act 1981 31, 33, 36, 182
company:
 appraisal of 27
 growth of 144-145
 purchase of own shares 31
 size of 115
competitiveness 41, 49-54
complexity 238
computer control 151
conglomerates/conglomeration 44, 57
conservatism 128
consultation 119, 126-127
control 52
convenor 117
Cooper, A.C. 60
co-ordination 19
corporate strategy/plans 6, 15, 142, 176, 194
corporatism 43
cost level/control 18
county bank 7, 32, 33
Coutts & Co 199
coverage ratio 155
Coyne, J. 10, 39, 40, 59, 81, 158, 236, 248
credibility 220
credit control 151, 181, 223-225
Creigh, S. 129
Curran, J. 58, 108
customers 137-141

Datronics Corporation Ltd 209, 211
Davies, E.W. 159

Index

Davis, K. 97, 108
deals 25
  marginal 26
  preliminary enquiries of 26
  syndicated 7, 33, 52
debtor control 150-151, 166, 191, 202
decentralisation 230
declining industries 17
Deeks, J. 94-95, 107, 108
delegation 49
Deloitte, Haskins and Sells, 40
Demsetz, H. 51, 61
Dennis & Robinson 12, 18, 22, 54, 57, 142, 194-207
Department of Trade and Industry 24, 154, 164, 182
depreciation 201
development 242-247
Dickens, L. 129
Dickson, T. 40, 129, 158
Dier Computer Corporation Ltd 209
dilution 51
discount 6, 15, 17, 23
diseconomies 55
disputes 121-122
diversification 57, 72-73, 186
diversity 80, 95
divestment 12, 18, 55, 57, 68-69, 99, 116, 118, 133, 243
dividend 51
divisionalisation 99
Dobbins, R. 61
Doran, A. 60
D.P.C.E. Holdings Plc 2, 12, 18, 52, 54, 105, 127, 208, 242
Drury, J.C. 153-154, 155, 159
Dun and Bradstreet 243
Dunlop Company 185, 190-191
Dunlop Energy Engineering 188

Dunn, S. 120, 129

Eastham 200
economic performance 8, 130-143, 172
economies of scale 44
economies, evolution of 41, 42-45
ECSC 35
EEC 35
EEC fifth directive 100
efficiency 41, 49-54, 131
Ellis, T. 94-95, 108
Elsheikh, F.H. 129
employee buy-out 3, 227-236
employee/management relations 226
employees: involvement of 36, 87
employee shareholders 228-236
employee share schemes 36
employee stake 126-127, 164-165, 170, 179, 216
employee trust fund 128
employment 131-137, 206
employment changes 132, 136
employment conditions of 117
employment in buy outs 75, 84
employment regions 134
'end game' 17
enterprise 4
Enterprise Board 33
entrepreneur 3, 48, 94
entrepreneurship 19, 38, 41, 45-49, 106-107, 190, 194, 217, 238
equity: dilution of 35
equity stake 21, 23, 37, 85-86, 88
Esmark Group 28
excess capacity 15
export markets 162, 173, 176-177, 201

251

Index

factoring 4, 37, 191
failure rates 65, 241
Fairley, A. 58
Fama, E. 61
family business 161
fashion 171
finance 4, 33, 34, 156-157, 163, 189, 199, 212, 223
Finance Acts 29, 35, 36-37
financial institutions 28, 31, 66, 87-88, 237
financial institutions: directorships 100
financial markets 244
financial package 31-37
financial performance 130, 143-151, 215, 241
financial structure 33, 153
financability 16, 22-25
financing 180
firm deaths 44
Firth, M. 53, 62
fixed assets 22
Fleet Street 115
flexibility 50, 53-54, 103, 123, 192, 225
Ford Motor Company 161
foremen 99, 167
France 43
freedom 239
Furniture Timber and Allied Trades Union (FTAT) 202

Garvin D.A. 10
gearing 52, 74, 143, 153, 155, 241
General and Municipal Workers Union (now GMBATU) 113
Gennard, J. 120, 129
George Angus Hose Company 186
Germany 43
Glube, R. 109
going concern 14

goodwill, 166
Goodyear 185
group strategy 142
Grovewood 200
growth 213
government philosophy 245
government policy 42, 47, 245-247
grants 164, 182
Gray, J. 158
Greenwood, M.J. 61
Greig, I.D. 109
Greiner, L.E. 218, 221
Grossman, S. 61, 63
Guidehouse Merchant Bank 33

Haggett, D.S. 40
Hanson Trust 20
Hardman, J.P. 30, 39, 40
Harrigan, K.R. 39
Hart, O. 61, 63
Hart, P.E. 58
'hawthorn effect' 101
Hayek, F.A. 46, 59, 60
high flyers 242
Hill, S. 109
hive down 2
Hoare-Candover fund 18
horizontal integration 185
Hull, F. 109
Hygena 200

IBM 210
ICFC (Industrial & Commercial Finance Corporation) 7, 31, 32, 33, 38, 65, 154, 159, 164, 198, 241
imports 200
incentives 48, 87
independence 20, 240
industrial distribution 111
industrial relations 110-129, 181, 229, 239
background of 110-111
issues 111-112
industries 77

Index

Industry Act 1972 35, 164
industry distribution 69-71
informality 128
information 126, 228
information distribution 126
Inland Revenue 36
innovation 47
insurance companies 52
interest 22
interest payments 150
interest rates 155
intermediaries 25
internal capital market 142
international lenders 244
investment 142-143
Ireland, N. 116, 129
Italy 43

Jaguar 12, 39
Jardin, A. 168
Jarrett, M.G. 39, 81, 107, 108, 159, 168
Jensen, M.C. 61
job losses 122-123
job saving 135
John Collier 20, 21
Johnson, P.S. 60, 108

Kaldor, N. 62
Keighley Foundries see BL-Austin-Rover
Kets de Vries, M.F.R. 109, 168
Kirzner, I.M. 46, 59, 60
KLM Royal Dutch Airlines NV 214
Knight, F.H. 60
Kuehn, D.A. 53, 62

Laing Group 138
Lanemark Thermal Systems 12, 142, 184-193
Law, W. 116, 129
leadership 101-102, 160
'leading light' 21, 97, 106, 197, 217
Lederman, L. 248

legal issues, 29
Lester, T. 107, 236
'leveraged' buy-outs 2, 43, 247
Levison, H. 168
life cycle 57, 103, 106, 174
liquidation 118, 162
liquidity 146
Littlechild, S.C. 59
Llewellyn, W. 61
Lloyd, J. 129
loan capital 87, 240
Loan Guarantee Scheme 24, 35, 44
loan repayments 192
local authority grants 35, 182
Lockley, H. 158
losses 224
Loveridge, R. 108
loyalty, 125

Macris, R.N. 248
Makeham, P. 129
management:
    changes 97, 98, 217
    characteristics 83
    consultants 100, 203
    control 168
    functions of 84, 90, 92-94, 170, 203
    local 57
    organisation 202-206, 218-219, 225, 240
    services 19
    skill 14, 19-22, 238
    stake 21
    structure 97, 166, 173, 180
    styles 100-105
    team 56, 82, 178, 198
        age of 91, 94
        experience of 92-93, 239
        size of 83, 84-86, 107, 189, 197
    veto 14, 16, 23, 29
    weaknesses 16
Manhattan Furniture 194, 200

253

Index

manning levels 121
Mansfield Shoe Co. 12, 105, 126, 170-183, 242
manufacturing 72, 76, 78-79, 111
Marchington, M. 108
Margerison, C. 109
Margison, P. 129
marketing 173-174, 190
market leaders 210
market restrictions 141
markets 137-141, 146, 209
   free 245
   new 208
   overseas 185
   segmentation 171
Marris, R. 61, 62, 63
Maslow, A.H. 108
Maughan, R. 40, 107
McGregor, D. 101
McKenna, E. 108
McLachlan, S. 236
Meadows, Keith 2
Means, G. 50, 60
Meatpak 28
Meeks, G. 59, 61
Mellish, M. 129
mergers 43, 44
MFI 200
Midgley, K. 61
Midland Bank 32
Midland Equity 7, 31, 32, 38
misinformation 56
Monopolies and Mergers Commission 193
Moracrest, see Midland Equity
morale 126
motivation 2, 101-102, 126, 166-168, 225
Moyle, J. 61
Mueller, D.C. 57, 63
Muir, C. 183
multiunionism 113-114

National Freight Consortium (NFC) 3, 12, 25, 32, 36, 66, 84, 92, 124, 127, 227-236

National Graphical Association (1982) 114
National Union of Footwear, Leather and Allied Trades (NUFLAT) 180
nationalised industries 227
negotiation/renegotiation 25-31, 82, 102, 112, 124, 156-157, 162-165, 197, 198-199, 211-213
net assets 153
new firms 94, 96, 135
new products 140-141

Oakeshott, R. 129, 236
objectives 14, 50, 103
O'Brien, D.P. 59
Office of Fair Trading 210
opposition 229
organisational hierarchy 41, 49, 56, 192
overheads 149
overmanning 118
over the counter market 4, 52
overtime bans 121
Owen, I. 39
owner/manager 105
ownership:
   change/transfer of 1, 29, 94, 137, 178
   dilution of 24, 235
ownership and control 50-53
   remarriage of 3

Panache Upholstery 12, 105, 123, 160-169
parent group/company 37, 55, 96, 138, 149, 211
Parkinson, J.R. 59, 193
participation 100-101, 103, 167, 229-230
Pearce, I. 60
Penrose, E. 62
pensions 23, 25
performance 180, 201-202,

254

Index

performance (continued) 213, 230-232, 241
  actual, 144
  expected 144
  of 2 cohorts 151-156
personal relationships 127
personal stake 196
Pirelli 186
pluralism 111
Porter, M. 81, 193
Prais, S.J. 50, 58, 60
price 17, 22, 74-75, 85, 88
price competition 210
price mechanism 55
Price Waterhouse 38
printing 115
privatisation 12, 227-236
procedural agreements 112
Procter and Gamble 202
product range 17
production: cessation of 141-142
professional advisers 189
profit/profitability 47, 143-146, 149, 201, 231
  changes in 154
  control 214
  factors affecting 145-146
  margins 213
  sharing 101
progress foundry 18
Prudential Assurance Co. 32
public relations 92
public sector 12

Qantas 209
quality circles 101

rates of return 153
rationalisation 42, 97, 141, 171, 173, 177, 188
re-buy-out 225
receiver/receivership 11, 12, 14, 18, 23, 29, 68, 89, 99, 170
redivestment 201
redundancy 122-123, 162, 174, 177, 191, 231
redundancy payments 24, 36, 165-166, 177
regional policy 77
regions 77-80
reinvestment 195-196, 241
re-nationalisation 229
reorganisation 131, 179, 184, 243
restrictive practices 54, 118
restructuring 77, 234
retailing 171
retirement 12, 68, 89, 99, 232
return on turnover 187
Rhodes, D.J. 108
rice trailers 188
Richard Shops 20, 21, 92, 97
risk 24, 48, 56, 96, 239
Roberts, E.B. 60
Rockness, H.O. 109

Sabin, S. 40
sale by tender 216
sales growth 144-146
Sarasota 52
Sargant Florence, P. 61
Say, J.B. 45, 59
Schumpeter, J.A. 43, 47, 58, 60
Sealink see British Rail
second marché 43
security 23
services 72
shareholders 50
  interests of 15, 24
  rights of 247
shareholdings 21
  institutional 50
share ownership 127, 229
share prices 127
shares: types of 31, 33, 34-35, 156, 216
Sharp Unquoted Midland Investment Trust (SUMIT) 28
shop stewards 117, 120, 167

Index

Singh, A. 53, 59, 62
Singlehurst Holdings 188
small claims court 223
small firms 44, 48, 53, 74, 135
   industrial relations in 111
   minister of 44
Smith, C.R. 129
Smiths Industries 57, 194, 198
Screw, Nut, Bolt and Rivet Trade Union (SNBRU) 117
Society of Graphical and Allied Trades (1982) 115
soil-less cultivation systems 188
Soloman, G.T. 108
Spicer and Pegler 21, 38, 40
spin off 2
standard industrial classification class (2 digit) headings - 1980 69, 81
Stanton-Staveley 234-235
Stanworth, J. 58, 108
stock control 181
stock exchange 18, 32, 176, 208, 216, 227, 232
stock market flotation 216-217, 220
Stockport Messenger Group 115
stocks 149
Storey, D.J. 107, 108, 109, 135, 158
strategic contracts 55
strategic objectives 186
strategic search 184
strategy 220, 242
strikes 110, 121-122, 206
subsidiaries 73
success 238
succession 94, 106, 161 218

Sumitomo 188
supplier/customer relationship 18, 138-139
suppliers 137-141
survey 65
survival 105

takeovers 44, 53, 224-225
target company 56
taxation 29, 36
tax liabilities 246
Technical and Supervisory Staffs (TASS) 117
technology 17, 115, 190
Thermalite 138, 142
Thompson Clive Investments 211-213, 216
Times Newspapers 115
Timpson Shoes 20
trade credit 138
trade indemnity 243
trade unions 54, 112, 113, 233,
   membership of 118
   opposition 124-125
   recognition 112, 115-119
   representation 112, 113, 120
   role of 125
trading dependence 139-140
transaction costs 55
transfer of undertakings (protection of employment) regulations 24, 36
transformation 242
Transport & General Workers Union (TGWU) 113, 117, 124, 229
trust fund 167
Tyne Ship Repairers 12

unemployment 80, 125
unionisation 111
Univac 209
United States experience 15, 22, 43

Index

Unlisted Securities Market (USM) 32, 52
Upton, R. 107
USI Engineering 186
Utton, M.A. 59

Vale, P. 158
vendor 26
vertical integration 185, 194-195
viability 16, 17-19, 68
Victaulic 3, 12, 32, 66, 84, 124, 227-236
Von Mises, L. 59
Vroom, V.H. 109

wages 121
Wainer, H.A. 60
Wallner, N. 40, 58
Warburg's Merchant Bank 198
Warrington, G. 3
Warwick Survey 120
Waters, C.R. 248
Weeks, B. 129
Welco 3
west midlands 6
West Yorkshire Enterprise Board 33
Wheelabrator Fry: see Progress Foundry
white collar unions 113
Whiting, B.G. 108
Whittington, G. 61
Williamson, O.E. 55, 61, 62, 142, 158
Wilson, N. 40, 81
Wood, R. 62, 109
worker co-operatives 4, 37, 164
working conditions 121
working practices 165-168
Wright, D.M. 10, 39, 40, 59, 62, 63, 81, 107, 108, 109, 158, 168, 236, 248
Wright, M. 120, 129
Wrighton, 200

Yeomans, K.A. 159
Yetton, P.W. 109

Young, M.R. 30, 39, 40